In Search of a
Future for Education
Readings in Foundations

STEPHEN C. MARGARITIS
Western Washington State College

Charles E. Merrill Publishing Company
A Bell & Howell Company
Columbus, Ohio

The Coordinated Teacher Preparation Series
under the editorship of
Donald E. Orlosky
University of South Florida

370.8
M 327i

Published by *Charles E. Merrill Publishing Company*
A Bell & Howell Company
Columbus, Ohio

International Standard Book Number: 0-675-09041-5
Library of Congress Catalog Card Number: 72-87151

74-3324

Printed in the United States of America

1 2 3 4 5 6 7 8—78 77 76 75 74 73

Preface

The accent in this book is on the exploration of what appear to be promising ideas and valid suggestions which might help insure a future for our schools. Never before in man's social existence have the schools been subjected to such intensive public scrutiny. Never before have educators been more confused and more interested in finding better ways for the process of education. Schools are in crisis and public trust is threatened. This crisis has been manifested primarily in the issues of the education of the culturally different, the effects of technology on education, student unrest, and teacher militancy.

In an age of unprecedented transitions and great departures such as ours, men of vision, wisdom, and compassion have expressed hope for human existence through positive educational rearrangements. Some of the best contemporary thoughts have been brought together under the four parts of this volume in the hope of generating interest and helping to serve the needs of those committed to the education of the young. Prospective teachers experimenting with such sensible modern approaches to learning as involvement, independent study, and reflective discussions will find this anthology of ideas an excellent facilitator.

Because the reader deserves to be presented with balanced information on controversial issues, extra effort is being made to include the works of individuals of different schools of thought. Their ideas and their recommendations are exciting and highly constructive. All articles—those specifically written for this publication as well as those previously published—have been solicited from outstanding people who have been very active in their professions and their lives.

Although I was moved by "crisis" considerations to produce this volume, the articles assembled and presented are of significant, permanent tenure. The limitation to four problem areas is intended to afford a more extensive exploration of secondary and related issues—in some direct or indirect way

any issue could be studied in association with one or more of these areas
—and a greater depth for total comprehension. In other words, the readings
were designed to provide an indepth presentation of selected issues and not
a comprehensive treatment of all issues.

These readings have been carefully selected so that the text will not suffer
from lack of cohesiveness and focus in carrying the student smoothly
through its study. In the overviews introducing the different parts of the
book, I have attempted to set the articles in context and meaningfully relate
them to basic philosophical assumptions and social considerations. Following each group of articles you will find specific questions for discussion and
selected references for further study. At the end of the book biographical
data are offered for better understanding of the contributors' philosophies
and appreciation of their works.

I would like to acknowledge gratefully the willingness of the authors and
publishers who offered and permitted the printing and/or reprinting of their
articles. To my students who enthusiastically joined me in the search of a
future for education in the four areas this volume covers, I am most appreciative; I trust they will continue the journey we have started together.

I am most thankful to Dr. Paul Woodring, whose constant advice and
encouragement were very instrumental to the completion of this publication; also, many thanks go to Drs. Thomas Billings and Mary Watrous who
read sections of the book and made constructive suggestions. Mrs. LaVerne
Larsen deserves the same for helping with typing services. Finally, I would
like to thank my son, Nicholas, whose youthful reactions to my writings I
found to be most refreshing.

It is my sincere hope that prospective teachers—perhaps all teachers—
studying Foundations of Education and other professional courses will
benefit as much as I and my students have from the stimulating thoughts
presented in this volume and the constructive suggestions as to the true
function of our schools.

Stephen C. Margaritis
Western Washington State College

Contents

v

Part 4

Teacher Militancy 195

to my wife Vivian

Part 1

Educating the
Culturally Different

Overview

The first section of this book includes articles offering positive ideas for teachers to use which should help them achieve greater cultural awareness and respect for the racial and ethnic groups represented in our schools. In a broad sense, through acceptance and understanding, teachers might be able to reach all students so that schools could become adequately responsible and responsive to all those they set out to serve.

Because philosophical positions greatly influence all phases of curricular development, educators should strive deliberately toward the creation of a unity or a synthesis of those diverse principles from various schools of thought which survive critical evaluation. The interdependent relationship between those philosophical principles and the theories and practices of education should be realized more completely. Philosophic interpretations have always helped to distinguish the better from the worse in modes of human living. The authors in this section look at the nature of man and his natural rights to personal identity and social role. What they see leads them to suggest a philosophy of education calling for profound reforms for better school effectiveness.

Some background information might be appropriate: World War II was followed by years of instability, uncertainty, and confusion. The war demonstrated the inhumanity of man in the destructive use of technological advancements, and released a cultural shock wave from which the world has not yet recovered. The slaughtering of people by the millions raised important ethical questions and led to a lasting pessimistic outlook on life. People lost touch with reality and started searching for big ideas that, taken together, could form a philosophy of life.

Although most educators in the immediate postwar period favored a nearly middle-of-the-road position, philosophically they tended more toward eclecticism, idealism, and traditionalism. It seemed for a while that the schools were adopting three different patterns. First were the modern experimental schools, dependent on empiricism, scientific method, skepticism, relativism, positivism, naturalism, and progressivism. Second were the traditional schools, dependent on Platonic idealism, scholasticism, Aristotelianism, essentialism, traditionalism. Third, were the in-between schools, dependent on idealism, scholasticism, essentialism, positivism, progressivism.

Because of its diversity, American public education has often been controversial and has suffered attacks from both conservatives and progressives. The conservative protest of the post-World War II period attracted many professors in the humanities as well as many lay critics. The uneasiness of the Cold War years on the one hand, and the needed changes in all institutions of society on the other hand, caused school people to seek relief in the essentialist philosophies of the Greeks with their permanent aims and values, or in new philosophies born out of crisis. The conservatives assembled around idealism and realism, but mostly around neo-Aristotelianism, with Robert Hutchins in the vanguard.[1]

Hutchins objected to the romantic character of naturalism being followed by the progressives. Interested in uniformity and stabilization in education, he wanted a philosophy of education based on the natural law. According to Aristotelians, however important the particulars may be, the universal and essential should never be pushed aside.

It was probably one of the few times that Aristotle was put so strikingly in opposition to another thinker, and this time it was Dewey. Taking essentialism a step further, Mortimer Adler asserted that the aims of education should be the same for all men regardless of time and place. Meanwhile, the Catholics found refuge in Thomism, and based their educational aims not on nature alone, but on the supernatural order of things.

Against the conservative efforts of traditionalists and their revival of the old philosophies arose new philosophies or systems to perpetuate the philosophic schism. Some progressives, including Brameld, found confidence in an educational philosophy advocating revolutionary changes. The *recon-*

---

[1]John Brubacher, *A History of the Problems of Education*, 2nd ed. (New York: McGraw-Hill Book Company), 1966.

structionists are convinced that progressive educational tactics are too slow in their effort to teach the skills and knowledge necessary for participation in a rapidly transforming society.

Other people who lost touch with modern life and felt alienated from it started raising fundamental questions as to the purpose of their very existence and turned to *existentialism.* The roots of existential philosophy go back to the nineteenth century, but it required a devastating global war to find many adherents for this philosophy in the United States. To existentialists, traditional philosophy and religion give no satisfying answers to the basic questions of human existence. Facing possible annihilation and not being sure as to the meaning of life, they look at the future with uneasiness. To find life meaningful they commit themselves to action and accept its consequences.

The one new philosophy or, better stated, system of thought which has been regarded as an important departure is *linguistic analysis.* It originated with the disappointment that some theorists felt in the inability of philosophy to reach consensus on basic assumptions after centuries of effort. Restricting syntactical statements of fact to severe standards, linguistic analysts impose limits on philosophy, as the positivists had done in the nineteenth century, by limiting philosophy to scientific statements.

These three systems were philosophies of crisis and, although their basic assumptions were old, the emphasis they received under the pressure of postwar anxieties elevated them to prominent positions of systematic thought. Reconstructionism, Existentialism, and, most important, Linguistic Analysis, profoundly stirred the minds of intellectuals. But until recently educators received little or no guidance in their efforts to reorganize school theories and practices, as necessitated by the demands of exploding population and ever-expanding knowledge. Only recently has linguistic analysis started making its impact on education; and it is still at the theoretical level.

The education of the young should be tailored to each individual's needs. All children are similar because they share human nature with all its mysteries and potentialities. Yet, they are different because they do not have the same start in life or the same experiences. The articles included here answer questions related to both the similarities and the differences found in children, as we are trying to meet their educational needs.

Earl Pullias' article, "The Education of the Whole Man," gives us direction, reorientation, and purpose in life. He states that the nature of man has been neglected, abused, and exploited. A clear conception of the nature and potential of man is necessary in order to educate the whole man effectively. At the present time, he asserts, our conception of man is fragmentary, confused, and often distorted and contradictory. Pullias suggests a harmonious treatment of the three elements of man's self—body, mind, and spirit —as the best education for man.

Carl Rogers also puts his emphasis on man, the learner. He sees the facilitation of learning as the only aim of education. For him the educated man is the one who has learned how to learn. In a drastically changing society nothing remains static; everything soon becomes outdated, and only the ability to learn receives permanent tenure. This ability rests upon certain attitudinal qualities to be found in the personal relationship between the facilitator and the learner.

In "In Learning, Begin Not Where You Expect to End," I show a major trend in the business of teaching and learning. Today, unlike previously, we have come to accept the notion that the child is more important than the knowledge we expect him to gain. It follows that the learning experiences we provide should be analogous to the needs of each individual student, and they should be offered on his own terms—that is, background, tastes, and abilities.

Sylvia Ashton-Warner, world-renowned for the humane and sensible methods she used to teach the Maori children in New Zealand, has expressed in her works the warmest feelings about man as a person. Her letter which I have selected is abundant in thoughtful and suggestive statements —all alluding to the significance of the human being. A worthwhile teacher, she says, is one of the blooms from the worthwhile person; she asks the questions: "Do you passionately examine yourself? . . . Do you agonize as I did between feeling and reason? . . . Do you retreat into solitude and consult your instinct when logic leaves you high and dry?" (See p. 31.)

Helen Schierbeck talks about education as the key tool of cultural politics for the dominant majority. In her personal point of view, the native Americans, as other minorities, are rising after years of poverty and repression to assert the dignity and quality of their own cultural heritage. She discusses Indian cultural characteristics important to learning and advocates community control of schools for Indian children. For the latter, Schierbeck elaborates on a few cases where pilot programs are under way.

The author of *Schools Without Failure,* William Glasser, is receiving national recognition for his challenging ideas about education. He suggests things that can be done without any revolutionary effort. In an atmosphere of failure, Glasser says, effort and interest seep away; problems become overwhelming, and people seem to "cop out." Schools should be primarily role-oriented: role first and then goal. We must accept students as potentially capable, not as handicapped by their environment. In his opinion students need involvement with educators who are warm and personal. They need teachers who will work with them until they finally learn to fulfill a commitment. And when they learn to do so, they are no longer lonely; they gain maturity, respect, love, and a successful identity.

Herbert Kohl seems to have been practicing the same ideas Glasser expounded, and he is trying to prove that great things can happen when the initiative comes from teachers and students and not from authority. Given the time and an atmosphere of trust, he says, young people often want to learn more than is usually expected of them. He implemented this idea in the open mini-school. Kohl discusses the need for teachers to work together to effect change and outlines strategies for creating open mini-schools within the existing schools. He also presents reactions by teachers who have experimented with new ideas in public schools.

Where Glasser believes that changes can be made within the existing school system, John Holt advocates radical changes. His ideas have scared some, confused a few, and excited many. Holt's philosophy of education allows the child to be the planner, director, and assessor of his own education. It encourages him with the inspiration and guidance of more experienced and expert people, and with as much help as he asks for, to decide what he is to learn, when he is to learn it, how he is to learn it, and how well he is learning it. He says we should convert our schools from jails for children into a resource for free and independent learning, which everyone in the community, of whatever age, could use as much or as little as he wanted.

EARL V. PULLIAS

The Education of the Whole Man

The nature of man is the central problem of education. Perhaps, in truth, what man is like, in reality and in potential, is the most significant issue in all of human life. The conception we, as individuals and as societies, have of man and the implications that flow from that conception are a major influence in determining the direction of all thought and action—in short, of civilization.

If man is conceived as merely a high order of animal, destined to snarl and fight his way to such advantages as he can attain; as a complex mechanism in a mechanistic universe devoid of meaning or love; as a cursed, sin-ridden changeling marooned on a muddy insignificant speck called earth; as a canny, somewhat intelligent but strangely selfish and often vicious organism to be controlled and if possible exploited; then the various aspects of a society reflect those conceptions. Education, law, economics, government, religion—the varied means of organized life—are built in terms of the way man is conceived.

If, on the other hand, man is conceived as a delicate combination of the physical and spiritual, perhaps unique in the universe; as a treasure of almost unlimited potential which proper processes can uncover; as a sensitive yet unbelievably durable instrument for the discovery, refinement and creative use of truth, beauty, goodness and love; as a remarkably versatile and energetic thinker, knower, builder, seeker who can be guided by love and truth; as a sacred being still in the process of creation, a part of which can now be self-directed; if these are the conceptions of man, then it follows somewhat as the night follows the day that man's thought and institutions —his attempts to order his life and find answers to his problems—will be given direction by these conceptions.

Revised from A SEARCH FOR UNDERSTANDING (Dubuque, Iowa: W. C. Brown Company Publishers, 1965), pp. 11-17. Reprinted by permission.

But the desire and need of the teacher are to know the truth about the nature of man, for man in all his complexity and variety is the "material" with which the teacher works. To complicate the matter further, the teacher himself is *man,* more or less mature, more or less whole, more or less self-actualized. So the teacher and the student and the relation between them are intricately involved in the problem of the nature and potential of the material (the human personality) which is both the means and the end of their efforts.

Yet man's knowledge of himself is still relatively slight and greatly confused. There is no lack of evidence about man. The account of his thought and endeavor is not complete but is abundant. In spite of frenzied orgies of destruction much remains from the efforts of man at his best. In recent times science (anthropology, psychology, sociology, etc.) has added much to the knowledge of man's nature and full potential. Still the story remains confused and the picture of the genuine nature of man is unclear and contradictory.

Perhaps the clumsy and often ugly practices of all civilizations which have arisen out of age-old struggles to survive and to secure and retain advantage make it almost impossible for us to examine objectively and sympathetically the nature of man which is being neglected, abused, or exploited by those practices. Even a mind of the quality of Aristotle's or Plato's, one supposes, could not face squarely the question of the nature and potential of man when the whole framework of the society rested on the exploitation of individual men in slavery. Could New England or Chicago families whose fortunes and favored positions resulted from the stunting labor of immigrant workers bear to study objectively the nature of man as man? Could the Southerner enjoying the benefits of cheap and servile labor ask the deep questions about the nature of man? To come uncomfortably closer home, do we as modern men have the courage to examine the varied evidence about the nature and potential of man in the face of our treatment and neglect of him as manifested in living conditions, work, recreation, nutrition, education, religion, medical care and all the rest? Such a view would be painfully self-condemning. It is so much easier to refuse to see the true nature of that which we neglect or destroy in ourselves and others.

We come then to a serious impasse in our thought about the education of the whole man: A clear conception of the nature and potential of man is necessary to the effective education of the whole man, but our conception of man is fragmentary, confused and often distorted and contradictory. Our processes of civilized life, including much of formal and informal education, reflect this state of affairs; that is, much of education is correspondingly fragmentary, confused, distorted and contradictory.

This situation does not surprise nor dismay the thoughtful student of man and his history. It simply suggests where we *now* are on the "immense journey." It profits little or not at all to curse our state and search irresponsibly to place blame. The demands and opportunities of the present and the future require better things of us.

Man is engaged in a prolonged and urgent search for an education that will realize his full potential—that is appropriate to the complex needs and abilities of his nature as man. It would be foolish to expect easy or quick answers for a problem of such depth and magnitude, yet the swift development of some aspects of civilized life since the Renaissance (particularly the areas of the natural sciences) makes effective education a prime necessity not only for a meaningful life but even for survival.

Man thus faces a crisis of first magnitude in education. Of one thing we can be sure: answers will not be found through mutual accusation or by going backward to some simpler time. The only hope lies in learning (1) to ask the right questions, and (2) to seek through every available means answers to those questions. Both the asking and the seeking must build upon all we have learned but must be free, unfettered by the fears and vested interests of the past and present. The times require questions which come fresh from the present and are oriented toward the new humanity and the new world civilization that must arise in the future; they require the best answers faith, reason, and science can provide.

If man can avoid destroying himself during this crucial transitional period, he will find constructive answers to this problem and will in the course of time move upward in his journey, perhaps coming very near to a genuine new world civilization. The working teacher must believe that man will have this needed time, for only then can his work have the zest and skill which such faith provides.

I wish to suggest four approaches that may help in this search. But first a word about my personal attitude toward man.

I am not ignorant of the dark history of man, nor unmindful of his long record of inhumanity to his fellow creatures. I am painfully aware of his gaudy and proud empires built on human misery, suffering, and exploitation; of his armies of helpless and ignorant men that "clash by night"; of his wide-flung brothels that traffic in bodies and souls; of his storied, ostentatious wealth side by side with grinding poverty and deprivation; of his indignities and cruelties to women, minorities and even his own children; of his irresponsible rape of the good and beautiful earth; even of his puny pride in his accomplishment, bringing him dangerously near a self-destructive cosmic irreverence—the *hubris* that *nemesis* ever follows.

But the potential of man is judged most meaningfully by what he has thought and done at his best. These high-water marks, largely individually achieved, give the true estimate of the nature of man; they suggest what he can be. I refer not only to the high points reached by so-called geniuses but equally to the best each of us occasionally reaches in dream or action. These "peak experiences" throw a quickly passing but revealing light, like a flash of lightning on a dark night, on the real potential of man.

Now to the four suggestions:

1) The remarkable abilities common to all normal men should be the center of the educator's concern, rather than the special abilities and talents of a few men. This principle does not suggest the neglect of special ability, but urges that emphasis upon what seems to distinguish a small percentage of persons not be allowed to distort our vision of the enormous potential of man, as *man*.

The educational scourge of our time (perhaps of most of the historical period of man) is the tendency, almost compulsive in nature, to fasten upon a certain percent of the population as the only ones capable or worthy of full education. I am suggesting that the difference between that group (whether it is the highest 5, 10, or 20 percent) and the general population is not nearly so significant as it is made out to be, certainly not so important as the abilities that distinguish man from all other living forms. The point here is that major emphasis on identifying and educating the elite has caused man seriously to neglect and misuse that reservoir of ability and talent common to all men.

As examples, let us think of language which requires such uncanny skill in perception, conception, memory, and delicate adjustment of the relationship of meanings. Yet all people under proper circumstances learn language quickly and well. Or consider sensory and muscular skills as manifested in seeing, hearing, and walking, not to speak of dancing, playing, and the varied achievements of creative work. Most impressive of all are the abilities and talents usually called spiritual: love, loyalty, sacrifice, appreciation of beauty, worship, kindness. Do we really know the extent, limit, and significance of these abilities which all men have in common?

It is my thesis that progress toward a genuine education of the whole man depends, in a crucial way, on a more adequate understanding and appreciation of the abilities and talents common to all men.

2) A central emphasis in education should be upon the unity or oneness of personality and upon the delicate interdependence of all aspects of the self. Or to put the principle more simply, education of the whole man requires a balanced attention to the three major aspects of the self: body, mind, and spirit.

I am aware that this ancient division of man into the physical, mental, and spiritual is, in an important sense, arbitrary and becomes meaningless and even confusing if pressed too far. The boundaries between these areas of the personality are not clear; indeed, there may be in actuality no such boundaries, for each aspect, at least in this life, partakes of and depends upon the others for its function and meaning. Such is the baffling complexity of the wholeness of man.

Still, it seems to me, for practical purposes, in planning the process of education we can best understand man if we think of him as body, mind and spirit. Assuming for the moment that these terms represent three significant aspects of human personality, then we can ask whether a particular educational program is designed to unfold or educe man's full potential in each of these aspects of self and, equally important, if an unbalanced emphasis upon one aspect or area hinders the proper education of the whole.

In essence, the questions would be these: (1) Are experiences provided throughout all levels of education that will realize the full potential of the remarkable human body to the end that it might approach its best in vibrant health, in skill, in joy, and in creative use? (2) Are optimum experiences provided to develop the full potential of the human mind that it may be informed, reasonable, flexible, imaginative, and curious? (3) Are experiences provided that will unlock and cultivate the aesthetic and moral qualities inherent in man that enable him to give and receive love and loyalty and to order his life after the ways of truth, beauty, and goodness? (4) Does the educational experience keep these three aspects of man's self in proper balance in such a way as to avoid distortion and to achieve wholeness?

3) The optimum education of the whole man is basically a matter of growth, and hence should not be rushed and crowded. The current fever to put more into the curriculum, to press for increased amounts of work at higher and higher speeds, and to lengthen the work day, week, and year could have reached such a pitch only by a refusal to remember the nature and goals of the educative process. It may be that a kind of quick result will be achieved by increasing the amount and concentration of stimulation, but I doubt that the best in human education can be secured in that way. Perhaps forced feeding, artificial light, chemical injections, and other commercial processes are successful in increasing egg production or plant growth or beef production, but the human personality is something of a very different order.

One of the greatest steps in the improvement of education would be the reduction of artificial pressures which threaten wholesome growth at its very roots. The urgent need is for ample provision for additional space and time in the entire process. Such breathing room might allow the most significant aspects of man's nature to take root and grow. Then perhaps some things might be learned deeply; crucial skills might reach rewarding and satisfying levels of excellence; reason, imagination, intuition might grow and flower.

4)Health should be a major concern in all education. By health I mean the optimum functioning of the human organism in all its complexity from the subtle process of metabolism to the most sensitive perception of beauty or truth or love. When any significant aspect of this functioning goes awry then the quality of human life is threatened. The extent of the threat depends upon the nature and degree of the malfunctioning. Advanced illness whether centered in body, mind, or soul rapidly destroys the effectiveness and meaning of all of life. These three aspects of man are so related and interdependent that serious malfunctioning in any one rapidly affects the others.

This truth is so evident that one marvels that any responsible educational effort could neglect it. The seriously unwell person loses all the best qualities of man: energy level is lowered, perception is narrowed, reasoning is more rigid, zest for living is reduced, imagination is dulled or confused, human relations are embittered, fear is increased, ethical judgment is warped. Aware of these facts, I have long been convinced that the part of education usually called Physical Education, including health and recreation, has a contribution of incomparable value to make to the education of the whole man. The current tendency to downgrade these phases of education in the face of the demands of modern life seems to me little short of madness.

Finally it should be noted that the problems related to the education of the whole person are greatly complicated by the special nature of modern life. It is very difficult to assess accurately the times through which we pass at present. It is natural for us to perceive the present in which we play our role in life as being special and more important than it really is. Even when we take this tendency into account, the evidence seems very strong that we are in the midst of a period of relatively rapid and perhaps profound change. The most important negative aspects of this period seem to be the following:

1) There is serious confusion in the area of values—of what matters most. This confusion has produced a loss of meaning which threatens every aspect of society, particularly by undermining the zest for life among the young, where it should be strongest. Many have no hypothesis or faith by which to live life. Probably basic to this condition is a profound distortion of the conception of the nature of man, manifested especially in much of contemporary art and literature.

2) Man is steadily being dehumanized. Both in thought and action the welfare of man has been moved from the center to the periphery of man's concern. The pervading question has come to be *can* this or that be done, not *should* it be done. The result is a toboggan, out-of-control effect in almost every aspect of life.

3) There is an increasing loss of individual and group restraint and self-control. This loss moves man away from the essences of the civilized life and toward barbarism. This attitude tends to cut man loose from his heritage.

4) There is a movement away from belief in gradual progress based upon intelligence, mutual good will, and persistent hard work to all-or-none, easy, quick solutions and slogans that oversimplify problems and nourish

frustration and disillusionment. Modern man does not understand or have faith in *process.*

5) There is a radical fragmentation of life characterized by a strong tendency to set parts of society against one another: youth against age, poor against the more affluent, students against teachers, race against race, etc.

6) Although the modern world is in a sense dangerous and full of risks and in some senses violent beyond any previous age, the excitement provided is gross, confused, and unaccompanied by deep purpose. Man sorely needs excitement to be his best—not the horrible, demoralizing excitement of television shows, cheap writing, or mechanized war, not the deadening excitement of business or educational competition. He desperately needs the wholesome, creative, inspiring excitement of festivals, games, and worship, limited and centered in deep purpose.

These then are a few thoughts on the intriguing topic of the education of the whole man. They are tentative thoughts put forth in the midst of a never-ending search for truth and wisdom about that most important of all problems, what is the best education for man?

The Interpersonal Relationship in the Facilitation of Learning

Though it may be considered unseemly for me to say so, I like this chapter very much, because it expresses some of the deepest convictions I hold regarding those who work in the educational field. The essence of it was first presented as a lecture at Harvard University, but that essence has been revised and enlarged for this book.

I wish to begin this chapter with a statement which may seem surprising to some and perhaps offensive to others. It is simply this: Teaching, in my estimation, is a vastly over-rated function.

Having made such a statement, I scurry to the dictionary to see if I really mean what I say. Teaching means "to instruct." Personally I am not much interested in instructing another in what he should know or think. "To impart knowledge or skill." My reaction is, why not be more efficient, using a book or programmed learning? "To make to know." Here my hackles rise. I have no wish to *make* anyone know something. "To show, guide, direct." As I see it, too many people have been shown, guided, directed. So I come to the conclusion that I *do* mean what I said. Teaching is, for me, a relatively unimportant and vastly overvalued activity.

But there is more in my attitude than this. I have a negative reaction to teaching. Why? I think it is because it raises all the wrong questions. As soon as we focus on teaching the question arises, what shall we teach? What, from our superior vantage point, does the other person need to know? I wonder if, in this modern world, we are justified in the presumption that we are wise about the future and the young are foolish. Are we *really* sure as to what they should know? Then there is the ridiculous question of coverage. What shall the course cover? This notion of coverage is based on

From *Freedom to Learn* (Columbus, Ohio: Charles E. Merrill Publishing Co., 1969), pp. 103–15. Reprinted by permission.

the assumption that what is taught is what is learned; what is presented is what is assimilated. I know of no assumption so obviously untrue. One does not need research to provide evidence that this is false. One needs only to talk with a few students.

But I ask myself, "Am I so prejudiced against teaching that I find no situation in which it is worthwhile?" I immediately think of my experiences in Australia, not so long ago. I became much interested in the Australian aborigine. Here is a group which for more than 20,000 years has managed to live and exist in a desolate environment in which modern man would perish within a few days. The secret of the aborigine's survival has been teaching. He has passed on to the young every shred of knowledge about how to find water, about how to track game, about how to kill the kangaroo, about how to find his way through the trackless desert. Such knowledge is conveyed to the young as being *the* way to behave, and any innovation is frowned upon. It is clear that teaching has provided him the way to survive in a hostile and relatively unchanging environment.

Now I am closer to the nub of the question which excites me. Teaching and the imparting of knowledge make sense in an unchanging environment. This is why it has been an unquestioned function for centuries. But if there is one truth about modern man, it is that he lives in an environment which is *continually changing.* The one thing I can be sure of is that the physics which is taught to the present day student will be outdated in a decade. The teaching in psychology will certainly be out of date in 20 years. The so-called "facts of history" depend very largely upon the current mood and temper of the culture. Chemistry, biology, genetics, sociology, are in such flux that a firm statement made today will almost certainly be modified by the time the student gets around to using the knowledge.

We are, in my view, faced with an entirely new situation in education where the goal of education, if we are to survive, is the *facilitation of change and learning.* The only man who is educated is the man who has learned how to learn; the man who has learned how to adapt and change; the man who has realized that no knowledge is secure, that only the process of *seeking* knowledge gives a basis for security. Changingness, a reliance on *process* rather than upon static knowledge, is the only thing that makes any sense as a goal for education in the modern world.

So now with some relief I turn to an activity, a purpose, which really warms me—the facilitation of learning. When I have been able to transform a group—and here I mean all the members of a group, myself included— into a community of *learners,* then the excitement has been almost beyond belief. To free curiosity; to permit individuals to go charging off in new directions dictated by their own interests; to unleash the sense of inquiry; to open everything to questioning and exploration; to recognize that every- thing is in process of change—here is an experience I can never forget. I cannot always achieve it in groups with which I am associated but when it is partially or largely achieved then it becomes a never-to-be-forgotten group experience. Out of such a context arise true students, real learners, creative scientists and scholars and practitioners, the kind of individuals who can live in a delicate but ever-changing balance between what is presently known and the flowing, moving, altering problems and facts of the future.

Here then is a goal to which I can give myself wholeheartedly. I see *the facilitation of learning* as the *aim* of education, the way in which we might develop the learning man, the way in which we can learn to live as individuals in process. I see the facilitation of learning as the function which may hold constructive, tentative, changing, *process* answers to some of the deepest perplexities which beset man today.

But do we know how to achieve this new goal in education, or is it a will-o'-the-wisp which sometimes occurs, sometimes fails to occur, and thus offers little real hope? My answer is that we possess a very considerable knowledge of the conditions which encourage self-initiated, significant, experiential, "gut-level" learning by the whole person. We do not frequently see these conditions put into effect because they mean a real revolution in our approach to education and revolutions are not for the timid. But we do . . . find examples of this revolution in action.

We know—and I will briefly describe some of the evidence—that the initiation of such learning rests not upon the teaching skills of the leader, not upon his scholarly knowledge of the field, not upon his curricular planning, not upon his use of audiovisual aids, not upon the programmed learning he utilizes, not upon his lectures and presentations, not upon an abundance of books, though each of these might at one time or another be utilized as an important resource. No, the facilitation of significant learning rests upon certain attitudinal qualities which exist in the personal *relationship* between the facilitator and the learner.

We came upon such findings first in the field of psychotherapy, but increasingly there is evidence which shows that these findings apply in the classroom as well. We find it easier to think that the intensive relationship between therapist and client might possess these qualities, but we are also finding that they *may* exist in the countless interpersonal interactions (as many as 1,000 per day, as Jackson[1] has shown) between the teacher and her pupils.

Qualities which Facilitate Learning

What are these qualities, these attitudes, which facilitate learning? Let me describe them very briefly, drawing illustrations from the teaching field.

Realness in the Facilitator of Learning

Perhaps the most basic of these essential attitudes is realness or genuineness. When the facilitator is a real person, being what he is, entering into a relationship with the learner without presenting a front or a façade, he is much more likely to be effective. This means that the feelings which he is experiencing are available to him, available to his awareness, that he is able to live these feelings, be them, and able to communicate them if appropriate. It means that he comes into a direct personal encounter with the learner, meeting him on a person-to-person basis. It means that he is *being* himself, not denying himself.

Seen from this point of view it is suggested that the teacher can be a real person in his relationship with his students. He can be enthusiastic, he can be bored, he can be interested in students, he can be angry, he can be sensitive and sympathetic. Because he accepts these feelings as his own he has no need to impose them on his students. He can like or dislike a student product without implying that it is objectively good or bad or that the student is good or bad. He is simply expressing a feeling for the product, a feeling which exists within himself. Thus, he is a person to his students, not a faceless embodiment of a curricular requirement nor a sterile tube through which knowledge is passed from one generation to the next.

It is obvious that this attitudinal set, found to be effective in psychotherapy, is sharply in contrast with the tendency of most teachers to show themselves to their pupils simply as roles. It is quite customary for teachers rather consciously to put on the mask, the role, the façade, of being a teacher, and to wear this façade all day removing it only when they have left the school at night.

But not all teachers are like this. Take Sylvia Ashton-Warner, who took resistant, supposedly slow-learning primary school Maori children in New Zealand, and let them develop their own reading vocabulary. Each child could request one word—whatever word he wished—each day, and she would print it on a card and give it to him. "Kiss," "ghost," "bomb," "tiger," "fight," "love," "daddy"—these are samples. Soon they were building sentences, which they could also keep. "He'll get a licking." "Pussy's frightened." The children simply never forgot these self-initiated learnings. But it is not my purpose to tell you of her methods. I want instead to give you a glimpse of her attitude, of the passionate realness which must have been as evident to her tiny pupils as to her readers. An editor asked her some questions and she responded: "A few cool facts you asked me for . . . I don't know that there's a cool fact in me, or anything else cool for that matter, on this particular subject. I've got only hot long facts on the matter of Creative Teaching, scorching both the page and me."[2]

Here is no sterile façade. Here is a vital *person,* with convictions, with feelings. It is her transparent realness which was, I am sure, one of the elements that made her an exciting facilitator of learning. She doesn't fit into some neat educational formula. She *is,* and students grow by being in contact with someone who really and openly *is.*

Take another very different person, Barbara Shiel, whose exciting work in facilitating learning in sixth graders has been described. . . . She gave her pupils a great deal of responsible freedom, and I will mention some of the reactions of her students later. But here is an example of the way she shared herself with her pupils—not just sharing feelings of sweetness and light, but anger and frustration. She had made art materials freely available, and students often used these in creative ways, but the room frequently looked like a picture of chaos. Here is her report of her feelings and what she did with them.

> I find it maddening to live with the mess—with a capital M! No one seems to care except me. Finally, one day I told the children . . . that I am a neat, orderly person by nature and that the mess was driving me to distraction. Did they have a solution? It was suggested there were some volunteers who could clean up . . . I said it didn't seem fair to me to have the same people clean up all the time for others—but it would solve it for me. "Well, some people like to clean," they replied. So that's the way it is.[3]

I hope this example puts some lively meaning into the phrases I used earlier, that the facilitator "is able to live these feelings, be them, and able to communicate them if appropriate." I have chosen an example of negative feelings, because I think it is more difficult for most of us to visualize what this would mean. In this instance, Miss Shiel is taking the risk of being transparent in her angry frustrations about the mess. And what happens? The same thing which, in my experience, nearly always happens. These young people accept and respect her feelings, take them into account, and work out a novel solution which none of us, I believe, would have suggested. Miss Shiel wisely comments, "I used to get upset and feel guilty when I became angry. I finally realized the children could accept *my* feelings too. And it is important for them to know when they've 'pushed me.' I have my limits, too."[4]

Just to show that positive feelings, when they are real, are equally effective, let me quote briefly a college student's reaction, in a different course:

> . . . Your sense of humor in the class was cheering; we all felt relaxed because you showed us your human self, not a mechanical teacher image. I feel as if I have more understanding and faith in my teachers now . . . I feel closer to the students too. . . .

Another says:

> ... You conducted the class on a personal level and therefore in my mind I was able to formulate a picture of you as a person and not as merely a walking textbook.

Another student in the same course:

> ... It wasn't as if there was a teacher in the class, but rather someone whom we could trust and identify as a "sharer." You were so perceptive and sensitive to our thoughts, and this made it all the more "authentic" for me. It was an "authentic" *experience,* not just a class.[5]

I trust I am making it clear that to be real is not always easy, nor is it achieved all at once, but it is basic to the person who wants to become that revolutionary individual, a facilitator of learning.

Prizing, Acceptance, Trust

There is another attitude which stands out in those who are successful in facilitating learning. I have observed this attitude. I have experienced it. Yet, it is hard to know what term to put to it so I shall use several. I think of it as prizing the learner, prizing his feelings, his opinions, his person. It is a caring for the learner, but a non-possessive caring. It is an acceptance of this other individual as a separate person, having worth in his own right. It is a basic trust—a belief that this other person is somehow fundamentally trustworthy. Whether we call it prizing, acceptance, trust, or by some other term, it shows up in a variety of observable ways. The facilitator who has a considerable degree of this attitude can be fully acceptant of the fear and hesitation of the student as he approaches a new problem as well as acceptant of the pupil's satisfaction in achievement. Such a teacher can accept the student's occasional apathy, his erratic desires to explore by-roads of knowledge, as well as his disciplined efforts to achieve major goals. He can accept personal feelings which both disturb and promote learning—rivalry with a sibling, hatred of authority, concern about personal adequacy. What we are describing is a prizing of the learner as an imperfect human being with many feelings, many potentialities. The facilitator's prizing or acceptance of the learner is an operational expression of his essential confidence and trust in the capacity of the human organism.

I would like to give some examples of this attitude from the classroom situation. Here any teacher statements would be properly suspect, since many of us would like to feel we hold such attitudes, and might have a biased perception of our qualities. But let me indicate how this attitude of prizing, of accepting, of trusting, appears to the student who is fortunate enough to experience it.

Here is a statement from a college student in a class with Dr. Morey Appell:

> Your way of being with us is a revelation to me. In your class I feel important, mature, and capable of doing things on my own. I want to think for myself and this need cannot be accomplished through textbooks and lectures alone, but through living. I think you see me as a person with real feelings and needs, an individual. What I say and do are significant expressions from me, and you recognize this.[6]

One of Miss Shiel's sixth graders expresses much more briefly her misspelled appreciation of this attitude: "You are a wounderful teacher period!!!"

College students in a class with Dr. Patricia Bull describe not only these prizing, trusting attitudes, but the effect these have had on their other interactions.

> ... I feel that I can say things to you that I can't say to other professors. ... Never before have I been so aware of the other students or their personalities. I have never had so much interaction in a college classroom with my classmates. The climate of the classroom has had a very profound effect on me ... the free atmosphere for discussion affected me ... the general atmosphere of a particular session affected me. There have been many times when I have carried the discussion out of the class with me and thought about it for a long time.

> ... I still feel close to you, as though there were some tacit understanding between us, almost a conspiracy. This adds to the in-class participation on my part because I feel that at least one person in the group will react, even when I am not sure of the others. It does not matter really whether your reaction is positive or negative, it just *IS*. Thank you.

> ... I appreciate the respect and concern you have for others, including myself. ... As a result of my experience in class, plus the influence of my readings, I sincerely believe that the student-centered teaching method does provide an ideal framework for learning; not just for the accumulation of facts, but more important, for learning about ourselves in relation to others. ... When I think back to my shallow awareness in September compared to the depth of my insights now, I know that this course has offered me a learning experience of great value which I couldn't have acquired in any other way.

> ... Very few teachers would attempt this method because they would feel that they would lose the students' respect. On the contrary. You gained our respect, through your ability to speak to us on our level, instead of ten miles above us. With the complete lack of communication we see in this school, it was a wonderful experience to see people listening to each other and really communicating on an adult, intelligent level. More classes should afford us this experience.[7]

As you might expect, college students are often suspicious that these seeming attitudes are phony. One of Dr. Bull's students writes:

> . . . Rather than observe my classmates for the first few weeks, I concentrated my observations on you, Dr. Bull. I tried to figure out your motivations and purposes. I was convinced that you were a hypocrite. . . . I did change my opinion, however. You are not a hypocrite, by any means. . . . I do wish the course could continue. "Let each become all he is capable of being." . . .[8]

I am sure these examples are more than enough to show that the facilitator who cares, who prizes, who trusts the learner, creates a climate for learning so different from the ordinary classroom that any resemblance is "purely coincidental."

Empathic Understanding

A further element which establishes a climate for self-initiated, experiential learning is empathic understanding. When the teacher has the ability to understand the student's reactions from the inside, has a sensitive awareness of the way the process of education and learning seems *to the student,* then again the likelihood of significant learning is increased.

This kind of understanding is sharply different from the usual evaluative understanding, which follows the pattern of, "I understand what is wrong with you." When there is a sensitive empathy, however, the reaction in the learner follows something of this pattern, "At last someone understands how it feels and seems to be *me* without wanting to analyze me or judge me. Now I can blossom and grow and learn."

This attitude of standing in the other's shoes, of viewing the world through the student's eyes, is almost unheard of in the classroom. One could listen to thousands of ordinary classroom interactions without coming across one instance of clearly communicated, sensitively accurate, empathic understanding. But it has a tremendously releasing effect when it occurs.

Let me take an illustration from Virginia Axline, dealing with a second grade boy. Jay, age 7, has been aggressive, a trouble maker, slow of speech and learning. Because of his "cussing" he was taken to the principal, who paddled him, unknown to Miss Axline. During a free work period, he fashioned a man of clay, very carefully, down to a hat and a handkerchief in his pocket. "Who is that?" asked Miss Axline. "Dunno," replied Jay. "Maybe it is the principal. He has a handkerchief in his pocket like that." Jay glared at the clay figure. "Yes," he said. Then he began to tear the head off and looked up and smiled. Miss Axline said, "You sometimes feel like twisting his head off, don't you? You get so mad at him." Jay tore off one arm, another, then beat the figure to a pulp with his fists. Another boy, with the perception of the young, explained, "Jay is mad at Mr. X because he licked him this noon." "Then you must feel lots better now," Miss Axline commented. Jay grinned and began to rebuild Mr. X.[9]

The other examples I have cited also indicate how deeply appreciative students feel when they are simply *understood*—not evaluated, not judged, simply understood from their *own* point of view, not the teacher's. If any teacher set himself the task of endeavoring to make one non-evaluative, acceptant, empathic response per day to a student's demonstrated or verbalized feeling, I believe he would discover the potency of this currently almost non-existent kind of understanding.

What are the Bases of Facilitative Attitudes?

A "Puzzlement"

It is natural that we do not always have the attitudes I have been describing. Some teachers raise the question, "But what if I am *not* feeling empathic, do *not,* at this moment, prize or accept or like my students. What then?" My response is that realness is the most important of the attitudes mentioned, and it is not accidental that this attitude was described first. So if one has little understanding of the student's inner world, and a dislike for his students or their behavior, it is almost certainly more constructive to be *real* than to be pseudo-empathic, or to put on a façade of caring.

But this is not nearly as simple as it sounds. To be genuine, or honest, or congruent, or real, means to be this way about *oneself.* I cannot be real about another, because I do not *know* what is real for him. I can only tell —if I wish to be truly honest—what is going on in me.

Let me take an example. Early in this chapter I reported Miss Shiel's feelings about the "mess" created by the art work. Essentially she said, "I find it maddening to live with the mess! I'm neat and orderly and it is driving me to distraction." But suppose her feelings had come out somewhat differently, in the disguised way which is much more common in classrooms at all levels. She might have said, "You are the messiest children I've ever seen! You don't care about tidiness or cleanliness. You are just terrible!" This is most definitely *not* an example of genuineness or realness, in the sense in which I am using these terms. There is a profound distinction between the two statements which I should like to spell out.

In the second statement she is telling nothing of herself, sharing none of her feelings. Doubtless the children will *sense* that she is angry, but because children are perceptively shrewd they may be uncertain as to whether she is angry at them, or has just come from an argument with the principal. It has none of the honesty of the first statement in which she tells of her *own* upsetness, or her *own* feeling of being driven to distraction.

Another aspect of the second statement is that it is all made up of judgments or evaluations, and like most judgments, they are all arguable. Are these children messy, or are they simply excited and involved in what they are doing? Are they *all* messy, or are some as disturbed by the chaos as she? Do they care nothing about tidiness, or is it simply that they don't care about it every day? If a group of visitors were coming would their attitude be different? Are they terrible, or simply children? I trust it is evident that when we make judgments they are almost never fully accurate, and hence cause resentment and anger as well as guilt and apprehension. Had she used the second statement the response of the class would have been entirely different.

I am going to some lengths to clarify this point because I have found from experience that to stress the value of being real, of *being* one's feelings, is taken by some as a license to pass judgments on others, to project on others all the feelings which one should be "owning." Nothing could be further from my meaning.

Actually the achievement of realness is most difficult, and even when one wishes to be truly genuine, it occurs but rarely. Certainly it is not simply a matter of the *words* used, and if one is feeling judgmental the use of a verbal formula which sounds like the sharing of feelings will not help. It is just another instance of a façade, of a lack of genuineness. Only slowly can we learn to be truly real. For first of all, one must be close to one's feelings, capable of being aware of them. Then one must be willing to take the risk of sharing them as they are, inside, not disguising them as judgments, or attributing them to other people. This is why I so admire Miss Shiel's sharing of her anger and frustration, without in any way disguising it.

A Trust in the Human Organism

It would be most unlikely that one could hold the three attitudes I have described, or could commit himself to being a facilitator of learning, unless he has come to have a profound trust in the human organism and its potentialities. If I distrust the human being then I *must* cram him with information of my own choosing, lest he go his own mistaken way. But if I trust the capacity of the human individual for developing his own potentiality, then I can provide him with many opportunities and permit him to choose his own way and his own direction in his learning.

It is clear, I believe, that the three teachers whose work was described in the preceding chapters rely basically upon the tendency toward fulfilment, toward actualization, in their students. They are basing their work on the hypothesis that students who are in real contact with problems which are relevant to them wish to learn, want to grow, seek to discover, endeavor to master, desire to create, move toward self-discipline. The teacher is attempting to develop a quality of climate in the classroom, and a quality of personal relationship with his students, which will permit these natural tendencies to come to their fruition.

Living the Uncertainty of Discovery

I believe it should be said that this basically confident view of man, and the attitudes toward students which I have described, do not appear suddenly, in some miraculous manner, in the facilitator of learning. Instead, they come about through taking risks, through *acting* an tentative hypotheses. This is most obvious in . . . Miss Shiel's work, where, acting on hypotheses of which she is unsure, risking herself uncertainly in new ways of relating to her students, she finds these new views confirmed by what happens in her class. I am sure [others] went through the same type of uncertainty. As for me, I can only state that I started my career with the firm view that individuals must be manipulated for their own good; I only came to the attitudes I have described, and the trust in the individual which is implicit in them, because I found that these attitudes were so much more potent in producing learning and constructive change. Hence, I believe that it is only by risking himself in these new ways that the teacher can *discover,* for himself, whether or not they are effective, whether or not they are for him.

I will then draw a conclusion, based on the experiences of the several facilitators and their students which have been included up to this point. When a facilitator creates, even to a modest degree, a classroom climate characterized by all that he can achieve of realness, prizing, and empathy; when he trusts the constructive tendency of the individual and the group; then he discovers that he has inaugurated an educational revolution. Learning of a different quality, proceeding at a different pace, with a greater degree of pervasiveness, occurs. Feelings—positive, negative, confused— become a part of the classroom experience. Learning becomes life, and a very vital life at that. The student is on his way, sometimes excitedly, sometimes reluctantly, to becoming a learning, changing, being.

NOTES

[1]P. W. Jackson, "The Student's World." (Unpublished ms., University of Chicago, 1966).
[2]Sylvia Ashton-Warner, *Teacher.* (New York: Simon and Schuster, Inc., 1963), p. 26.
[3]Barbara J. Shiel, "Evaluation: A Self-Directed Curriculum." (Unpublished ms., 1966).
[4]*Ibid.*
[5]Patricia Bull, "Student Reactions, Fall, 1965." (Unpublished ms., State University College, Courtland, New York, 1966).
[6]M. L. Appell, "Selected Student Reactions to Student-Centered Courses." (Unpublished ms., State University of Indiana, Terre Haute, Indiana, 1959).
[7]Bull, *op. cit.*
[8]*Ibid.*
[9]Virginia M. Axline, "Morale on the School Front," *Journal of Educational Research,* 1944, pp. 521–33.

STEPHEN C. MARGARITIS

In Learning, Begin Not
Where You Expect to End

Our middle-class-oriented school system has not succeeded in preparing all children to live useful and happy lives. We probably know how to educate those whose cultural background matches that of the school, and perhaps a few others who, for some good reason, come to school highly motivated. We are beginning to know how to educate children from different cultural backgrounds under the pressure of their own legitimate demands.

But who are the youngsters telling us that our ways of teaching do not match their ways of learning? They are not newcomers, nor are they strangers. For many years they have attended our schools; the only difference is that they now come in greater numbers and they openly raise disturbing questions.

Here I do not intend to apologize for my teaching flaws and those of my colleagues (although I regret them profoundly), or to suggest any untried new ideas for the elimination of all educational ills. I will, however, share with you some personal thoughts and some feelings which have come to me over the years through some strange process of "chronic educational osmosis."

Lack of sensitivity and limited wisdom on the part of educators has resulted in long years of abuse and ineffectiveness. Enamoured of middle class ideologies, few teachers, if any, recognize that economic deprivation and cultural difference generate serious handicaps to learning. Beginning where they expect to end, teachers seldom make the effort to relate what is being taught to what the child already knows and needs to know. This failure is understandable. Very few people can rise above the level of role expectations set by the system in which they operate. Notwithstanding their initial station in life, most teachers aspire to middle class status and behave accordingly once they become professionals.

This article was written especially for this volume.

24

Their many years of schooling condition teachers to become subject-oriented. And it is only recently that the emphasis seems to be shifting from subject to student—first to groups and, more recently, to individuals. Teachers are discovering that people learn in many different ways, and that a multicultural approach seems more desirable than a monocultural approach. Let's face it—children do not share a single way of life! Their cultures have different sets of experience and different maps of reality. The power of cultural habit is enormous, and it should not be ignored. Children lose heart and become either apathetic or hostile in a world that has no tolerance, no understanding, and no compassion for them. Rather than make the student conform to the school system, we should make learning experiences relevant to the needs of the student and build from there.

The beginning of learning for any student is rooted in his existing situation. With some degree of sensitivity and a minimum of educational statesmanship, teachers should be able to diagnose the needs of their students and their levels of performance before any real learning experience is provided. One of the richest resources for learning is the learner himself. Learning is highly unique and individual; it is the kind of experience which occurs inside the learner, and ideally is directed by the learner himself.

The basic needs of food, clothing, health, and affection must be satisfied if school experiences are to have real meaning to a child. If these needs are not met by the family, society and the school must meet them in ways that allow the child to preserve his dignity. Every effort should be made to promote cultural pride. Our society needs all the happy, friendly, cooperative, free and independent people it can get. If a child is hurting, his whole system is hurting, and his learning activities will be shallow and insignificant. If he feels good about himself, he will feel good about the system and learn well. Many students drift through school because they have to be there; they are unmotivated and apathetic.

It is vitally important to understand the child's values and behavior and realistically appraise his personality. Traditional methods should be set aside in favor of activities more meaningful to each student. Assignments should be individualized as much as possible and should be related to the real life style of the student. The child who comes from a poor environment needs stimulation through which he may explore and discover himself and his world on his own terms. The fact is that outside the school the child is frequently given little real opportunity. Commonly he discovers only the cruelties of life. Remember, knowledge for knowledge's sake is insignificant; knowledge which will provide direction and purpose for life is of utmost importance. A school should be a place in which children learn what they most want to learn. Nothing is learned unless a person has the desire to do so. Meaningful learning takes place when motivation springs from within the learner and when learning is a personal experience. Children with active imaginations can accomplish all sorts of monumental things. In this respect teachers can stimulate them to unlock some of their hidden potential.

A schoolroom resembles a miniature world where emotionally fragile human beings come with different interests, different abilities, and unique personalities all their own. People need to relate to others; loneliness is frost to a child's heart. We should get the students' vibrations and allow them to receive ours. We should give them affection and tenderness. For a teacher to deny affection and understanding is to deny a child respect and an education. We should make them feel wanted and secure, truly care about them, be sensitive to their needs, invite them to express their feelings and thoughts, and listen to them.

There is a popular old misconception that teachers should talk and students should listen. Being more mature and knowledgeable than their students, teachers feel that students should do what is expected of them. But teachers, too, need to engage in the art of listening. Through listening comes understanding and communication, and the door can open to another great art of social living or meaningful human existence—the art of sharing: sharing of thoughts, sharing of feelings, sharing of experiences.

Teachers must possess a special ability to relate genuinely to children since communication is the key to cooperation. Too many students worry about the right answer when they should concentrate on expressing themselves in creative ways. Fear often causes them to go to any extent to find acceptable answers and please their teachers instead of taking the risk of exploring new frontiers, following their natural curiosity. If we can remember that failure is not a sin but a valuable learning instrument, then our students will be more likely to grow from their mistakes instead of shrinking from them. A thoughtful person is more likely to express his thoughtfulness if he is exposed to experiences that place a premium upon questions rather than answers. We should present material in interesting and refreshing ways; we cannot afford to stand still in education; we must make waves.

Teachers must not refuse to spend extra time with students. It is vitally important that the teacher-pupil ratio be reduced to functional levels. In the meantime, teachers should try to make the best use of their time, to spread themselves thinly enough to cover most students and deeply enough to help them. With parental cooperation and involvement teachers can better help foster the aspirations of children. This kind of help is especially needed since culturally different children often have to relate to instructions given in a different dialect.

We usually do things for the convenience of the school. Teachers and administrators must reevaluate their operations and become pace-setters of a truly significant environment. A child's creative flow can be stifled and even halted entirely through negative reinforcement. We should not chain their imaginations. Children are curious; let us capitalize on that.

Being treated as an individual and watching others receiving the same treatment, the child will grow to learn self-discipline and help promote the best learning atmosphere. One of the most counterproductive hang-ups we have in the profession is the tendency to classify and label people. We must master the difficult task of maintaining the student's unique individuality, his personal identity, and at the same time developing his social identity and ability to participate in a group.

Fear of failure must be eliminated. The best approach is to minimize failures and maximize successes. It doesn't take a child long to experience defeat and discouragement and to internalize a sense of frustration, inadequacy, and inferiority. If we teach children to fail, they will learn to fail; but if we expect success, we will get success. In a number of ways schools inhibit the process of self-development. A low personal opinion results in low academic achievement. Teachers must encourage students to take risks in exploring, thus becoming more responsible for their actions. They will be learning in their own way and they will be enjoying it.

To a Young Teacher

My dear:

Far too good an opportunity to overlook, replying to you between the covers of a book. Thank you very much for your letters. I like articulate people who know what they think and how to say it. You may even get as far as New Zealand some day to say in person what you think, over coffee or in the sun. Some Americans see the Pacific as no more than a paddling pool when it comes to getting where they want to; just pick up their skirts and wade across.

You are young and I like young company, from the cradle up. I've liked your letters over the years since I wrote *Spinster* and *Teacher*. You remind me how to listen again, an art overlooked when I was young. We all talk at once when we are young, isn't that so? We all know everything about anything at all . . . we are certain of it! Everything except correction. For one thing, talking flat out, we don't hear anyway, and for another we haven't got time to hear and if we should hear accidentally we don't agree with a word. Which from your end may sound pretty bad but from my end looks irresistible.

An exclusive art, listening . . . if I may digress so early in a letter. Until my late thirties I don't think it occurred to me to listen to anyone much and then only because I had to. Working on the Key Vocabulary I found that unless I listened, heard clearly, understood and felt what the children were saying I couldn't do what I wanted, whereas I'm a great one to do what I want if possible, even more so when impossible. An expensive exercise that, learning to listen, but worth it: expensive in patience but worth it in interest. Since then I've listened to everyone within earshot, to the five small

From *MYSELF* (New York: Simon and Schuster, Inc., 1967), pp. 7–13. Reprinted by permission of Monica McCall–International Famous Agency. Copyright © 1967 by Sylvia Ashton-Warner.

children in this house including the new baby who says a lot and often. Without that discipline of listening to children during the Key Vocabulary I could have been deaf still; might not have been answering your letters but talking to myself.

Which brings me to the astonishing thing in your letters: you appear to have heard what I said. Being the reason I send this old manuscript along because *I* heard what *you* said. Wistful business, isn't it? this casual dialogue between mutually unintelligible generations like a separated seminar; letters jetting over continents and crossing oceans and far forgotten years.

I've been surprised at the humility in your letters. Not that humility does not make an excellent foundation on which to build a philosophy, a sound pad from which to blast off into unknown spaces; to equip yourselves for Operation Life humility could be the best storehouse of all. But my reaction has been that there could be more pride about, not only as an ambassador of your profession but in simply representing youth. "The widespread pride of man," from Whitman.

Of course I might be wrong. Pride might be there all the time but blurred by awe of me, yet I doubt if I'm awe material. I'm quite tame—at least I am now. I'm not saying I haven't picked up a few things that you have not been able to, being ahead of you along the road, but that doesn't make me awesome. If you saw me in the garden in my old clothes . . . if you saw me at my table in something loose, my writing table or if you heard me crooning to this new baby, my daughter's, you'd forget about the awe. Actually I find I know less as I go along this part of the track, and that others know much more. In fact there are many senior teachers in other countries as well as in my own, from New York to Bangkok, London to Buenos Aires, to the west coast of Africa, who are better than I ever was, and it will do you good, at least clean up the awe, to read just what I was like when young—the original of *Teacher*. Not marvelous at all . . . frightful!

In this manuscript I admit much I don't like admitting, that I was anything but an example. Not a good teacher, not much of a person and a dead loss as a listener. I'm even risking my reputation by recording that I was not above loving with passion in forbidden directions, in several places at once, though honorably within the vows of marriage: on paper it looks selfish, but love was my big trouble when I was young—still is, to be frank; I should say love to me is still big but no longer trouble. My need of and dependence on it. I couldn't breathe without love in the air. I'd choke. I ceased to exist when not in love. The radiance within blotted out so that nothing would happen inside, nothing exploded into action. I can quite truthfully say that I never lifted a hand unless *for* someone: never took up a brush or a pen, a sheet of music or a spade, never pursued a thought without the motivation of trying to make someone love me.

But the hardest of all to expose to you is the violence that was in my character ever lapping and threatening near the surface, showing up in my nightmares. I could manufacture multitudes of magnificent and convincing excuses but excuses are boring, take too much time and use up too much paper.

For all that, I'm sending it along to—what I'm sending it for really is to —let me see . . . I'd like to say it is wholly a manner of answering all you have written to me, not from the wisdom of seniority which is not quite fair but from the stance of youth, putting you and me for once on the same age level, supplying a medium of comparison that is fair between us. Actually, I doubt that these revelations will help you as a teacher—nothing new professionally in them but insofar as there is inspiration from talking things over youth to youth confessing our mad mistakes, pontifically advising each other, lecturing each other on what we think and what the other should do, you may be supported as a young person possibly, as I would have been at that time. That's what I'd like to say and get away with it, but I suspect that is not the whole reason, nor the main one. The real reason lies else-where: as in everything I do, even in this, I want to win your indulgence and a smile for that person over twenty years ago. Not for the middle-aged me that I am but for that young person. That's what she wanted so terribly then. It's not too late.

Not that I assume for one moment that you are as confused as I was then, personally or professionally, but whatever our differences, however opposed our ways of seeing things, of going about doing a thing, there do remain codes in youth by which we understand each other, and it is in this area of the common hells and heavens of young people living it out, of young people trying to chart a course through the arduous terrain ahead; through the gullies, over the mountains and across the bleak plateaus, noting the voluptuous error of side-tracking glades and dells . . . it is on this blindfold track of blindfold decisions that it will give you something, this written memory, even if that something is only my own young company. At least you will know the language of the place.

I did however just in time get hold of one truth on my own when trying to plot my route: that not just part of us becomes a teacher. It engages the whole self—the woman or man, wife or husband, mother or father, the lover, scholar or artist in you as well as the teacher earning money so that a worthwhile teacher is one of the blooms from the worthwhile person, even though in my twenties and thirties I could neither isolate the different facets of the person nor balance them. They overlapped, merged and affected each other, infected each other often, with teaching itself the sounding board. If I was unhappy the schoolroom paid, if happy the schoolroom won. If I thought my husband wasn't pleased with me I didn't teach in tune but if he had kissed me before school in the morning I did teach in tune. When my own children were well the class was well but if one was sick I'd leave and go home. If I'd had time for early morning study I'd understand what I was doing but if I hadn't I wouldn't. Even what a lover said yesterday qualified the tone of the room and my finding out of all this was what sent me so deeply into study of myself and of the whole human self in order to try to become, not specifically a worthwhile teacher, but a worthwhile person first.

All that study I did on my own for years in isolation, that fierce attack on books. From those distant pages my youth thrusts questions: Do you study much? Do you passionately examine yourself, ruthlessly analyze yourself, do you agonize as I did between feeling and reason? Do you know the need to sit in silence over a thing, to follow a line of thought to a firm conclusion, then write down that conclusion? Do you retreat into solitude and consult your instinct when logic leaves you high and dry? Are you as confused as I was then, are you as bad as I was, as selfish, as foolish? I'd feel better about it if you are.

Do you too aim to be a worthwhile person or only a worthwhile teacher? How do you see teaching—as a source of income or as a work of global status? I wonder if you'll think, when you read through this, that I was moving in the right direction, if indeed I moved at all, or in the wrong direction—if you will think as I did then that war and peace might . . . only might . . . be in our hands, conceived in the early years of children, the classroom, the incubator. Or will you think I was wrong?

So here is this long letter of over two hundred pages in answer to all of yours. As a book it is unsound artistically on account of the balance disturbed by loving. Saul runs away with this story of a school; I know it and I could rectify it but I'll leave it because that's how it *was.* I could prune the references to him, in the interests of art, but it would no longer be how it was, for just as Saul unbalances this book so did my love for him unbalance my life when teaching on the River as possibly . . . even probably . . . a love in your own life at this moment disturbs your teaching. Besides, his inclusion is justified; our upsetting love enriched me as a person and therefore enriched the teacher.

Are you going to "go off" her—that young person—on account of her behavior: demanding from one man, running to the other? Please do not. Observe, yes, that she appears on paper selfish and willful, but understand and be faithful to her, allow for her vagaries, for if you in your youth do not, who will? Who knows—observed from the outside, confessed on paper, you may be as bad yourself? But Saul remains a gamble.

At my table looking out the windows I wonder what to say to you . . . to a young teacher. Across the spring garden, above the cineraria, through the trunks of the towering trees; over the silk water of the inner harbor I see the ships' entrance, beyond which is the tall Pacific and beyond that, your country. Only to find I have no advice.

I look back on fifty years, you look forward on fifty years. This world is yours, not mine. It was mine when I was young and I strongly knew it. True, there's a war on now but there was one on then; the world still belongs to you. For ever the world belongs to youth. Do you also strongly know it?

From fifty I have no advice. But from thirty I have! In the splendid authority of youth to youth I quote from those blurring pages, written in fierce swift pencil-passion: "You must be true to yourself. Strong enough to be true to yourself. Brave enough, to be strong enough, to be true to yourself. Wise enough, to be brave enough, to be strong enough, to be true enough to shape yourself from what you actually are. What big words, O my Self: true, strong, brave and wise! But that's how it is, my Self. That's how it must be for you to walk steadily in your own ways, as gracefully as you feel, as upright as you feel, a ridiculous flower on top of your head, a sentimental daisy. For therein lies your individuality, your own authentic signature, the source of others' love for you."

Thank you again for your letters, my dear. I wish you a difficult year.

SYLVIA ASHTON-WARNER

September 29, 1966
New Zealand

HELEN SCHIERBECK

Education = Cultural Politics

For many years the six great gardens of the earth shed few flowers. Seeds would spring forth from the soil, but their plants were stunted and never grew full. Many of nature's children perished prematurely; others lived but their branches were sapped of energy. The sun was being kept from them by a dark cloud which kept the children from absorbing the sun's food and using it to sprout beautiful flowers. Then one day the dark cloud began to weaken and the sun's rays could be seen peeking through and spreading nourishment to the gardens. This was the beginning of a great awakening. The more sun the children of the gardens could absorb, the more they were able to fight the cloud.

The last decade has marked the blossoming of nature's children in many parts of the world. From Asia to Africa to the Americas, people are beginning to grow and leave behind the harmful effects of long years without nourishment from the sun's rays. Many in the United States are involved in this tumultuous social dynamic. Black people, Mexicans, Puerto Ricans, and native Americans are all rising to meet the sun despite years of poverty and repression fostered by the cloud of the dominant society and to assert the dignity and quality of their own cultural heritage. The cloud takes many shapes and forms, but one of its most important forms has been the educational system presented by the one culture to the other. Indeed, education has been the key tool of cultural politics for the dominant society.

As the recent report of the U.S. Senate Subcommittee on Indian Education put it:

From the first contact with the Indian, the school and the classroom have been a primary tool of assimilation. Education was the means whereby we

---

From *Inequality In Education* (Cambridge, Mass.: Harvard Center for Law and Education, February 10, 1971), 7, p. 3. Reprinted by permission of the author and the publisher.

33

emancipated the Indian child from his home, his parents, his extended family, and his cultural heritage. It was in effect an attempt to wash the 'savage habits' in the 'tribal ethic' out of the child's mind and substitute a white middle class value system in its place.

A Ponca Indian testifying before the Subcommittee defined this policy from the standpoint of the Indian—"School is the enemy."

Why "the enemy"? The role of the educational system in American society has been consistently to reduce cultural diversity among various cultural and racial groups, along with its responsibility to transmit cognitive skills. To the immigrants who fled to the United States to escape various forms of persecution in Europe, the new values and cultural identity acquired in the schools were useful. The new Americans were being equipped to move upward in the economic and social structure of the society. Assimilation to them meant a chance to share in the wealth of the country and that's what they came for in the first place. For the American Indian, assimilation meant something entirely different. He had not come to America; America had come to him. Indian values did not stress the acquisition of wealth. Preservation of the values themselves was much more important. The educational system was not viewed as a mechanism for developing upward mobility, but rather as a subtle weapon of subjugation. Education was presented as an either/or proposition: Either learn the ways of the whites or remain poverty stricken. But Indians, and other minorities, are beginning to realize that the alternatives are considerably more varied than they had been presented. If the suffering of the American Indian means anything at all, it means that the Indians value their culture and that it cannot be taken away from them by white decree. But Indians have begun to grasp the idea that they do not have to relinquish their values and heritage in order to be educated. What is clearly no longer desirable is the interference of a white educational system. Once this is realized, education can become the device which will help Indians preserve their communities and live their own lives.

The three basic foundations of values for any group of people are their tradition, their environment, and new ideas and ways of doing things brought from the outside, but the Indian experience has taught him to resent and even to despise the latter two of these modes of value orientation. The environment of the contemporary Indian is one that was forced on him after he was torn from lands he loved and lived in harmony with. New ideas from outside became white ideas devised for the sake of the white man's political and economic advantage, or simply for the sake of establishing the supremacy of the white way. Schools for Indian children have always held classes on rigid schedules; students are encouraged to compete with their peers as the prime form of motivation; native languages are suppressed and

English is the language for teacher and student in all subjects; behavior is controlled through harsh discipline. All of this is foreign to the Indian value system, but it is probably the key to transforming the Indian school into a center for Indian learning. For tradition, the third foundation of values, has remained strong.

Take Care of Your Feet

The following narrative both illustrates and embodies the Indian tradition and the Indian way of making a point:

> Part of the reason our parents say so little is that that's their way. They don't teach like white people; they let their children make their own decisions. The closest they got to formal teaching was to tell a story. Let me give you an example. We had been out picking blueberries one time and while sitting around this guy told us this story. The idea was that he wanted to get us to wash our feet because we had been tramping through the brush all day long. He talked about a warrior who had a really beautiful body. He was very well built and he used to grease himself and take care of his body. One day this warrior was out and he ran into a group of other people he had never seen before. They started to chase him. He had no problem because he was in such good shape. He was fooling around and playing with them because he was such a good runner. He ran over hills and rocks teasing them. But then he ran into another group. The first group gave up the chase, but now he had to run away from this other group, and he was fooling around and doing the same thing with them. All of a sudden he ran into a third group. He ran real hard and all of a sudden he fell. He tried to get up and he couldn't. He spoke to his feet and said, 'What's wrong with you? I'm going to get killed if you don't get up and get going.' They said, 'That's all right. You can comb your hair and grease your body and look after your legs and arms, but you never did anything for us. You never washed us or cleaned us or greased us or nothing.' He promised to take better care of his feet if they would get up and run, and so they did.
>
> This is one of the stories we were told and we went up and washed our feet right away and then we went to bed. Whether this happens among other ethnic groups, I don't know, but this is the kind of learning we have. I will never forget the kinds of things we learned, because to me it all belongs to me. It isn't something that someone says is so: it's mine.
>
> I'd want to go hunting and the guys would know I couldn't get across a stream because it was flooded, but they wouldn't say anything. They'd let me go and I'd tell them that I'd see them later where the rocks are, and they'd say okay, knowing all the time I couldn't get through. But they wouldn't tell me that. They'd let me experience it. And I'm grateful to these people for allowing me to have this kind of exploration/learning situation. Secondly, of course, the fact is that maybe I could've gotten across where they couldn't,

discovered something different, a method that was new. I think this kind of learning situation is one of the really important things that Indians could contribute to the society that we have today, that is, a learning situation for *people,* instead of teaching, or information giving.

While this story of beautiful warrior who ignored his feet is not suited to a unit on personal hygiene in a health curriculum, it is well suited to conveying the same sort of information. Which of us who were educated conventionally remembers any lesson in personal hygiene so vividly and warmly? Almost all Indians have similar memories of similar lessons, but such pedagogy has always been practiced outside the formal school situation.

This is not to suggest that astronomy could be taught through recalling Indian beliefs about the sun, moon, and stars, or that tales of wily tricksters can replace "formal" instruction in any field. It is to suggest, however, that where a culture's view of the role of knowledge differs, it follows that different methods of imparting knowledge may be more suitable.

Of course, Indians are not alone in expressing doubts about the value of American education, with its rigid and dogmatic subject requirements starting in kindergarten and running through college graduation. Many feel that this education produces adults with narrowly based knowledge and contributes immeasurably to the alienation of Americans from all learning. Values are beginning to shift away from the divisive competitiveness that has played such a profound part in the American experience. Fears of mass conformity and technological domination are widespread. Indians have *always* felt this way. Indians have *always* felt that cooperation between people is a more human form of social organization. Indians have *always* wanted community controlled schools. Thus, the coming arrival of *Indian* education can be as important to the rest of the society as it is to the Indians.

Rocky Boy

Let us look at this thrust for return of Indian education to Indian hands in a concrete situation. This movement is very young, though the desire is very old. At present, there are three important community controlled Indian schools, at Rough Rock, Arizona, Ramah, New Mexico, and Rocky Boy, Montana. [The establishment of these schools is discussed in a separate article in this issue of *Inequality in Education.*] I would like to quote rather extensively from documents produced by the Rocky Boy community before they won their fight to control their own school, for these materials clearly indicate the realities of white dominated education for Indians and the vision that Indians have of education.

Excerpts from the proposal follow; these constitute a case study in the theoretical underpinnings of Indian community control as seen from the point of view of an Indian community which has never had that control.

Purpose. The parents of Rocky Boy feel that the purpose of their school should be to develop a general curriculum for Indian children in a context germane to their experience.

Instrumental to the development of such a program is the involvement of all facets of community life in the education process. Further, the school should be a model of Indians controlling their educational destiny, a unique occurrence in this society.

Objectives. 1. Improve the self-concept of low-income Indian children through relevant educational programs. A recent report of the Senate Subcommittee on Indian education finds that white controlled education of Indians has failed. One of the reasons for failure has been the inability of white administrators and school boards to appreciate the cultural differences between themselves and their students. Attempts have been made to turn Indian children into "white men" and drive out Indian cultural patterns. No attempt has been made to teach the Indian cultural heritage. History is taught from the white point of view. The Indian fighting to defend his homeland is portrayed in history books as the enemy of progress, holding back the settling of the frontier. This approach has a devastating effect on Indian children; they cannot be white men and they are not allowed to be Indians. This pattern held true when the Rocky Boy community was included in the Havre school district. Havre's white administrator of the Rocky Boy school said on numerous occasions, "I don't see why Indian culture should be taught here. Nobody ever taught me my culture." Parents complain that their children are ashamed that they are Indians. The juvenile delinquency rate is high. Children watch cowboy-and-Indian movies on television and cheer for the cowboys. The low self-esteem fostered by the curriculum and the attitudes of the administrators is reinforced by the fact that the Indians see their schools run by whites. It is as if the white man is saying to the Indian children, "We have to do this for you because your people can't do it themselves." The effects of cultural bias in the school system on the self-image of the child are compounded by the effects of poverty. The 1960 census showed that 84 percent of the Rocky Boy families receive less than three thousand dollars a year.

The creation of the Rocky Boy school district will have beneficial effects on the self-image of the Indian children. Through the experience of operating the school, the entire Indian community should gain self-confidence. This community feeling will be communicated to the children. Children will see their parents exercising responsibilities for their schools. Indian administrators and teachers will be sought out to provide models for Indian children. The new school board will incorporate changes into the curriculum gradually, to give the children a sense of the history and contributions of their own people while, at the same time, providing the skills needed in the world outside the reservation.

2. *Improve academic achievement of low income Indian children.* The creation of the Indian controlled Rocky Boy school district will result in improved academic achievement of the children. Central to academic success are the self-concept of the child, the attitude of teachers and administrators toward the children and the community, and the attitude of the parents and the community leaders towards the school. The Rocky Boy school board will hire teachers who have a positive attitude toward Indian children and the Indian community. Through this project, the Rocky Boy teachers will be immersed in the community and therefore become cognizant of parent and community attitudes and problems. The Senate subcommittee reported that in most Indian communities the school is an alien institution over which people feel they have little control. This is true for the Rocky Boy community. If the parents are resentful toward the school, their attitude is bound to be reflected in the academic performance of their children. These attitudes will change as the school becomes part of the community and is controlled by the community.

3. *Integrate the school and the teachers into the community.* It will be the strong desire of the new school board and the Rocky Boy people that the teachers participate in their community life. At present, most teachers live at Havre and are not familiar with the Rocky Boy community. No attempt is made to introduce the teachers to the local community. Last year there were two teachers who did become part of the community, attending Indian dances and ceremonies, taking Indian children into their homes for long periods, and becoming friends of many of the parents. These two teachers were fired by the Havre school board.

Two approaches currently being considered to involve teachers more actively in the community include: scattering teacher housing throughout the reservation, and an orientation program to acquaint them with the Rocky Boy community. The transfer of control makes the school itself part of the community. This fact will help to reinforce efforts by teachers and community people who seek to improve parent-teacher communication. As the teachers gain an understanding of the community, they will also gain an understanding of the children. Improvements in the children's academic performance and self-esteem should also follow.

If the Rocky Boy effort is successful, their example may be followed by other Indian groups, and the impact of their experience will extend far beyond the boundaries of the reservation.

Description of Activities. An environment in which the parents view the school as a foreign and alien place, in which students view education as an exercise in schooling rather than learning, and in which Indian leadership has traditionally been excluded from the decision-making process is hardly conducive to the above-stated objectives. Achievement of these objectives requires not only an intensive effort, but a unique one. The role of the classroom teacher is critical, for she must now serve an educating function that extends beyond the classroom to the entire community.

The essence of community involvement is the degree to which parents and community leaders understand the educational process, for knowledge must precede decision-making. Hence, since education of Indian children requires involvement of Indian parents, the classroom teacher must explain the educational process to parents and involve them in it, or achievement will remain low and we will have failed.

In recognition of the burden that this places on the teacher's time, we propose that the classroom teaching load be arranged so that the teachers have more time to work with community people and raise the achievement of the students. By adjusting the pupil-teacher ratio from 30-to-1 to 20-to-1, with the addition of five teaching positions, each teacher's classroom load will be reduced by one-third, with the following conditions resulting:

1. *Fewer students per teacher,* allowing more individualized instruction;
2. *Fewer parents per teacher,* allowing for more intimate and detailed consultation;
3. *More time for community involvement,* allowing more time for community meetings and home visitations.

Each teacher will spend ten hours a week in regularly scheduled parent consultation. This will allow a teacher to consult with each of the parents twice a month. Monthly community meetings will also be held by the professional staff of the school. The purpose of these meetings will be to involve all interested community people, including those that are not parents of students.

This vision of what a school could be has come true, not in every detail, but it has come true in Rocky Boy. The same vision can be found in almost all Indian communities; may these come true as well.

The role of the federal government, however, must undergo drastic changes if it is to be of assistance in the development of an effective Indian educational system, by which I mean, a system run by Indians for themselves. Indeed, the changes have begun. The present administration has thus far paid much more than lip service to the idea of Indian self-determination. I am most familiar with the activities of my own associates in the Education for American Indians Office that has been developed within the U.S. Office of Education. EAIO is an advocate office; it will assume a role of responsibility and commitment to all educational ventures affecting Indian communities and Indian people. EAIO, which was established in 1966 and has a staff of seven people, two of them Indians, has several major functions:

Assisting Indian communities and organizations in developing and promoting a coordinated federal approach that will best serve their interests and needs.

Communicating with regional and local Indian groups to spread knowledge about developments in Indian education and to receive constant feedback on the operation of the programs.

Assisting in the maintenance of liaison between federal and other programs with functions in Indian education.

Acting as consultants and advisors in whatever efforts concerning Indian educational policies and procedures that arise, including conferences and task forces as well as ad hoc community efforts.

Talking to the tribes, the organizations, the Indian groups in the field so that EAIO will be constantly aware of their educational problems, priorities, needs, and areas of concern.

This is what we hope to do. But the problems of the Indians cannot be solved through edicts from Washington. The federal government can provide certain financial and programmatic assistance and also perhaps moral leadership. The Indians can provide the desire and the will to follow through on self-determination, but even this will not be enough. Two questions of crucial importance must be answered. Can the resources necessary to accomplish the task be mobilized and chanelled through an entrenched political apparatus still resisting change? Can institutional and individual racism be eliminated or neutralized to the level that will allow Indians to learn as Indians without being hampered by outsiders? If we are to make meaningful gains, attitudes and power relationships must undergo change at the local level. This means that every community that harbors Indians, and this includes most communities, is involved. Every citizen must be prepared to help avoid increased frustration and more intense polarization. The solution of the ills of education, like other social ills, requires radical approaches. We must have the courage to try.

WILLIAM GLASSER

Reaching the Unmotivated

Lack of success, more than any other one thing, contributes to non-motivation. In an atmosphere of failure, effort and interest seep away; problems become overwhelming, and people seem to "cop out." I say "seem" because, even in alienation and withdrawl, the individual is trying to say something. What are our unmotivated youngsters in schools trying to tell us? What does non-motivation reflect of the life they experience in school?

Everyone has a basic concept of himself, whatever that concept may be. Each of us not only has such a concept, but we are continually evaluating ourselves. This ongoing process is true of all of us. It is as though, over our heads, we have a little radar that is constantly passing back signals to us. If the signals come back continually: *The work you do is no good. You are not worth very much. I don't care much for you,* one's self-concept is bound to become a concept of failure.

When I began to work as a consultant in schools where there were large groups of unmotivated students, I realized that these were indeed the signals that are coming back to most of the boys and girls in the school. Their reaction is the same as anybody's reaction to such signals. They are upset; and they will not do anything that the people who are giving them these signals are telling them to do. If we want something from people—not something they give to us, but something from them in terms of their attention, in terms of at least beginning to study a curriculum that we designed for them—then we must scrutinize very carefully the kind of information we feed into their self-evaluation system.

If our information is that they are not worth very much, they begin to believe they are not worth very much—unless they can find someone else who puts in information that they are worth much more than our message says.

If you ask youngsters who aren't doing well in school:

From *The Science Teacher* (March, 1971), pp. 18-22. Reprinted by permission of the author and the National Science Teacher Association.

41

What do you believe about yourself in relationship to school? and they answer:

Well, I guess I'm not very good. I'm not very competent. I'm not doing very well, you can't expect them to be very motivated. If you tell them they are doing great, that would be phony, so you are in a bind. Ordinarily, if you want to tell people something nice about themselves, they have to do something that gives you some reason to send out this kind of positive message.

In school what we have to do is devise a way to get the students to do some work so we can give the input that they are doing something that is worthwhile. If I tell any of you, "I think you are pretty smart, pretty worthwhile, and I think you are proceeding in the right direction," there is a good chance that you will at least listen to what I have to say. This is basic to the whole procedure. This is what you must do with students. Get involved with them; help them become friendly; create some warmth and some interaction in the classroom. This is a basic minimum for getting them to listen to *you* and then, hopefully, to listen to *what* you are attempting to teach them.

If you say, *Whether we're friendly or not, learn this stuff,* youngsters won't learn. Most teachers of about my age don't really understand why this is so. Most of us can look back and see that we didn't always have teachers who were friends. We didn't always have teachers who cared about making the subject relevant. We had some pretty dull, dry teachers; but still we learned, and we didn't give the teachers a hard time while we were at it. Even when what I was told to learn didn't make much sense to me, I still gave it a try, because I thought I had to do it or because I didn't have the nerve to be obstreperous. Sometimes today, I hear principals lamenting that kids are no longer frightened. Principals today can't scare kids. I was scared into learning some things. But today's students aren't scared, and we are still unwilling to do the things that will get them to learn when they are not scared. This leaves us quite powerless.

Why aren't they scared? This has puzzled me for some years. In public schools, students are doing all kinds of disruptive things; and they are paying very little attention to teachers. Yet still we try to use the old scare tactics: *I'm going to punish you. I'll call your mother. You won't go to college. You'll fail. You'll be unsuccessful in life.* This works almost not at all in most communities today.

I believe that this being impervious to such threats relates to change. We are living through a time of cultural change. An entire generation is changing its basic social attitude toward our institutions and how they operate and toward goals for individuals and for society. Suddenly we find that institutions that have worked well for hundreds or thousands of years are no longer effective.

Many people have been explaining change. Some have said, "Our society has gone bad; our institutions are no longer working properly." But they have not explained why. *Why,* for instance, do schools no longer fit our young people? Obviously, they don't fit because so many youngsters are doing badly. But why? What has been happening? I think one very good clue comes from a Marshall McLuhan interview in the March 1969 *Playboy* magazine. In it McLuhan said that students are searching for a role not a goal. Think about that. Then think about your schools. What are schools set up to provide for our students? Our schools are set up to reinforce goals. McLuhan says students are searching for a role, not a goal. I'd like to paraphrase that, for I won't go quite that far. I'll say that students are searching for a role first, and then they are willing to search for a goal. If anything, school is destructive to role reinforcement.

Role is the person's identity, the person's feelings that "This is me, I'm a separate person—hopefully a distinctive person, a person that stands for certain things, a person that wants to be accepted." This is almost a wish to be accepted "for me, regardless of what I do." That is an over-statement, but it means not being judged solely for what one does but being accepted for one's own basic humanity. This is what I call identity.

When I was in school, and probably for most of us, our concern was in learning what we were supposed to learn, getting some security, getting a home, and so on. We thought, "I'll get this knowledge, this degree, this job, then I'll start concerning myself with who I am." First, security; then, who I am. Find your niche, earn a secure place for yourself, then work for some individuality, for some kind of human expression.

But suppose, somehow, security was already at hand. It seems to me that our present society gives this security. In a sense, youngsters feel secure when they come to school. True, many of them may be starving and don't have clothes, and their homes are chaotic. But somehow they believe that they will have something to eat, that they will ultimately have a car, a job, and the possessions they want. Even if our system hasn't given people security, it has given them a powerful illusion of security. Even in a central city, where kids are absolutely poverty-stricken, they still don't believe that they are not going to be secure. They still feel that somewhere they are going to get the Mustangs. They are going to get the sharp things. They are going to do things that secure people do. Television has fostered this illusion by hammering over the message: "You are going to have it; don't worry about it; you'll get these things somewhere," though it doesn't mention how to get the things or all the work involved. But it does get across the illusion of security.

Therefore, we are now dealing with a student who can't be frightened. He doesn't care whether he learns science or algebra or chemistry, because he feels somehow or other, it is going to be OK. It doesn't matter whether he comes from a rich home or a poor home. He feels that things are going to work out. The old scare tactics won't work because his basic aim doesn't include the old goals that we still try to make him think he won't reach if he doesn't do as we say. Young people today are seeking identity as human beings; they want to be assured that they will get this kind of acceptance.

Somehow or other in education, we must give children a positive identity reinforcement. We must make them feel that while school believes the goals are important, the school system and we as teachers also believe, *You are a human being. We care for you. We will express it to you by being friendly and being interested in you.* If we can do this, the youngster will say, *Well, I ought to begin listening to you. Maybe I ought to begin to learn some of the things that you, who are my friend and who care about me, say I should learn.*

This is a shift. In the old system, we didn't care about the human part. That was an extra. Today's youngsters want some of this extra right now.

This is easy to verify. A dialogue with a teen-aged girl might go something like this—and I've asked at least 300 the same question and gotten the same answer.

What's the most important thing to you? Really the most important? *I want to be myself.* Only five words: *I want to be myself.* If you probe a little deeper, you get: *I want to be me. I want to be accepted. I want to have friends. I want to stand for something.*

And then what they say almost invariably is, *I want to be accepted for me, just for me.* If I ask, *You mean regardless of what you do?* they'll say, *Not regardless of what I do but kind of separate from what I do.* Almost, *Accept me for me, but let's not worry about what I'm going to do. I have basic value just because I am a human being.*

If we are a society which is no longer going to worry in the traditional sense about security goals but seeks first to gain reinforcement as human beings, this calls for a vast change in our teaching.

As I have described in *Schools Without Failure,* we can use class meetings in the lower grades and discussion with students in the upper grades so that the students begin to say, *The teacher talks with us. He listens to us. He interacts with us.* In effect they are saying, *He does the things that help to reinforce me. That makes me feel worthwhile as a person.*

This is no longer optional. This is no longer what we must do only if we have spare time. I believe that this is what we must do if we are going to have any teaching. For many of you, your job is to teach science to youngsters who are relatively unmotivated, youngsters who have felt failure.

Remember that in this new social need for identity, there is nothing that says it has to come out positive. We try to gain a successful identity for ourselves. We hope to get reinforcement and care from other people which confirm good feelings about ourselves. But there is another option also. The other option is that if we are not able to identify ourselves as a success, we identify ourselves as a failure. We identify ourselves as a person all right, but as a person who fails. And we behave in a way which reinforces failure. If you analyze how the students that you can't teach behave, you will find that they behave according to two patterns. One is antagonistic, anti-social; they don't care; they constantly agitate. The other way is to withdraw. These students just check out. In talking to them you are talking to the wall. You can't get through to them. Their bodies are in the class, but their minds aren't. What students are doing in both these behaviors is reinforcing their opinion of themselves, their "I am a failure" identity. They express this view actively through antagonism and passively through withdrawal. Neither of which allows any way to reach them effectively.

How do you reach an antagonistic person? Every time you reach out your hand, he only slaps it. You may sit up nights figuring out a nice lesson—something that really ought to excite and interest these youngsters, but they come in with a sour expression, *Aw! Same old thing!* It is not the same old thing, but they won't bother to look at it. They believe they are failing anyway. It seems to them that they can't do anything, so why in the world would you want to get in touch with a failure? Why would you want to sit up nights with their lessons? They can't conceive of your doing this. The job of reaching out to them is the primary job. Somehow or other, they must hear you saying: *Look, Kid, we must get acquainted—get friendly. We must make some contact with each other.* Anyway that you can emphasize this is all right, but you must do it systematically—in three steps that I think will help keep the youngsters from failing and start them believing they can be successful.

Number one: We ought to stop failing kids. We ought to make it impossible for children to fail in school. Let me define failure. Failure occurs when the options are closed. That's what failure is all about.

If you are fishing 25 miles off shore, and you drop your camera overboard —that is failure. The options are all over. In 2,000 feet of water, that camera is gone. There is no way you are going to get it back. That is what failure is like. All paths to success are closed.

In school, when the child takes a test and gets a low grade, and the teacher says, *That's it.* And the child says, *Gee, can I make it up? Can I do something, can I restudy it? I don't understand it.* And the teacher persists, *That's it. That's your grade. That's your place. That's every word.* That is a failure system. The grading system is one way schools practice failure. The outside world doesn't operate on a failure system nearly as much as schools do. The world operates on a fairer system—one which says that it is possible not to succeed, but usually not to have complete failure either. We must get rid of every possible way that students can identify themselves as failures in school. We can't change their homes or their roles —at least not directly, but we can change what we have control over in our own classes.

To teach science to youngsters who have been turned off by school, you will have to let them know that, *There is no failure here. We are here to learn science. I will give you credit for what you learn. If you learn a little, I'll give you credit for it. If you learn a lot, I'll give you credit for that.*

Long ago, when I entered medical school, the dean announced on the first day, "No one is going to fail." He said that the teachers were there to take care of the students; all tests would be fair and reasonable; if there were any problems they'd be straightened out. And it *was* like that for four years— four years of pure joy in school. That gave me my first inkling that all students could find school like that.

The only way to approach disadvantaged students is to say to them, *You're here to learn. We're not here to fail you. If you're up against something you don't understand, we'll explain it to you. We'll give tests— tests are important if you are going to evaluate yourself. But if you don't pass the test, take it again, take it home and study it. Work on it. Ask another kid about it. We don't care if you look at papers in this class. Trade information back and forth. Keep your books open. All we want you to do is learn.*

Teaching is not testing; it's not monitoring students. It's letting them know they can learn, and letting them know that the hardest thing to do in class is not learn. *We won't fail you.*

My philosophy of education is: *Come to school. We like you. We're interested in teaching you something, and we will give you credit for what you've learned. Come to class. We'll get involved. You'll not only get to know me, you'll get to know other kids. We'll talk to each other.*

Science is the best possible subject for this kind of teaching. No subject lends itself better than science to figuring things out and for throwing questions for inquiry and discussion back and forth.

The important thing is not to "down" anybody in these discussions. It's very critical with disadvantaged students who are used to being downed that you don't down them. Don't act judgmental in class discussion. If you ask a student something, and he gives an irrational answer—let it go. Don't pick up immediately and say, "That's wrong." Ask another student, "What do you think of that?" Let the class kick it around. At the end of the day, if they haven't discovered the exact answer to things as you see them, let it go for another day. In science the exact answer may be somewhat doubt-ful anyway. Take the problem home and think about it. Ask yourself "How can I get this across? How can I develop a lesson where they begin to believe that it is possible for other ideas to be entertained?"

Even if you don't teach anything else in science, you ought to teach the fact that there is not one answer for everything. There are many ways to skin a cat. There are other ideas worth considering. Finally, the students will get the feeling that, *Here my ideas, my brains, and my application of the knowledge as I see it are worth something. It's worthwhile for me to listen to other people and for other people to listen to me.* Finally you achieve the reinforcement which convinces a person that he can succeed. Successful identity is gained through involving yourself with other people, through listening, through intellectually involving yourself, talking back and forth and arguing, but not being put down. We can change identities from failure to success through this method. Get the class involved; eliminate all of the options for failure. If you leave even one option for failure open, these failing youngsters will find it and use it. Plug all the failure options so they can't fail. *Sorry, kids, you can't fail. It's impossible, just can't do it. That's all there is to it.*

If the student says, *I won't come to class,* reply, *That's your choice. If you won't come to class, I can't teach you. But if you come here, you'll learn, and you won't fail.*

All that the student should have to do is come, at least in the beginning. Make sure he gets to school. Through this system of involvement and of eliminating failure, he will be motivated, because it feels good to learn things. If it didn't feel good to learn, to think, and to discuss things that are interesting and exciting and intellectually important, nobody would learn anything. In science you are especially fortunate to be teaching something you can make fairly exciting.

This brings us to the second point in feeling worthwhile. The student feels worthwhile if he can relate the material to his life. Of course, if you are teaching really bright students, really gung-ho kids, you can teach them far-out stuff, and you don't necessarily have to relate it to their lives. But the less motivated youngsters are interested in what you're saying that might possibly pertain to their lives. If what you are teaching doesn't seem to relate to their lives, they turn off very quickly. Once they turn off, it's very hard for them to turn on again. So far as possible, relate what you teach to their lives, to what they know and understand so that they can recognize that this is the kind of thing that happens to them.

For example, if you are trying to teach them the normal distribution, let them roll a pair of dice, and they will find out that there is such a thing as a normal curve. Most of them have shot enough craps to know that there is some kind of curve operating. If you are explaining how a siphon works, use the example of siphoning gas from a car if you're out of gas. You'll lose these students if you talk about siphoning a liquid from one bottle to another. They are not interested in bottles of water in a laboratory, but they are interested in siphoning in relation to cars and gasoline.

The third important point—after getting the students involved and teaching relevant material—is to get them to think. Thinking and the kind of goal-oriented education which has been going on in the schools and colleges and graduate schools for a long period of time are antagonistic to each other. We must get rid of this antagonism. We must make thinking pay off—not just occasionally, but pay off in a major way, because it's fun to think. In any situation where you are stimulated, where people get you really intellectually stimulated, and where you suddenly realize that you have thought of something new or discovered a possibility that relates to you, you will find it extremely exciting. This kind of thinking is what we have to stimulate the students to do. And that means, for one thing, no memorizing. Make it an absolute rule in your class that students don't have to memorize anything. Whatever is important enough to be memorized is important enough to be learned. Put it on the board in big letters, or on charts, or give it to the students in mimeographed notes. Tell the class, *This is something that ought to be learned; but for goodness sake, whenever you need it, refer to it, and use it. It's right here.*

If you ask unmotivated youngsters to memorize something that makes no sense to them in the first place, they'll turn off the whole thing. You close one of the failure options if they can never get stuck, never fail, never get stymied, because they didn't know something that was to be committed to memory. Memorizing is not a reasonable use of our brains anyway. Our brains aren't built to memorize things, and we force them into all kinds of convolutions when we memorize things.

My son has an excellent chemistry teacher who keeps important information on the board and doesn't ask the class to memorize anything. What happens is that the students do learn a great deal by heart—when they realize that this saves looking up what they use over and over. People do memorize information they use every day—their phone number, address, car license number, and the like. This is what smart people do. They don't commit things to memory unless they use them all the time. But don't memorize the things that are used in science. These things can be looked up or figured out. With students, dispel the notion that when they read a page, if they haven't got it committed to memory, they fail. They won't commit it to memory, anyway. Say, *We're going to use this. We're going to figure it out. You can always open the book and look up what you need.*

After you get students involved; do relevant things; get them to thinking, get rid of certainty, get rid of memorization; you next stop measuring students against each other. This kind of measuring is always very destructive. Get across the idea that, *We're interested in teaching you. This other kid may be better or worse—we don't care—its what you're learning that counts.* Success breeds success; we build success upon success. We always tend, especially with youngsters who are behind, to go too fast. Suppose you start in the fall with a class of students that aren't doing as well as they should. Very carefully set up your lesson for the first week, and then say to yourself, "I'll take nine-tenths of it away and teach this much." However, once they succeed they'll want a little bigger bite the next time. You can't teach in tiny increments all along, but do start with them. As soon as the students understand the first few lessons, give a little test that they can all succeed on. Then compliment them and let them know what is planned for the next day. Never start too big. I can well recall teachers who went too fast—teachers who were going to cover the whole text whether the class did or not. They'd turn the pages in the book, skip 40 pages, and say to go on from there. You can't skip those 40 pages and go ahead. Your job is not to get to the end of the semester, covering the unit on A, and the unit on B, and the unit on C. Your job is to teach as much as you can to the class and then make a careful record of where they are for the next teacher. The class should succeed up to this point. You've got to keep these youngsters saying,

I can. It's important to me. Others are listening to me. The teacher cares about me. There is absolutely no way I can fail if I count. I may not do as well as the next guy. That's possible. Somebody may learn more than me, and somebody may learn less, but I can learn things in this class, and I will not fail.

This is about where we are now in our ideas about schools without failure. We have pretty well established some things that can be done in an elementary school. We are starting in secondary schools and learning how to apply these principles systematically in secondary schools. We have a few schools that believe enough in these ideas that they are going to cooperate with us to see whether together we can solve the problem of the unmotivated students. That kind of cooperation is the key to education. No one can come into your school and say, "Do it this way; it'll work." The only people who can really make it work are the faculty of the school. They can accept good ideas and give them a try. I hope you will try out these ideas in your classes, but obviously it needs more than one class. If you can get ideas like this going throughout a school so that they fit and apply to your school—that's when the real changes start. When a student walks through the door to that school he begins to feel

Here, I don't fail. Not only in science class, I don't fail any place in this school. I don't get credit for things I don't do, but they don't fail me, and I do get credit for what I do.

HERBERT KOHL

A School Within a School

I. *You don't have to find your way alone. There are other teachers who want to try new things. And there are ways to find them and begin together.*

Rigid and authoritarian administrators—and some teachers—have little tolerance for open classrooms and often are not even willing to observe and discover what is actually going on in them. Any breach of what they consider order threatens. I have known teachers who were quite literally ostracized for fraternizing too much with the students or for allowing students to talk with each other in class and walk about the room. Throwing out the rigid, structured standard curriculum is often regarded as sinful.

An open classroom is often threatening to teachers. They fear that it may turn the heads of their pupils and make control and discipline more difficult. In some ways these teachers' fears are justified.

Students who see, by the example of an open classroom in their school, that a sterile form of school life is not necessary may begin to demand that things change. Too often their defiance will be punished summarily. And the matter may not stop there. The innovative teacher may be blamed for his students' actions. And he, too, may meet with various subtle restraints.

Sooner or later, the teacher interested in opening things up will have to confront uptight teachers with his work and fight to make it possible for his type of teaching to exist within a public school setting. This is extremely difficult if you are completely alone in a school.

There are other pitfalls in trying to develop an open classroom on your own. You have to be constantly responding to the needs of individual

From *Grade Teacher* (September, 1969; October, 1969; March, 1970). This article was originally printed as three separate articles. Copyright © 1969, 1970 by Herbert Kohl. Reprinted by permission of the Robert Lescher Literary Agency.

students and getting resource material and people as well as developing your own ideas. Your students become hungry to learn and the textbook will not provide fully for their needs.

When let go, students want to learn so many different things that it is almost impossible for any one adult to keep up with them. Many teachers fear that students will be lazy when allowed freedom. Actually, given the time and an atmosphere of trust, young people often want to learn more than educational theorists claim they are capable of learning.

You will face other problems in the confinement of a single classroom. At any given time there are different activities that students will be involved in. Some will require movement and noise, others the presence of music, and still others relative silence and solitude. If the classroom is to resemble life, all of these activities must be permitted to go on simultaneously and not be arbitrarily structured so that some forms of activity are permitted and others (usually the more spontaneous and physical as well as the solitary ones) are prohibited.

It is also difficult to force upon young people the necessity of relating to one and only one adult during a school year. Some adults relate better with active rather than passive children. Others appreciate boys more than they do girls, or athletes instead of intellectuals. Students also have their preferences among adults. Within a single classroom, neither the adult nor the children have a choice. They must relate to each other, like it or not, and this often gives rise to conflicts that could have been avoided if the teachers and students had a choice of people to work with.

There is a final problem I would like to mention, one which has particularly distressed me. What happens if one succeeds in opening up the classroom and enabling students to pursue what they consider relevant and relate to you as a person and not as a teacher? What about the next year, what happens to the children if they pass back into a rigid, hostile situation where creativity and honesty will be looked upon as defiance? I do not think this is a valid reason for one to adopt an authoritarian pretense, but it is a question to worry about.

Four-Room Mini-School

None of these problems is so difficult if you are not alone. Four of us worked together in my elementary school. We didn't talk much about our work with the rest of the faculty and they didn't seem particularly interested. What we tried to do was get our rooms placed together at the end of a hall and then use the four rooms and the hall space as a separate school within our school. The students in the four classes were free to move from one room to another or use the hall as part of our mini-school.

It would have been ideal if there was a set of swinging doors that separated us from the rest of the building, or if we had been placed in four adjoining portable classrooms in a remote part of the schoolyard. But we did the best we could at one end of a long hallway.

We looked out for each other's students and tried to help each other out. I was concerned with writing, another teacher with athletics, a third with history and sociology and the last with soul music. We just made a beginning and didn't realize the possibilities we had for creating an alternative open school within our existing school without having to ask anyone for any extra money.

This year I will be working with small groups of teachers trying to develop open mini-schools within existing schools. I am sure it can be done, that all of us can do it, though not without hard work and resistance.

Sounding-Out Process

Your first step is to sound out other teachers, asking them what they think about education in general. Only broach the question of what they think about your school after you have a general feeling that they may be discontented with the way things are.

Meet with interested teachers, away from the school building. If you think it might help, give them this article or any other material that might move them along. Perhaps a pot-luck supper or a picnic would be a good occasion to begin discussions.

Once you have identified a few people it might be possible to work with, there are many ways to proceed, according to the nature of your school, the number of people interested, the kind of community support you are likely to get, etc. . . .

II. *You have found other teachers interested in effecting change in your school's approach to education. What next? Here are some suggestions . . . and some cautions.*

When I was teaching in the New York public schools there was always talk about innovation and change. I taught in both a Higher Horizons School and a Special Services School, while some of my friends worked in a More Effective School. We were all supposedly involved in education innovation. Our schools, however, really didn't differ much from each other or from the supposedly non-innovative schools.

We still had to follow a set curriculum, the students had to perform or be punished, and the supervisors spent most of their time handling discipline problems and making sure there was no unfavorable publicity for the school. The "innovations" we were part of consisted primarily of receiving prettier and slicker textbooks, having smaller classes, and getting more relief people around to cover our classes for a few hours a day while we smoked in the teachers' lounge. Admittedly some of these changes made our lives as teachers easier (and all of them, of course, cost the school system a lot of money). However, they had nothing to do with teaching, learning, or the lives of the students.

These innovations had another self-defeating characteristic. They came from above—from experts at some university, or from the union's central office or the curriculum division of the board of education. They were filtered down to us teachers through the principal, who was sent a series of "guidelines for innovation." None of us was consulted on how a specific change would fit in with our particular school, the needs of our kids or with ideas we valued. We were treated like soldiers who must obey orders from above, however questionable their value. Innovations were pasted onto our ongoing programs and soon melted into the regular program. These innovations designed for *all* schools fit none, and therefore had little effect.

New Structure

I don't believe innovations commanded by experts from above and imposed upon teachers will produce significant change within the existing schools. I'm especially doubtful about this if the innovations merely introduce quantitative changes without creating new structures. It is the spatial, temporal, and personal life that is lived within the schools that needs to change.

Fundamental changes must arise out of the specific needs and problems of individual students and teachers. They cannot be packaged. Let me give a few examples of specific qualitative changes that can open things up and lead to the development of open mini-schools:

1. Spatial restructuring can take place by eliminating fixed and assigned seating in the classroom. On the first day of school let the students sit where they choose and let them change seats at will throughout the year. Disputes about seating can be dealt with as practical problems to be solved by the persons involved rather than as discipline problems requiring punishment.

2. Temporal change can take place by abandoning the notion of spending fixed periods of time on individual subjects. Reading can go as long as people are involved in it; math can be forgotten for a few weeks and then returned to; history can take up a few weeks to the exclusion of other subjects and then be dropped for a while. More radically, punctuality could be given up as a moral concept. Students could come to school between 8 and 10 and leave anytime from 2 to 4. If school is interesting, students will stay. If not, they ought not be confined.

3. You, the teacher, can give up the power to punish or grade students, can give up lecturing all the time, and instead spend time discovering interesting things to add to the classroom environment.

While these three types of innovation cost nothing financially, they do require a great deal of your time, work and patience before they begin to work well. Once they take root, however, life in school just might be more fun and richer for everyone concerned.

From the Ground Up

An open school within an existing school probably has the best chance of succeeding if it starts from the ground up, from the teacher and the students who must live with it, and therefore it cannot be imposed from above. You cannot tell people, "Be open," and expect anything but a mockery of a free situation to develop.

Teachers and students who are interested in opening things up must start by considering how they can do it in their school with the specific conditions they face. For example: How many students are willing to try something new? How many supportive parents are around? How much support can be expected from the administrations? From other teachers?

There are other specific questions to be considered: What part of the school is most isolated and will provide the mini-school with the privacy it might need? How much cooperation will be gotten from janitors, school secretaries, parent aides, special teachers? You must estimate the strengths and weaknesses of your specific situation.

In some schools it is easiest to develop an experimental program with "special" students whom the school has given up on. In other cases, all students are so ready for change that you would hardly know where to begin. You must spend time assessing the specific nature of your school in order to develop a strategy for change. It is not enough to have good ideas or good intentions.

An Element of Risk

I want to add a cautionary note: Too many good-willed attempts to change public schools are destroyed because the teachers and students involved believe that the rightness and humanness of their ideas is sufficient to eliminate opposition and open things up. It doesn't usually work out that way. People in power do not like to give up their power even though their positions may be intellectual and humanly untenable.

There are several general strategies that I would like to end with. They have been evolved by a number of people who have gone through the agonies of trying to restructure their public schools:

1. At the beginning, it is usually unwise to cut off completely people who claim to be interested in innovation, and yet are not trusted or are not personal friends of members of the core group.

2. All reasonable objections to your plans must be met reasonably and patiently.

3. Plans ought to be kept out in the open.

4. The project needs to be open to intelligent evaluation.

5. If all these conditions are met and there is still serious opposition to change, you ought to be willing to go ahead anyway, even if it means taking risks.

III. *The Mini-School Revisited*
   A few imaginative teachers have implemented the school-within-a-school idea. . . . Here's an eye-opening progress report.

Early this year I wrote two columns on developing open mini-schools within existing schools . . . Since then, I have heard from a number of readers who have been trying out some of my suggestions. I have also been working with teachers in the San Francisco Bay area who are attempting to create their own open mini-schools. There are things we all learned that might help other teachers organize open alternatives within their own schools.

Most of the mini-schools I have heard about were started by three or four teachers who believe that it was necessary to allow their students greater choice and independence within the school. For the most part, these teachers had not worked together on a day-to-day basis, but had shared ideas and done much of the same reading. Usually, but not always, they were on the same grade level. In some instances, they represented all of the grade levels in the school.

Once these teachers decided they wanted to share their rooms and develop a school-within-a-school, they had the task of persuading their supervisors to approve the experiment. This was not always easy. For example, if there was no tenured member of the staff within the group, the principals were usually very negative. Some groups went ahead anyway without letting on publicly what they were doing. This, however, invariably led to confrontation with the administration.

Proof of Responsibility

Other groups were told that before they could begin they would have to document their aims and goals, as well as develop an evaluation of their work. In other words, they would have to prove to the administration that they were "responsible." I have seen documents produced by some of the teacher groups and they are impressive. Many of the documents have drawn upon the excellent, annotated bibliography of works on open schooling, "Informal Education," appearing in *The Center Forum,* Vol. 3, No. 7, July, 1969, published by the Center for Urban Education, a regional educational laboratory in New York City.

These documents contain sections which list the options the teachers hope to provide for the students and other sections which discuss the prospects of developing a rich environment within their classrooms. The more specific the documents are, the more effective they have been in convincing the administration that the effort was worth making.

Other strategies have been tried to get past administrative objections. One group of teachers decided that their mini-school would take all of the "difficult" students in the school, thereby taking a "problem" off the administration's hands. Another group started out by offering a special after-school class for students and another class for parents, entitled "Innovation in Education." The children in the class were from grades 3 through 6, and their parents were invited to the adult group. The parents read John Holt's *How Children Fail* (Pitman), Jonathan Kozol's *Death at an Early Age* (Bantam) and my own *36 Children* (New American). They visited free schools and experimental schools in their area and ended up planning their own mini-school. Then the teachers took the joint student-teacher-parent plans to the administration and the PTA where they made a very convincing case for letting the mini-school grow naturally out of this after-school class.

Most of the teachers who were determined to have open mini-schools managed somehow to get administrative sanction, though not necessarily administrative approval. In some cases it took several months of persuading, documenting, meeting, planning, and general haggling to get the school off the ground. The persistence usually paid off.

Togetherness Problems

Once the schools got started, however, new problems arose. Although the teachers involved in the mini-schools had shared ideas and spent time talking with each other, they had not worked together. They were not used to sharing materials, exchanging information about students, learning about each other's strengths and weaknesses and, most important, learning how to criticize each other without creating personal animosity. There was another problem. The format of the usual school faculty meeting didn't apply to the mini-school. There was no principal to set the agenda, run the meeting and generally keep things under control. The mini-schools were supposed to be run democratically with all teachers participating in making all the major decisions. Yet it was not clear how meetings were to be run or whether people should vote on all issues or just talk them out until a consensus was reached. Some teachers wanted to assume the principal's role even in the mini-school, and many enlightened teachers found themselves involved in the same political maneuvering and battling for power that exists in the larger school.

I don't know how the problem of developing a small democratic institution that functions smoothly can be solved. However, the staff at Other Ways (the mini-school where I work) has found two types of meetings to be useful. Once a week we meet in school to deal with specific problems. For example, we talk about individual students, about problems of teaching or about developing our school environment. This meeting takes place in the school and may end with our repainting a classroom or trying to design a new reading program or finding out how to get good volunteers. These meetings are open to students.

Another type of meeting we have takes place away from the school, usually in the home of one of the staff members. Often we'll start with dinner or drinks. It is important that the atmosphere be relaxed and that we are free to continue as long as necessary. At these home meetings we talk through most of our problems until some decision is reached. We have developed ways of criticizing each other and being honest (even if it is painful sometimes) about the work we do. At these meetings we talk about fundraising, the future of the school, our relationship to the rest of the school system, and about complaints and grievances that have developed during the week.

Two long meetings a week are time-consuming and exhausting, but we find them necessary. One way of fitting in these meetings is to set aside one afternoon a week for the students to be on their own and for the teachers to have an all-purpose meeting.

First-Year Problems

In addition to problems with the administration—and with oneself—teachers can anticipate problems with students and parents during the first year of an open mini-school. There will be some students who are very enthusiastic at the beginning but who get bored during the middle of the year and then do nothing.

There will be others who ask to return to a more rigid form of schooling because they are frightened by the responsibility of making choices for themselves. Though not insurmountable, these problems require immense patience and flexibility on the part of teachers. The main difference between embarking on an open experiment in education and other types of educational experimentation is that there is no map to follow on the open road. Teachers must constantly make judgments, depend upon intuition and institute changes when the needs arise.

For this reason, it is very important for teachers to document what goes on in their school. Diaries, films, drawings, tapes—all the material possible, in fact—ought to be collected and periodically ordered and reviewed. In this way a certain perspective will be maintained.

Recently the staff of Other Ways got together and looked over the material we had collected. At that time we were tired and discouraged. We were so close to the situation that we had lost sight of the progress being made by the students and the sense of community developing in the staff. Looking back on all the material we collected gave us a renewed sense of our work leading somewhere. We could see changes in students' attitudes and feelings. Seeing our work in this perspective renewed our energy.

This documentation serves another purpose. Many of the students' parents want to know what we are doing. They support our work generally, but they are uneasy with the notions of freedom and choice. They want to be reassured that their children are doing something. The more concrete and specific work parents can be shown, the better they will feel about their students learning in an open context. Therefore, we try to use the documents we collect as reports to the parents. Once parents have specific examples of learning in an open context in their mind, it's easier for them to accept a new way of being in school for their children.

Why We Need New Schooling

Knowledge is increasing so fast, a recent ad said, that the problem of education is to find better ways "to pack it into young heads." This popular belief is wrong, and causes much of what is so wrong with our schools. For years, it is true, learned men used their brains to store and retrieve information. Today, the child who has been taught in school to stuff his head with facts, recipes, this-is-how-you-do-it, is obsolete even before he leaves the building. Anything he can do, or be taught to do, a machine can do, *and soon will do* better and cheaper.

What children need, even just to make a living, are qualities that can never be trained into a machine—inventiveness, flexibility, resourcefulness, curiosity and, above all, judgment.

The chief products of schooling these days are not these qualities, not even the knowledge and skills they try to produce, but stupidity, ignorance, incompetence, self-contempt, alienation, apathy, powerlessness, resentment and rage. We can't afford such products any longer. The purpose of education can no longer be to turn out people who know a few facts, a few skills and who will always believe and do what they are told. We need big changes, and in a hurry. Here, in no particular order, are some things to change:

We must get rid of the notion that education is different and separate from life, something that happens only in school. Everything that happens to us educates us, for good or for bad. To answer "What makes a good education?" we must ask, "What makes a good life?"

Teachers must have, like doctors with patients, the professional freedom to work with their students as they think best. Only the child himself should

From *Look* (January 13, 1970), p. 52. Copyright © 1970 by John Holt. Reprinted by permission of the Robert Lescher Literary Agency.

have more to say than the teacher about what is learned, and when, and how; today, in most places, only the child has less. So, out with lesson plans, fixed schedules, so many hours a week per subject, prescribed texts, grades, normal curves, censorship, supervisors—the whole deadening, humiliating, intimidating regime under which too many teachers have to work.

Children and their parents should not have to submit, for lack of choices, to school experiences that seem degrading, painful or harmful. School is neither jail nor the Army. People should be free to find or make for themselves the kinds of educational experiences they want their children to have. Anything in law that makes this impossible or even very difficult should be changed.

In most of history, children have been educated by the whole community, the whole society they lived in. Nothing else makes any sense. We must get as much as possible of the outside world into our schools, and get the schools and the children into the outside world, as in the Parkway project in Philadelphia, where hundreds of students use the city itself as their classroom.

Abolish compulsory attendance laws. We cannot measure growth and learning by the day or hour. A child, finding out what he wants to find out, fully alive and alert, learns more in an hour than most students learn in school in weeks or months. Schools are only one place, among many, where people can learn about and grow into the world. Let them compete with other educational resources for the time and attention of children.

Abolish all certification requirements for teachers. They don't make teachers better, often make them worse, and keep or drive out of teaching many excellent people. Let the people who run a school use as teachers anyone they think can help the children.

Teachers, or teachers and parents, should run schools, not specialists in school administration. Whoever pays the bills and sees that the floors are swept and the windows washed should be under the teachers, not over them.

Abolish the required curriculum. Children want to learn about the world and grow into it; adults want to help them. Let them get together, and the proper curriculum will grow out of what the children need and want, and what the adults have to give.

Abolish all compulsory testing and grading. If a student wants his teacher to test his knowledge or competence, so that he may know how to improve, fine. All other testing and grading is destructive and inexcusable. Students should organize to refuse to take tests for other people's purposes, and teachers should organize to refuse to give them.

Abolish the required use of so-called intelligence tests and other psychological prying. Such tests should only be given with the consent of parent and child, and the results should belong to them *exclusively*. Establish by law that *any and all* records of what a child does in a school shall go with him, as his exclusive property, when he leaves that school.

In all educational institutions supported by tax money, or enjoying tax-exempt status (with the possible exceptions suggested below), abolish all entrance exams or other selective admissions requirements. An educational institution, like a library, museum, lecture hall, park or theater, should be open at least until full, to any and all who want to use it. A few exceptions might be made for institutions where performance skill is involved, as in the performing arts, crafts, skilled trades, or in flying, surgery, perhaps some sciences. But even here, the institutions should have to show that selection is really needed, and not just a concession to institutional vanity, or a way, as in some professions and trades today, to keep the cost of services high by limiting the number of people able to provide them.

Abolish all requirements for schools. *Parents and parents alone* should decide whether a school is right for their children; it is no one else's business. Health and safety? Let parents decide. Our cities do not enforce health and safety codes in the homes of the poor. Why should these codes be used to harass poor people's schools, or to prevent people from trying to solve their problems?

Every school charging no tuition and open to all should be considered an independent public school and entitled to tax support per pupil-day on the same basis as state-run schools in its district. Why should the state have a monopoly on public education?

As Peter Marin and others have suggested, we should radically revise all laws that deny children the right to work, travel, and live independently. The laws once passed to protect children now oppress more than they protect. We ought not to deny any child the right to take part in society as fully as he wishes and is able.

Students of any age should get academic credit, as some college students now do, for holding down a job. Better yet, schools should get out of the business of granting credentials as the proof, and only proof, of job-worthiness.

As Christopher Jencks and others have suggested, the best way to finance education might be to give every child an education allowance, for him to spend on his education as he chooses. Parents and their children might in many places develop forms of education vastly more efficient than our present schools.

Too many of our schools are too big to be human. Instead, we could have, in any of our giant school buildings, a number of small schools, each independently run and using its own ideas and methods, and all sharing whatever facilities needed to be shared.

Let students, whose time is taxed by the schools, and who really know and care about them, vote in school-board elections.

Give more time, money and space in all schools for all the arts and for developing physical fitness, strength and skill. Sports, games, athletics are too important to be for just the varsity.

For part of people's lives, we tell them they can't get out of school, and once they're out, we tell them they can't get back in. Let people, of whatever age, go in and out of school when they see fit, using it when it seems most useful to them. Let the learner direct his own learning.

Discussion Questions

1. Why has education failed miserably in the case of the culturally different?

2. Do the ends and means of unicultural schools coincide with the aspirations and habits of culturally different children? Can we diversify our educational system to the extent of enabling it to meet the needs of all children?

3. Should schools strive to integrate everyone into one big happy family or should they try to promote group pride and minority identity? In a society such as ours, should the education of minority groups be different than that of the majority? If yes, in what ways?

4. What school experiences can provide meaning to the life of children who are struggling to find their roots which are buried in poverty and discrimination?

5. How can teachers demonstrate, in tangible ways, greater cultural awareness and respect for the racial and ethnic groups represented in our schools?

6. What types of experience and preparation would enhance our chances of success in the education of the culturally different? Should courses be required of the student of education in the fields of culture differences, poverty, and racial tensions?

7. Do individuals with cultural backgrounds similar to those of their students become better teachers than individuals with backgrounds different from their students?

8. What steps can teachers take to help the culturally different overcome the handicaps their environment may have imposed on them?

9. How can teachers overcome communication problems caused by children from different cultural backgrounds? In what ways can teachers encourage cultural understanding between students of varying backgrounds? How do we teach acceptance of individual and group differences, and how can we help culturally different children trust and identify with one another?

10. To what extent do teacher expectations and/or prejudices affect the performance of students?

11. How much should teachers know about their students in order to help them help themselves? How far should they probe into the private lives of students?

12. What programs have been tried, governmental or otherwise, for the education of the culturally different children? How successful have they been?

13. To what extent should students be allowed to use their language or dialect (other than English) as well as other cultural traits? Should English be used as a second language by children entering school and speaking a different language?

14. Will "bussing" be effective in producing an educational system free of shame and discrimination? What are some of the *pro* and *con* arguments to bussing?

15. How can teachers elicit and secure parental and community cooperation?

Project: Considering the different philosophies, thoughts, feelings, suggestions, and implementation of ideas offered by the authors of this section of the book, would you stay with the public school system or would you go out of the system to make your reforms? In either case, what positive steps would you take to enable the school to meet its challenge? Discuss your educational design.

Selected References

Ackerman, Nathan, *et al., Summerhill: For and Against* (Miami, Florida: Hart Publishing Co., Inc., 1970). This book is composed of 15 essays which are reactions to *Summerhill.* They range from blind praise of Neill and his views to a blind criticism.

Coleman, J. S. *et al., Equality of Educational Opportunity* (The Coleman Report) (U.S. Department of Health, Education and Welfare, Office of Education, 1966). This study attempted to assess the effect of segregation on the quality of education. One significant conclusion was that a child's performance in school could be predicted by the family's income independently of innate ability.

Glasser, William, *Schools Without Failure* (New York: Harper & Row, Publishers, 1969). The author presents a challenging program based on increased involvement, relevance, and thinking instead of mere memory drill. Schools should develop programs that will help children succeed and become involved in responsible human relationships.

Goodman, Paul, *Compulsory Mis-Education* (New York: Vintage Books, Random House, Inc., 1970). The author holds that schools are among those institutions responsible for and contributing to the ills of society.

Gross, Ronald and Beatrice Gross, *Radical School Reform* (New York: Simon and Schuster, Inc., 1969). This is a book of readings that brings together the thoughts of radical educational reformers.

Holt, John *How Children Fail* (New York: Pitman Publishing Corporation, 1964). This book presents a disquieting dissection of why schools often fail to meet the needs of students. Children who try to protect themselves against failure only succeed in cutting themselves off from living, growing, and learning. His other books, *How Children Learn* (Pitman, 1969), *The Underachieving School* (Pitman, 1969), and *What Do I Do Monday* (Dutton, 1970), carry a powerful message for effective learning. They formulate more precisely what Holt deems wrong with the schools and what we must do to make them viable places for our most important commodity—the students.

Illich, Ivan, *De-Schooling Society* (New York: Harper & Row Publishers, 1970). Illich tries to draw a line between schooling and education, and puts his emphasis on the notion of returning the freedom and the responsibility of education to the individual. He discusses some interesting ideas, one of which is the redistribution of educational resources through a credit-card approach.

Kohl, Herbert, *36 Children* (New York: New American Library, 1967). Kohl gives a reflection on his experiences in the New York schools and a plea for the liberation of children from the deadening rote and discipline of "closed" classrooms. Schools can be effective if teachers want to try. In his other book, *The Open Classroom* (The New York Review, 1969), he discusses methods which will bring about desired changes.

Krishnamurti, J., *Education and the Significance of Life* (New York: Harper & Row Publishers, 1953). The author discusses freedom, understanding, love and the meaning of life. Teachers, he says, should be truly free and aware of themselves before making the commitment to teaching.

Leonard, George, *Education and Ecstasy* (New York: Delacorte Press, 1968). Leonard asserts that when joy is absent, the effectiveness of the learning process falls and falls until the human being is operating hesitatingly, grudgingly, and fearfully at only a tiny fraction of his potential. The educator should seek out the possibility of delight in every form of learning. The skillful pursuit of ecstasy will create the pursuit of excellence, not for the few, but for the many, what it never has been—successful.

Montessori, Maria, *The Montessori Method* (New York: Schoken Books, Inc., 1964). Montessori offers a systematic method for facilitating cognitive development.

Neill, A. S., *Summerhill: A Radical Approach to Child Rearing* (Miami, Florida: Hart Publishing Co., Inc., 1960). Neill put his emphasis on extensive freedom for children. His book caused a powerful and strange appeal among teachers and laymen alike for its stimulating, exciting and challenging message. In another book, *Freedom - Not License!* (Hart, 1966), Neill offers direct answers to questions from parents.

Piaget, Jean, *The Science of Teaching and the Psychology of the Child* (New York: Grossman Publishers, Inc., The Viking Press, Inc., 1970). This book is a classic in the area of child development.

Silberman, Charles, *Crisis in the Classroom: The Remaking of American Education* (New York: Random House, Inc., 1970). Silberman's information is based on a study sponsored by the Carnegie Corporation. Based on studies of literature, visitations of schools, and interviews, Silberman found that schools operate on irrelevant curricula, too much control and distrust. He suggests changes for an "open" and "informal" education.

Part 2

Technology's Impact on Education: Reflections

Overview

Strangely enough, the school in contemporary America has been held accountable for the inability of her people to cope with problems of enormous magnitude. Instead, these problems were brought about by new forms of relationships between humans and their environment. The schools cannot be any better or any worse than the society they represent: they reflect both its strengths and its weaknesses. We must realize that education is a shared responsibility between those directly involved in the very tasks of teaching and learning and those beyond who take part in school decisions and set the priorities for social arrangements. If there is any future for education, our whole perspective should be based on the apparent strengths of our schools. Many promising attempts to improve schools have been made by individuals and institutions of learning, and signs of success have already appeared on the wall. Some people of great ambitions believe that the school might reach the "height of the time"—to use Jose Ortega's phrase—and fulfill its obligations in a not too distant future.

In Part 1 several practical ideas were offered for the improvement of teaching and learning. Our difficult task of educating the culturally different (and for that matter, all children), would undoubtedly be helped through proper use of technological devices. This part of the book centers on the impact technology has had on the nature of society and on the role of our educational institutions. The authors offer assurances as to the effectiveness of wise and proper use of instructional technology. Humanistic fears are discussed and gently discarded.

As early as 1960, Jerome Bruner discussed the teaching machine in relation to other aids to teaching and also in relation to the teacher and the entire business of learning. He states that it is still far too early to evaluate the eventual use of technological tools in education, and it is highly unfortunate that such exaggerated claims have been made by both proponents and opponents.

Edgar Friedenberg's "Effects of the Technological Mystique on Schooling" is a shortened version of a paper that was one of the support papers for *To Improve Learning, A Report to the President and the Congress of the United States by the Commission on Instructional Technology.* Friedenberg discusses the advantages of improved educational technology with specific references to disadvantaged children, administrative procedures, and the quality of communication. Technological improvement in education cannot induce school people to do a better job than they want to do, he says; it is concerned with means, not ends. It can, however, help them do their present job more effectively.

No one has put so much faith in science for determining man's behavior as has B. F. Skinner. He departs from the traditional views on the nature of man, society, and values, and proposes the utilization of scientific technique to engineer a happy man in a happy society. This type of thinking led him to programmed instruction and the teaching machine. In "Teaching Science in High School—What Is Wrong?" Skinner discusses his behavioristic views by pointing to the need of and the advantages offered by programmed instruction.

In his answers to a *Playboy* interview, Marshall McLuhan expresses his widely publicized ideas about the impact technology has had upon man and his environment. For all his abstractness, McLuhan has found positive humanistic meaning and the color of life in technological developments man is using. He sees societies being shaped more by the nature of the media through which men communicate than by the content of their communication. In his opinion one of the things which will happen in the immediate future is the deliberate programming of environments instead of curriculums, the deliberate programming of environments as teaching machines.

Kenneth Melvin takes the lead among McLuhan's critics. He states that McLuhanism is a pretentious foray that demonstrates dramatically what the ancient heresy of methodology can presume under this newest ink-wet cybernetic. Melvin has abstracted several of McLuhan's ideas and commented on them with biting criticism. He agrees that today's technology is probably the most important advancement since the invention of the movable table, but for the educator concerned with the formation of worthy character, as distinct from retrieval and fact finding, it is ominous.

Patrick Suppes has found that the use of computer technology in education has enormous potential for improving quality, especially in the area of individualized instruction. He discusses important issues that have raised controversy and concludes that the problem is to learn how to use machines well.

A more optimistic view is expressed by David Engler. As he sees it, only a new instructional technology can change the existing ecological balance in education; the tools and techniques are available. He believes that the use of technology can further humanize education; he sees no conflict between humanism and instructional technology. Where the machine can satisfy the factual part of learning, the teacher can perform his humanitarian task. Engler calls for getting on with the use of technology to further humanize education and to achieve the goals of supporters of the humanities.

In my article "Teachers and Machines Must Learn to Live Together," I have reflected on points which should not fail to attract the attention of those who honestly want proper use of technological means for the education of our youth. I call for a distinction between the teacher and his tools, for a systematic approach, and for administrative rearrangements based on informed knowledge and trust. I am convinced that technological devices are not in themselves good or bad; it is the *manner* of their use that determines their value.

JEROME BRUNER

Aids to Teaching

There has been a great deal of discussion in recent years about the devices that can be employed to aid in the teaching process. These devices are of many kinds. Some of them are designed to present material to the student of a kind that would not be available to him in his ordinary school experience. Films, TV, microphotographic film, film strips, sound recordings, and the like are among the devices ordinarily employed in such work. Books also serve in this role. These are the tools by which the student is given vicarious though "direct" experience of events. It does not serve much to dismiss such materials as "merely for enrichment," since it is obvious that such enrichment is one of the principal objectives of education. Let us call these *devices for vicarious experience.*

A second type of teaching aid has the function of helping the student to grasp the underlying structure of a phenomenon—to sense the genotype behind the phenotype, to use terms from genetics. The well-wrought laboratory experiment or demonstration is the classic aid in such activity. A closer look at our efforts to get students to grasp structure indicates that there are many other devices and exercises that have the same function. The effort to give visible embodiment to ideas in mathematics is of the same order as the laboratory work. The Stern blocks, Cuisenaire rods, and Dienes blocks, as well as the demonstrations of Piaget and Inhelder . . . have the same function. So too do certain kinds of charts and representations, either in animated or still form. Models, such as a model of the molecule or an idealized model of the respiratory system, serve a comparable function. Needless to say, films and television as well as adroitly illustrated books can be adjuncts to the effort at producing clarity and concrete embodiment.

Reprinted by permission of the publishers from Jerome S. Bruner, *The Process of Education* (Cambridge, Mass.: Harvard University Press), Copyright, 1960, by the President and Fellows of Harvard College.

But there are other, more subtle devices that can be and are being used to lead the student to a sense of the conceptual structure of things he observes. Perhaps the best way to characterize them is to call them "sequential programs." There are certain orders of presentation of materials and ideas in any subject that are more likely than others to lead the student to the main idea. The courses being devised by the University of Illinois Committee on School Mathematics, the School Mathematics Study Group, the Physical Science Study Committee, and others are excellent instances of the well conceived sequence designed to lead the student to an understanding of basic ideas and structures.

The whole range of aids from the laboratory exercise through the mathematical blocks to the programmed sequence we shall, for convenience, speak of as *model devices.*

Closely related to these are what might be called *dramatizing devices.* The historical novel that is true in spirit to its subject, the nature film that dramatizes the struggle of a species in its habitat, the exemplification of an experiment executed by a dramatic personality, exposure to greatness in government by a documentary on the life and service of a Winston Churchill—all these can have the dramatic effect of leading the student to identify more closely with a phenomenon or an idea. Undoubtedly, this "aid" in teaching can best be exemplified by the drama-creating personality of a teacher. But there are many additional dramatic aids upon which teachers can and do call—and one wonders whether they are called upon often enough.

Finally, the past decade has witnessed the emergence of various *automatizing devices,* teaching machines, to aid in teaching. While such devices vary quite widely, they have certain features in common. The machine presents a carefully programmed order of problems or exercises to the student, one step at a time. The student responds selectively in one form or another to the alternatives presented in a problem or exercise. The machine then responds immediately, indicating whether the response was or was not correct. If a correct response is made, the machine moves to the next problem. The progression in difficulty from problem to problem is usually quite gradual in order to keep the student from the discouragement of excessive failure.

What one teaches and how one teaches it with the aid of such devices depends upon the skill and wisdom that goes into the construction of a program of problems. The art of programming a machine is, of course, an extension of the art of teaching. To date, most of the programming has been intuitive and has been entrusted to a teacher of known reputation. It has been remarked by teachers who have written tapes for teaching machines that the exercise has the effect of making one highly conscious of the sequence in which one presents problems and of the aims of the sequence

—whether, for example, one is trying to get children to memorize material or use material cumulatively in doing progressively more difficult problems.

Perhaps the technically most interesting features of such automatic devices are that they can take some of the load of teaching off the teacher's shoulders, and, perhaps more important, that the machine can provide immediate correction or feedback to the student while he is in the act of learning. It is still far too early to evaluate the eventual use of such devices, and it is highly unfortunate that there have been such exaggerated claims made by both proponents and opponents. Clearly, the machine is not going to replace the teacher—indeed, it may create a demand for more and better teachers if the more onerous part of teaching can be relegated to automatic devices. Nor does it seem likely that machines will have the effect of dehumanizing learning any more than books dehumanize learning. A program for a teaching machine is as personal as a book: it can be laced with humor or be grimly dull, can either be a playful activity or be tediously like a close-order drill.

In sum, then, there exist devices to aid the teacher in extending the student's range of experience, in helping him to understand the underlying structure of the material he is learning, and in dramatizing the significance of what he is learning. There are also devices now being developed that can take some of the load of teaching from the teacher's shoulders. How these aids and devices should be used in concert as a system of aids is, of course, the interesting problem.

The matter of "integration" is nicely illustrated in a report on the teaching films used by the Physical Science Study Committee.

> Until quite recently, most educational films were enrichment films, designed primarily to introduce phenomena or experiences that would otherwise be unavailable inside the classroom. Such films are necessarily self-contained, since the producer is ignorant of what his audience has previously learned or what it will go on to learn; he can neither build upon the student's immediate past nor lay the groundwork for his immediate future. In the last few years, another kind of educational film, stimulated to a large extent by television, has made its appearance. These films present the entire substance of a course, and are designed to minimize the need for a teacher. Clearly, it is possible to make extremely useful films in either of these forms, and such films have indeed been made.

Stephen White, who has had a major part in producing the films used in the high school physics course prepared by the PSSC, then goes on to say in his report on the film work of that group, "Every film produced by the PSSC must meet two conditions. It must (1) further the presentation of the PSSC course as a whole, and (2) set the tone and level of the course. For the PSSC film is part of a complex that includes also the text, the laboratory, the classroom, the student, and the teacher."

White describes some of the problems of making the film fit.

The film must fit into this complex and never disrupt it. Obviously, this principle imposes serious restrictions on the producer. The most important of these for the PSSC films lies in the relation between the film and the laboratory. Only at his peril may the producer include in a film experiments which the student should and could do in the laboratory. Occasionally such an experiment will be included because it is essential to the logical development of the film's theme, in which case it is done briefly and allusively. More often, it is considered desirable to repeat on film, with more sophisticated apparatus, an experiment that is suitable for the school laboratory; in such cases the film is made in a manner which indicates clearly that it should be shown *after* the student has done the lab work, and the teacher is strongly urged to defer it until that time.

Other elements in the complex must also be taken into account.

Other restrictions on the film require it to follow the logical development, the spirit, and the vocabulary (where it exists) of the text. Finally, the film must always respect the position of the teacher; it must leave for him those activities which are necessary for him if he is to retain the respect of his class. All these are negative, but the film makes positive contributions to the complex as well. It serves the classroom by directing attention to those aspects of the subject which will best stimulate classroom discussion. Thus, the PSSC film on "Work and Mechanical Energy" deliberately calls attention to the temperature rise in a nail on which work is being done, and thus opens discussion of thermal energy, which the class will meet next. And the film, wherever possible, serves the individual student directly by suggesting work he himself can carry on outside the school; it is for this reason that many PSSC films contain sophisticated experiments performed with simple apparatus.

The writer discusses a second function performed by the integrated teaching film:

The second condition that every film must meet—that of setting level and tone —may well be the most important contribution that the film medium can make. By directing attention to the important questions and the important problems, the film can help assure that all the great mass of fact and concept and theory and application that constitute any field of knowledge will fall into a coherent pattern in which the more important aspects will be clearly differentiated from the trivial. This is most difficult to achieve with the printed word; on film it can be accomplished at times with a gesture. Beyond meeting these two conditions, PSSC attempts in each film to make other substantial contributions to the learning process. Each film shows a real scientist in action, presenting him not as a disembodied intellect but as a normal, active, occasionally fallible human being, dealing rigorously and respectfully with real problems and deriving not only satisfaction but at times excitement from the intellectual pursuit in which he is engaged. It is in this implicit fashion that the films attempt to elucidate the nature of scientists and of the scientific life. . . . The films are scrupulously honest. Experiments that are seen on the screen were carefully performed and are accurately reported. The temptation to use the legerdemain inherent in film processes has been steadily resisted, and in those rare cases where it is used to produce a desirable effect, the student is told explicitly how it is used and why.

The task of the PSSC—the creation of a single high school course in physics—was a specialized one, and the particular problems of the course may not relate to all forms of curriculum construction. Yet there is always a question as to the purpose of any particular device—be it a film of paramecia or a slide projection of a graph or a television show on the Hoover Dam. *The devices themselves cannot dictate their purpose.* Unbridled enthusiasm for audio-visual aids or for teaching machines as panaceas overlooks the paramount importance of what one is trying to accomplish. A perpetual feast of the best teaching films in the world, unrelated to other techniques of teaching, could produce bench-bound passivity. Limiting instruction to a steady diet of classroom recitation supported only by traditional and middling textbooks can make lively subjects dull for the student. The objectives of a curriculum and the balanced means for attaining it should be the guide.

A discussion of teaching aids may seem like an unusual context in which to consider the teacher's role in teaching. Yet, withal, the teacher constitutes the principal aid in the teaching process as it is practiced in our schools. What can be said of the teacher's role in teaching?

It takes no elaborate research to know that communicating knowledge depends in enormous measure upon one's mastery of the knowledge to be communicated. That much is obvious enough—whether the teacher uses other aids or not. It is also quite plain from recent surveys that many primary and secondary school teachers are not, in the view of various official bodies, sufficiently well trained initially to teach their subject. It is also the case that, with the present high turnover in the teaching profession, even relatively well prepared teachers do not have sufficient opportunity to learn their subjects in that special way that comes from teaching it. For teaching is a superb way of learning. There is a beautiful story about a distinguished college teacher of physics. He reports introducing an advanced class to the quantum theory: "I went through it once and looked up only to find the class full of blank faces—they had obviously not understood. I went through it a second time and they still did not understand it. And so I went through it a third time, and that time *I* understood it."

There are certain measures that must be taken to improve the quality of teachers, steps that have been proposed many times and that need no elaboration here. Better recruitment and the possibility of better selection, better substantive education in teacher training institutions, on-the-job training of younger teachers by more experienced ones, in-service and summer institutes, closed-circuit television to continue the education of teachers, improvement in teachers' salaries—all of these must obviously be pursued as objectives. But equally important is the upgrading of the prestige of the teaching profession. This upgrading will depend upon the degree to which we in America are serious about educational reform and the degree to which efforts are made to improve not only the facilities and salaries available to teachers but the support they can count on from the community and from our universities.

One special matter concerning the teacher as communicator of knowledge must be mentioned: the training and qualifications of the elementary school teachers. Several references have already been made to the training of children concretely and intuitively in logical operations that will later be taught more formally in upper primary and secondary school. Such teaching requires special training, and it is not clear what the most effective form of training is. Special emphasis should very likely be given to such work— research on how to train teachers for such teaching along with research on the actual teaching of younger pupils.

The teacher is not only a communicator but a model. Somebody who does not see anything beautiful or powerful about mathematics is not likely to ignite others with a sense of the intrinsic excitement of the subject. A teacher who will not or cannot give play to his own intuitiveness is not likely to be effective in encouraging intuition in his students. To be so insecure that he dares not be caught in a mistake does not make a teacher a likely model of daring. If the teacher will not risk a shaky hypothesis, why should the student?

To communicate knowledge and to provide a model of competence, the teacher must be free to teach and to learn. We have not been sufficiently mindful of the ways in which such freedom can be achieved. Notably, we have been neglectful of the uses to which educated parents can be put. Various schools have experimented successfully with plans that use parents for the semiprofessional tasks that keep teachers pinned down. Parents can certainly help in supervising study halls, in grading routine quizzes, in preparing laboratory materials, and in the dozens of routine operations necessary in a school. The effect would be to free the teacher for teaching and study. If the teacher is also learning, teaching takes on a new quality.

The teacher is also an immediately personal symbol of the educational process, a figure with whom students can identify and compare themselves. Who is not able to recall the impact of some particular teacher—an enthusiast, a devotee of a point of view, a disciplinarian whose ardor came from love of a subject, a playful but serious mind? There are many images, and they are precious. Alas, there are also destructive images: the teachers who sapped confidence, the dream killers, and the rest of the cabinet of horrors.

Whitehead once remarked that education should involve an exposure to greatness. Many of us have been fortunate. But there is no simple plan for attracting greatness to the teaching profession. Emphasis on excellence is still the slow but likely way. Might it not be the case, however, that television and film might expand the range of identification figures—models of greatness—within the special limits imposed by one-way communication? We know relatively little about effective identification figures for children at different ages and in different circumstances. Are Olympian models the only ones or the best ones for engaging a child's sense of competence or greatness? Perhaps promising high school students as guest teachers from time to time would do better? They might also lure more talent into teaching.

In sum, then, the teacher's task as communicator, model, and identification figure can be supported by a wise use of a variety of devices that expand experience, clarify it, and give it personal significance. There need be no conflict between the teacher and the aids to teaching. There will be no conflict if the development of aids takes into account the aims and the requirements of teaching. The film or television show as gimmick, the television system without substance or style in its programs, the pictographically vivid portrayal of the trivial—these will help neither the teacher nor the student. Problems of quality in a curriculum cannot be dodged by the purchase of sixteen-millimeter projection equipment. The National Defense Education Act provides considerable sums of money for the development of audio-visual aids. The intelligent use of that money and of other resources now available will depend upon how well we are able to integrate the technique of the film maker or the program producer with the technique and wisdom of the skillful teacher.

Effects of the Technological Mystique On Schooling

Liberal democracy is so firmly committed to the idea that public education is unquestionably good for the individual and society that [the] enormous expansion of the education industry is assumed to be a notable national achievement and an unalloyed blessing. Education does not share with the military its access to unlimited funding—bond issues and tax increases for educational purposes are often quite strongly resisted—but it does share, as no other public venture does, its immunity to popular *radical* criticism. There is constant complaint, certainly, that the schools are not doing as good a job as they might. . . . But except—again as with the military—from intellectuals, there is hardly ever a voice raised to suggest that what the schools are doing may be not only poorly done but undesirable, and may violate the interests of quite legitimate minorities in the society—especially those of youth itself—while it serves others; and that increased efficiency and indefinite expansion of the educational enterprise may result in a further loss of diversity and encroachment on civil liberty. Yet, I believe that this is so; and that in exploring the question "Cui bono?" I have dealt sufficiently with "Quo warranto?" as well. For the mandate under which the schools operate is essentially a conservative mandate; a mandate to keep the place of youth—our last disfranchised minority—in society defined and limited as it is. And what is expected of new instructional technology, surely, is primarily that it keeps them happy enough to prevent trouble, but not so happy as to arouse the envy and suspicion of their elders; and, above all, that it reach and involve "disadvantaged" children before they abandon the educational system altogether as a proper channel for their aspirations and begin, instead, to aspire toward goals which the educational system does not accept and to develop extramural and possibly antisocial means of achieving them. . . .

Excerpted from *To Improve Learning* (New York: R. R. Bowker Company, 1970), pp. 13-23.

There are . . . consequences of the use of improved instructional technology that will, I believe, contribute on balance to making education freer, more humane, and less bound to shabby-genteel norms. These consequences are not sought for their own sake and would not arouse the enthusiasm of school personnel if they were fully anticipated. They are rather in the nature of side effects. But the side-effects of communications technology, as McLuhan has stressed, are often far more significant than the intended consequences; and this is likely to be as true in school as out. Some of these will, I think, be very desirable. . . .

The first of these desirable effects is a greater centralization of resources for curriculum construction, which is likely to have several beneficial consequences—as well as some not so beneficial which in most situations will, I think, be less important. Obviously, the takeover of the preparation of curricular materials by the mass media from smaller and more parochial publishing firms which are less able to resist the parochialism of the school systems themselves, will permit a more costly production job to be done. This will make the new materials slicker, and the new technologies more elaborate—which is not good. But it will also permit the hiring of more skilled people with a higher level of scholarship and ingenuity to work on their preparation in the first place; and these people, though they must ultimately appeal to their institutional clients, are surely less exposed to local but often violent community pressures to narrow or emasculate their materials.

As the newer instructional technologies prevail more and more, the effect on instruction will probably be comparable to the spread of Howard Johnson's restaurants and motels on the general quality of food and lodging available in the country; or of the establishment of flight kitchens for airlines in major airports. The results will never be either as good or as responsive as a first rate chef or inn-keeper would provide; local variation will be superficial and whimsical if, indeed, it occurs at all; there can be considerable built-in flexibility in what is offered, but no spontaneity. Nevertheless, in most towns with a Ho-Jo's, the food and accommodation are better than could be obtained anywhere else for miles around; and it would usually be unwise for a first class passenger in a transcontinental airliner to seek equally good food and service—poor as he may be getting aloft—in the drive-in immediately beneath him, even if it *is* very popular with truck-drivers. Ho-Jo's and the airliner have better equipment to work with, both in food preparation and distribution and in cost accounting; they can deliver a better product per unit of cost. Moreover, they are much less ignorant and slightly less contemptuous of the tradition they work in: Howard Johnson's Beef Bourguignon won't make anybody think of Dijon, but the food technologists who devised it did, I think, have a fair Platonic conception of the real thing and were influenced by it in a civilized direction. You should only have anything as good in a school cafeteria; you better believe it.

The same thing will, I believe, happen with books, films, tapes, extra-sensory irradiations—whatever the medium, the message should be a bit richer; just as network TV, ghastly as it is, is better than what comes on local option time. This will seem a curious statement from a person who favors, as I do, school decentralization. But that is necessary in order to protect the autonomy of the client, which is the first consideration. Decen-tralization would not, certainly, contribute in the same way to the improve-ment of the curricular devices and services offered him.

Will this reduce the teacher to the status of a plastic *geisha,* as it has airline stewardesses—who initially were qualified R.N.'s with a quite differ-ent conception of their role? It will surely tend in that direction; but is this not also on balance a good thing? Airline stewardesses today come from about the same social class as schoolteachers; they are not notably less well educated; and they do not behave altogether differently. Notice how they handle passengers—especially in the more crowded Y-class section—who don't want to watch the movie on transcontinental flights; observe how readily they summon an officer from the cockpit to deal with a drunken passenger, and how unenthusiastically they greet the demands of an occa-sional passenger for a little unscheduled diversion, as of the aircraft to Havana—surely one of the most interesting cities in North America at the present time and one which, in the ordinary course of business, they would never get to visit. What keeps stewardesses from becoming oppressive is neither their *elan vital* or their devotion to their clients—both are often obviously limited—but the mutual understanding between the stewardess and her client that her role is actually carefully defined and largely limited to supplying him with preprocessed comforts and services to which his ticket, as a contract, entitles him. Granted a minimal civility, then, her personality really doesn't matter very much; and the occasions when one feels that one is thereby missing something are fewer than those on which one is grateful to be spared. Similarly, if centralized technology limits the scope of the dedicated teacher, it will also limit the effective lethal range of the vulgar-minded martinet.

There is already evidence, indeed, that "teaching machines" prove partic-ularly effective with schizophrenic children who, in the ethnocentric lan-guage of the institutions that classify them "cannot relate to other people"; but who must, themselves, surely experience these other people as unbear-ably threatening or intrusive. We must, to be sure, beware of expecting too much on the strength of observations which may reflect nothing more than the primitive quality of present equipment. It would hardly challenge the art to devise a machine which would respond to wrong answers not by a neutral message but by a painful shock; the unit might even include a photo-electric cell to determine whether or not its pupil was black so that the shock could be diminished or intensified according to the political climate of the school district. Since the introduction of impunitive devices might seriously disrupt the routines of control and lead to the breakdown of law and order, it would perhaps be fruitless even to attempt to sell machines to major urban school districts until these refinements could be incorporated within them. Nevertheless, as of now, seriously disturbed children are less frightened of the machines than they are of teachers; and there must be many more children who, while not so disturbed but that they can relate to school personnel, would find machines more humane and easier to get along with.

The advantages I have attributed to improved educational technology in my discussion so far have been related to the quality of communication which it will help to supply to pupils. But there will be, I think, administrative advantages as well. The engines of contemporary technology are much better at keeping accurate, neat records, than people are; and while such record keeping adds to their operating costs it does not add to their operating time. For this reason, their widespread introduction into schools will either tend to relieve teachers of their horrible present burden of paperwork or, according to Parkinson's law, require a new rationale for its expansion. While, in any social situation, status factors tend to prevail over technological innovation so that administrators might merely find new kinds of busy-work for their staffs, the possibility of eliminating this tedium is still worth taking. A more fundamental administrative advantage of shifting some of the curricular load from teaching staff to programmed devices may be derived from the very casual attitude of Americans to machinery of all kinds. We expect equipment to be quickly obsolescent, and design it for replacement rather than repair. We do not, in short, give it tenure; and can scrap it when it becomes a drag on the enterprise. This is not an irrelevant attraction to a school system.

Most of the arguments I have read for the adoption of advanced instructional technology rest primarily on the expectation that the new media will permit the curriculum to be enriched by bringing a wider range of phenomena into the classroom and help the school to transcend its boundaries and its students to transcend their provincialism and limited social and geographical mobility—especially if they are "culturally disadvantaged." The new technology is expected, that is, to give them broader and higher horizons. I doubt this very much. It is more likely to add to their passivity by making even more of their experience of life either into a show that one watches or a game that one plays with a friendly computer. The life of the American masses is like that already in relation to the events that affect it; there must be very widespread resentment that the sponsor of our political assassinations, if there is one, has not managed to schedule these events more regularly, and on prime evening time; so that one might plan one's viewing. Moreover, McLuhan is right; the medium, not its content, is the message. There is no such thing as being present at an event through the medium of TV though there are many events to which TV gives an observer more intimate access than he could gain by being present. What one learns, instead, is that intimacy can be—and is at best—vicarious. One of the many comforts that Truman Capote must have afforded to poor Richard Hickok and Perry Smith during their last hours was the implication—inescapable from the very nature of his participation in social reality—that what they were really doing was working on a script for a movie the young men had begun, which they would all see together later.

There are severe limits, moreover—though educators are, as a profession, reluctant to acknowledge them—on the degree to which education, however technically ingenious, can impinge on the experience of persons who find it cognitively dissonant, whether because its idiom or its format is inappropriate to persons of their social class, or for more idiosyncratic reasons. Reality, itself, does not work much better. Foreign travel, notoriously, does not broaden the horizons of soldiers; it usually antagonizes them by showing them that the world is even more full of gooks than they had supposed, all of whom, in President Johnson's deathless phrase, "want what we've got; and we aren't gonna give it to 'em!" So I am not going to rest any claim for the desirability of improved instructional technology on the imputation that it offers improved communication. I'm not so sure; and, in any case, the curriculum of the school has always seemed to me largely the pretext on which students were obliged to submit to its routines, which are the real educative experience; and their function is not benign. The fundamental function of the schools is not to liberate; but to extinguish alternatives to socialization; and a lively, vital, probing curriculum would do this less effectively. From the point of view of a conservative, mass society, the ideal school functions like a domineering and unattractive wife who *derives* her authority from her stupidity; who would never acknowledge that she even comprehended that she might be abandoned if she did not become more loving—or at least more tactful; and who punished infidelity by suspension of the dubious privileges of the bedchamber but never—no, never—by divorce. Its relationship to the evolving potential of its students is, roughly, that of Lucy to the evolving potential of Charlie Brown.

Technological improvement in education cannot induce school authorities to do a better job than they want to do, though it may enable them to do their present job more effectively, for it is concerned with means, not ends. For this reason, it is to be feared. Yet, it is also a source of hope for administrative and structural change which will alter the locus of decision and simply bypass the dingiest and most pettily provincial forces that affect curriculum.

B. F. SKINNER

Teaching Science in High School – What Is Wrong?

(As originally published, the paper begins with a statement of the problem of science teaching, an analysis of traditional instructional methods, and discussions of "discovery" and "aversive control.")

Programmed Instruction

Programmed instruction is primarily a way of using recent advances in our understanding of human behavior. We want to strengthen certain kinds of behavior in our students and so far as we know, there is only one way of doing so. Behavior is strengthened when it is followed by certain kinds of consequences. To be more precise, a response which produces a so-called positive reinforcer or terminates a negative is more likely to occur again under similar circumstances. We use this principle of "operant conditioning" to strengthen behavior by arranging reinforcing consequences—by making available reinforcers contingent on behavior. This is often said to be nothing more than reward and punishment, and there is certainly a connection. But the traditional concepts of reward and punishment are about as close to operant conditioning as traditional concepts of heat, space, or matter are to contemporary scientific treatments. Only a detailed experimental analysis of contingencies of reinforcement will supply the principles we need in the design of effective instructional practices.

Teaching is the arrangement of contingencies of reinforcement which expedite learning. Learning occurs without teaching, fortunately, but improved contingencies speed the process and may even generate behavior

Excerpted from *Science, 159* (February 16, 1968), pp. 704-10. Copyright 1968 by the American Association for the Advancement of Science.

which would otherwise never appear. Programmed instruction is designed to solve a special problem. We cannot simply wait for our student to behave in a given way, particularly in the complex ways characteristic of a scientist, in order to reinforce him. Somehow or other we must get him to behave. Our culture has devised relevant techniques for other than educational purposes. We resort to verbal instruction, for example, when we simply tell the student what to do, or we show him what to do and let him imitate us. If we induce the student to engage in terminal behavior in that way, however, he will be much too dependent upon being shown or told. He will not have learned. We begin instead with whatever behavior the student has available—with behavior which does not call for much help. We selectively reinforce any part which contributes to the terminal pattern or makes it more likely that the student will behave in other ways which contribute to it. The devices we use to evoke the behavior can then be easily withdrawn, so that the terminal behavior appears upon appropriate occasions without help. A high degree of technical knowledge is needed to do this.

Many instructional programs have been written by those who do not understand the basic principle, and it is an unhappy reflection on the state of education today that they are still probably better than unprogrammed materials, but they give a wrong impression. Even a good program may be misleading to anyone who is already proficient in a field because he cannot easily appreciate its effect on a new learner. Anyone who wants to get the feel of programmed instruction should try his hand at a good program in an unfamiliar subject. A colleague whose work had begun to move in the direction of biochemistry worked through an excellent program in that field. "In 3 days," he told me, "I knew biochemistry!" He was exaggerating, of course, as we both knew, but he was expressing very well the almost miraculous effect of a good program.

A further misunderstanding has arisen from the fact that industry and the Armed Services have taken up programmed instruction much more rapidly than schools and colleges. There are some obvious reasons. For one thing, teaching techniques in these organizations can be easily changed. For another, there are people in industry and the Armed Services whose job it is to see that no possible improvement in teaching is overlooked. Unfortunately they have no counterparts in school and college administrations. Explanations of this sort have not prevented the erroneous conclusion that there is another reason why instruction is particularly suited to industry and the Services. Instruction there is said to be of a special nature, a matter of training rather than teaching. This is a very dubious distinction. Training once meant nonverbal instruction, usually through the use of training devices, but that is no longer true. Industry and the Services teach many of the things taught in schools and colleges, although the terminal behavior admittedly comes in smaller packages. The important thing is that it can be more easily specified. The traditional distinction comes down to this: when we know what we are doing, we are training; when we do not know what we are doing, we are teaching. Once we have taken the important first step and specified what we want the student to do as the result of having been taught, we can begin to teach in ways with respect to which this outworn distinction is meaningless.

In doing so we need not abandon any of our goals. We must simply define them. Any behavior which can be specified can be programmed. An experimental analysis has much more to offer in this direction than is generally realized. It is far from a crude stimulus-response theory and is not committed to rote memorizing or the imparting of monolithic, unchanging truth. It has as much to say about solving problems, inductive or deductive reasoning, and creative insight as about learning facts. We have only to define these terms and a technology of teaching becomes applicable. Specification, of course, is only the first step. Good programs must be constructed. At the moment only a few people have the necessary competence, but this is one of the points at which educational reform should start. Scientists, as subject matter specialists, must play a major role.

Classroom Management

Another important application is in classroom management. The teacher who understands reinforcement and is aware of the reinforcing effects of his own behavior can control his class. Those who are interested in the intellectual side of education have tended to neglect classroom discipline, but at great cost. Much of the time of both student and teacher is now spent in ways which contribute little to education. Students who are particularly hard to manage are often in effect abandoned, although there are probably geniuses among them.

It is here that the transition from older aversive practices is most conspicuous. Many educational reformers—Admiral Rickover among them, for example—look with envy on the disciplined classroom of European schools. It appears to be a background against which the student uses his time most profitably. But punitive techniques have objectionable by-products, and we are led to explore the possibility of creating an equally favorable background in other ways. Special skills on the part of the teacher are needed, not only in maintaining discipline but in teaching the kinds of nonverbal behavior which figure so prominently in such fields as laboratory experimentation. It is a particularly difficult problem because we must compete with other contingencies in the student's daily life involving sex, aggression, competitive sports, and so on. Too often the good student is simply one who is unsuccessful in other ways. He responds to our instructional contingencies only because he has not come under the control of others. The result, of course, is poor selection. We need to recruit scientists from those who could be successful in any walk of life. To do so we must take the design of classroom behavior seriously.

Effective instructional contingencies in the classroom are more difficult to arrange than those in programmed instruction. Curiously enough, the nature of the enterprise is clearest with respect to a more difficult kind of student. Institutions for the care of autistic or retarded children and training schools for juvenile delinquents have begun to make effective use of operant conditioning. Because of either their heredity or their early environments, certain people do not respond well to normal contingencies of reinforcement. A special environment must be constructed. Ogden R. Lindsley has called it a prosthetic environment. Eyeglasses and hearing aids are prosthetic devices which compensate for defective sense organs, as crutches and artificial limbs compensate for defective organs of response. A prosthetic environment compensates for a defective sensitivity to contingencies of reinforcement. In such an environment reinforcers may be clarified; many institutions reinforce students with tokens, exchangeable for other reinforcers such as sweets or privileges, which can be made contingent on behavior in conspicuous ways. Many of these defective people will always require a prosthetic environment, but others can be brought under the control of the reinforcers in daily life, such as personal approval or the successful manipulation of the physical environment, and can thus be prepared for life outside an institution.

Contrived reinforcers intended to have a similar effect are by no means new in education. Marks, grades, diplomas, honors, and prizes, not to mention the teacher's personal approval, are seldom the natural consequences of the student's behavior. They are used on the assumption that natural consequences will not induce the student to learn. Several objections may be leveled against them. In the first place, as conditioned reinforcers they are likely to lose their power. This is even true of personal reinforcers if they are not genuine. When our telephone says to us, "I'm sorry. The number you have reached is not in service at this time," we may respond at first to the "I'm sorry" as if it were spoken, say, by a friend. Eventually, we may stop to ask, *"Who* is sorry?" and look forward to the day when machines will be permitted to behave like machines. The computers used in computer-aided instruction are particularly likely to "get personal" in this way. They call the young student by name and type out exclamations of delight at his progress. But the natural consequences which made these expressions reinforcing in the first place are not forthcoming, and the effects extinguish. What is not so obvious is that personal approval may be equally spurious. George Bernard Shaw is responsible for a principle which may be stated in this way: never strike a child except in anger. A complementary principle in the classroom is this: never admire a student except when he is behaving admirably. Contrived admiration is self-defeating.

But the objection to grades, prizes, and synthetic personal approval is not that they are contrived, but that the contingencies in which they are used are bad. An experimental analysis is most valuable at just this point. To bring a class under control, the teacher must begin by making available reinforcers explicitly contingent on the desired behavior. Some students may need reinforcers as conspicuous as tokens or points exchangeable for goods or privileges. Money is a token reinforcer which should not be ruled out of account. (It could solve the high school dropout problem if the contingencies were right.) But once a classroom has been brought under control, a teacher must move to more subtle contingencies and eventually to those inherent in the everyday physical and social environment of the student.

Techniques of reinforcement are now available which can replace the aversive techniques which have dominated education for thousands of years. We can have students who pay attention not because they are afraid of the consequences if they do not, or because they are attracted by fascinating if often meretricious features, but because paying attention has proved to be worthwhile. We can have students who are interested in their work not because work has been chosen which is interesting or because its relation to interesting things has been stressed, but because the complex behavior we call taking an interest has been abundantly reinforced. We can have students who learn not because they will be punished for not learning, but because they have begun to feel the natural advantages of knowledge over ignorance. We can have students who will continue to behave effectively after instruction has ceased because the contingencies which have been used by their teachers find counterparts in daily life.

Above all, we can have dedicated students who will become dedicated men and women. Many interesting aspects of human behavior, often attributed to something called motivation, are the results of various schedules of reinforcement to which almost no attention has been given in educational theory. A common criticism of programmed instruction, for example, is that frequent reinforcement leaves the student unprepared for a world in which reinforcers may be scarce, and this would be true if the possibility were neglected. But programming techniques are available which permit us to sustain the behavior of the student even when reinforcers are very rare indeed. One of the most powerful schedules, the so-called variable-ratio schedule, is characteristic of all gambling systems. The gambler cannot be sure the next play will win, but a certain mean ratio of plays to wins is maintained by the system. A high ratio will not take control if it is encountered without preparation, because any available behavior will extinguish during a long run, but a low ratio will be effective and can be "stretched" as the behavior builds up. This is the way a dishonest gambler hooks his victim. At first the victim is permitted to win fairly often, but as the probability that he will continue to play increases, the ratio is increased. Eventually he continues to play when he is not winning at all. The power of the schedule is most obvious when it produces a pathological gambler, but pigeons, rats, monkeys, and other lowly organisms have become pathological gamblers on the same schedule.

And so have scientists. The prospector, the explorer, the investigator, the experimenter—all meet with success on a variable-ratio schedule. The dedicated scientist continues to work even though the ratio of responses to reinforcement is very high, but he would not have become a dedicated scientist if he had started at that ratio. It would not be correct to say that we can always arrange a program which starts with frequent successes and leads inevitably to a high ratio, but at least we know the kind of schedule needed. In any case, the extraordinary effects of scheduled reinforcements should not be overlooked. In designing a laboratory course, for example, if we keep an eye on the student's successes and particularly on the way in which they are spaced, we are more likely to produce a student who not only knows how to conduct experiments but shows an uncontrollable enthusiasm for doing so.

The new materials which have been made available for teaching science in high school are genuinely exciting, but the fact remains that classroom practice has not really changed very much. The forces which make practices traditional make them easy to transmit to new teachers. The relations between student and teachers demanded by such practices arouse no anxiety. The practices can be justified to parents, policy makers, supporters of education, and students themselves. They call for no extensive changes in administration. And of course they have their occasional successes—particularly with good students or in the hands of good teachers. All this favors the *status quo.*

The change which is needed must overcome many handicaps. Much more is known about the basic processes of learning and teaching than is generally realized, but we need to know still more. What is known has not yet been put to use very effectively. The design and construction of methods and materials is a difficult enterprise which demands a kind of specialist who is, at the moment, in short supply. New practices need to be thoroughly tested. And when, at last, we have devised more effective methods, we must convince educators that they should be used. Extensive administrative changes must be made. (The changes required simply to permit the individual student to progress at his own rate are prodigious.) Teachers need to be retrained as skillful behavior engineers. The common complaint that new materials do not work because the teachers are incompetent is not only unfair, it shows a failure to recognize another point at which the improvement of teaching might begin. Materials are good only if they can be used by available teachers. It is quite possible that materials can be designed which will permit teachers to teach well even in fields in which they have no special competence.

The Improvement of Teaching

Scientists are wary of being asked about their "values." They hesitate to speak of progress because they are likely to be asked, "Progress toward what?" They are uneasy in suggesting improvements. "Improvements in what sense?" The current fashion is to speak only of educational *innovation.* All that is claimed for a new practice is that it is new. We need a much more positive attitude. The efficiency of current methods of teaching is deplorably low. The change which occurs in a student as the result of spending one day in high school is discouragingly small. We need to improve education in the simple sense of making it possible to teach more in the same time and with the same effort on the part of teacher and student. It is a difficult assignment —possibly as difficult, say, as the control of population or resolving the threat of nuclear war, but there is no more important problem facing America today because its solution will advance all other solutions.

It is the sort of challenge that scientists are accustomed to accept. They, above all others, should appreciate the need to define objectives—to know, in this instance, what it means to teach science. They should be quick to recognize the weaknesses of casual experience and of folk wisdom based on that experience. They, above all others, should know that no enterprise can improve itself to any great extent without analyzing its basic processes. They should be best able to gage the importance of science in the immediate and distant future and therefore the extent of the disaster which will follow if we fail to recruit for science large numbers of our most intelligent and dedicated men and women. It is no time for half-hearted measures. The improvement of teaching calls for the most powerful methods which science has to offer.

Playboy Interview:
Marshall McLuhan

Playboy: A good deal of the perplexity surrounding your theories is related to the postulation of hot and cool media. Could you give us a brief definition of each?

McLuhan: Basically, a hot medium *ex*cludes and a cool medium *in*cludes; hot media are low in participation, or completion, by the audience and cool media are high in participation. A hot medium is one that extends a single sense with high definition. High definition means a complete filling in of data by the medium without intense audience participation. A photograph, for example, is high definition or hot; whereas a cartoon is low definition or cool, because the rough outline drawing provides very little visual data and requires the viewer to fill in or complete the image himself. The telephone, which gives the ear relatively little data, is thus cool, as is speech; both demand considerable filling in by the listener. On the other hand, radio is a hot medium because it sharply and intensely provides great amounts of high-definition auditory information that leaves little or nothing to be filled in by the audience. A lecture, by the same token, is hot, but a seminar is cool; a book is hot, but a conversation or bull session is cool.

In a cool medium, the audience is an active constituent of the viewing or listening experience. A girl wearing open-mesh silk stockings or glasses is inherently cool and sensual because the eye acts as a surrogate hand in filling in the low-definition image thus engendered. Which is why boys make passes at girls who wear glasses. In any case, the overwhelming majority of our technologies and entertainments since the introduction of print technology have been hot, fragmented, and exclusive, but in the age of television we see a return to cool values and the inclusive in-depth involvement and participation they engender. This is, of course, just one more reason why the medium is the message, rather than the content; it is the participatory nature of the TV experience itself that is important, rather than the content of the particular TV image that is being invisibly and indelibly inscribed on our skins.

Playboy: Even if, as you contend, the medium is the ultimate message, how can you entirely discount the importance of content? Didn't the content of Hitler's radio speeches, for example, have some effect on the Germans?

McLuhan: By stressing that the medium is the message rather than the content, I'm not suggesting that content plays *no* role—merely that it plays a distinctly subordinate role. Even if Hitler had delivered botany lectures, some other demagog would have used the radio to retribalize the Germans and rekindle the dark atavistic side of the tribal nature that created European fascism in the Twenties and Thirties. By placing all the stress on content and practically none on the medium, we lose all chance of perceiving and influencing the impact of new technologies on man, and thus we are always dumfounded by—and unprepared for—the revolutionary environmental transformations induced by new media. Buffeted by environmental changes he cannot comprehend, man echoes the last plaintive cry of his tribal ancestor, Tarzan, as he plummeted to earth: "Who greased my vine?" The German Jew victimized by the Nazis because his old tribalism clashed with their new tribalism could no more understand why his world was turned upside down than the American today can understand the reconfiguration of social and political institutions caused by the electric media in general and television in particular.

Playboy: How is television reshaping our political institutions?

McLuhan: TV is revolutionizing every political system in the Western world. For one thing, it's creating a totally new type of national leader, a man who is much more of a tribal chieftain than a politician. Castro is a good example of the new tribal chieftain who rules his country by a mass-participational TV dialog and feedback; he governs his country on camera, by giving the Cuban people the experience of being directly and intimately involved in the process of collective decision making. Castro's adroit blend of political education, propaganda and avuncular guidance is the pattern for tribal chieftains in other countries. The new political showman has to literally as well as figuratively put on his audience as he would a suit of clothes and become a corporate tribal image—like Mussolini, Hitler and F. D. R. in the days of radio, and Jack Kennedy in the television era. All these men were tribal emperors on a scale theretofore unknown in the world, because they all mastered their media. . . .

The overhauling of our traditional political system is only one manifestation of the retribalizing process wrought by the electric media, which is turning the planet into a global village.

Playboy: Would you describe this retribalizing process in more detail?

McLuhan: The electronically induced technological extensions of our central nervous system, which I spoke of earlier, are immersing us in a worldpool of information movement and are thus enabling man to incorporate within himself the whole of mankind. The aloof and dissociated role of the literate man of the Western world is succumbing to the new, intense depth participation engendered by the electronic media and bringing us back in touch with ourselves as well as with one another. But the instant nature of electric-information movement is decentralizing—rather than enlarging— the family of man into a new state of multitudinous tribal existences. Particularly in countries where literate values are deeply institutionalized, this is a highly traumatic process, since the clash of the old segmented visual culture and the new integral electronic culture creates a crisis of identity, a vacuum of the self, which generates tremendous violence—violence that is simply an identity quest, private or corporate, social or commercial.

Playboy: Do you relate this identity crisis to the current social unrest and violence in the United States?

McLuhan: Yes, and to the booming business psychiatrists are doing. All our alienation and atomization are reflected in the crumbling of such time-honored social values as the right of privacy and the sanctity of the individual; as they yield to the intensities of the new technology's electric circus, it seems to the average citizen that the sky is falling in. As man is tribally metamorphosed by the electric media, we all become Chicken Littles, scurrying around frantically in search of our former identities, and in the process unleash tremendous violence. As the preliterate confronts the literate in the postliterate arena, as new information patterns inundate and uproot the old, mental breakdowns of varying degrees—including the collective nervous breakdowns of whole societies unable to resolve their crises of identity—will become very common.

It is not an easy period in which to live, especially for the television-conditioned young who, unlike their literate elders, cannot take refuge in the zombie trance of Narcissus narcosis that numbs the state of psychic shock induced by the impact of the new media. From Tokyo to Paris to Columbia, youth mindlessly acts out its identity quest in the theater of the streets, searching not for goals but for roles, striving for an identity that eludes them.

Playboy: Why do you think they aren't finding it within the educational system?

McLuhan: Because education, which should be helping youth to understand and adapt to their revolutionary new environments, is instead being used merely as an instrument of cultural aggression, imposing upon retribalized youth the obsolescent visual values of the dying literate age. Our entire educational system is reactionary, oriented to past values and past technologies, and will likely continue so until the old generation relinquishes power. The generation gap is actually a chasm, separating not two age groups but two vastly divergent cultures. I can understand the ferment in our schools, because our educational system is totally rearview mirror. It's a dying and outdated system founded on literate values and fragmented and classified data totally unsuited to the needs of the first television generation.

Playboy: How do you think the educational system can be adapted to accommodate the needs of this television generation?

McLuhan: Well, before we can start doing things the right way, we've got to recognize that we've been doing them the wrong way—which most pedagogs and administrators and even most parents still refuse to accept. Today's child is growing up absurd because he is suspended between two worlds and two value systems, neither of which inclines him to maturity because he belongs wholly to neither but exists in a hybrid limbo of constantly conflicting values. The challenge of the new era is simply the total creative process of *growing up*—and mere teaching and repetition of facts are as irrelevant to this process as a dowser to a nuclear power plant. To expect a "turned on" child of the electric age to respond to the old education modes is rather like expecting an eagle to swim. It's simply not within his environment, and therefore incomprehensible.

The TV child finds it difficult if not impossible to adjust to the fragmented, visual goals of our education after having had all his senses involved by the electric media; he craves in-depth involvement, not linear detachment and uniform sequential patterns. But suddenly and without preparation, he is snatched from the cool, inclusive womb of television and exposed—within a vast bureaucratic structure of courses and credits—to the hot medium of print. His natural instinct, conditioned by the electric media, is to bring all his senses to bear on the book he's instructed to read, and print resolutely rejects that approach, demanding an isolated visual attitude to learning rather than the *Gestalt* approach of the unified sensorium. The reading postures of children in elementary school are a pathetic testimonial to the effects of television; children of the TV generation separate book from eye by an average distance of four and a half inches, attempting psychomimetically to bring to the printed page the all-inclusive sensory experience of TV. They are becoming Cyclops, desperately seeking to wallow in the book as they do in the TV screen.

Playboy: Might it be possible for the "TV child" to make the adjustment to his educational environment by synthesizing traditional literate-visual forms with the insights of his own electric culture—or must the medium of print be totally unassimilable for him?

McLuhan: Such a synthesis is entirely possible, and could create a creative blend of the two cultures—if the educational establishment was aware that there *is* an electric culture. In the absence of such elementary awareness,

I'm afraid that the television child has no future in our schools. You must remember that the TV child has been relentlessly exposed to all the "adult" news of the modern world—war, racial discrimination, rioting, crime, inflation, sexual revolution. The war in Vietnam has written its bloody message on his skin; he has witnessed the assassinations and funerals of the nation's leaders; he's been orbited through the TV screen into the astronaut's dance in space, been inundated by information transmitted via radio, telephone, films, recordings and other people. His parents plopped him down in front of a TV set at the age of two to tranquilize him, and by the time he enters kindergarten, he's clocked as much as 4000 hours of television. As an IBM executive told me, "My children had lived several lifetimes compared to their grandparents when they began grade one."

Playboy: If you had children young enough to belong to the TV generation, how would you educate them?

McLuhan: Certainly not in our current schools, which are intellectual penal institutions. In today's world, to paraphrase Jefferson, the least education is the best education, since very few young minds can survive the intellectual tortures of our educational system. The mosaic image of the TV screen generates a depth-involving *nowness* and simultaneity in the lives of children that makes them scorn the distant visualized goals of traditional education as unreal, irrelevant and puerile. Another basic problem is that in our schools there is simply too much to learn by the traditional analytic methods; this is an age of information overload. The only way to make the schools other than prisons without bars is to start fresh with new techniques and values.

Playboy: A number of experimental projects are bringing both TV and computers directly into the classrooms. Do you consider this sort of electronic educational aid a step in the right direction?

McLuhan: It's not really too important if there is ever a TV set in each classroom across the country, since the sensory and attitudinal revolution has already taken place at home before the child ever reaches school, altering his sensory existence and his mental processes in profound ways. Book learning is no longer sufficient in any subject; the children all say now, "Let's *talk* Spanish," or "Let the Bard be *heard,*" reflecting their rejection of the old sterile system where education begins and ends in a book. What we need now is educational crash programming in depth to first understand and then meet the new challenges. Just putting the present classroom on TV, with its archaic values and methods, won't change anything; it would be just like running movies on television; the result would be a hybrid that is neither. We have to ask what TV can do, in the instruction of English or physics or any other subject, that the classroom cannot do as presently constituted. The answer is that TV can deeply involve youth in the process of learning, illustrating graphically the complex interplay of people and events, the development of forms, the multileveled interrelationships between and among such arbitrarily segregated subjects as biology, geography, mathematics, anthropology, history, literature and languages.

If education is to become relevant to the young of this electric age, we must also supplant the stifling, impersonal and dehumanizing multiversity with a multiplicity of autonomous colleges devoted to an in-depth approach to learning. This must be done immediately, for few adults really comprehend the intensity of youth's alienation from the fragmented mechanical world and its fossilized educational system, which is designed in their minds solely to fit them into classified slots in bureaucratic society. To them, both draft card and degree are passports to psychic, if not physical, oblivion, and they accept neither. A new generation is alienated from its own 3000-year heritage of literacy and visual culture, and the celebration of literate values in home and school only intensifies that alienation. If we don't adapt our educational system to their needs and values, we will see only more dropouts and more chaos.

Playboy: Do you think the surviving hippie subculture is a reflection of youth's rejection of the values of our mechanical society?

McLuhan: Of course. These kids are fed up with jobs and goals, and are determined to forge their own roles and involvement in society. They want nothing to do with our fragmented and specialist consumer society. Living in the transitional identity vacuum between two great antithetical cultures, they are desperately trying to discover themselves and fashion a mode of existence attuned to their new values; thus the stress on developing an "alternate life style." We can see the results of this retribalization process whenever we look at *any* of our youth—not just at hippies. Take the field of fashion, for example, which now finds boys and girls dressing alike and wearing their hair alike, reflecting the unisexuality deriving from the shift from visual to tactile. The younger generation's whole orientation is toward a return to the native, as reflected by their costumes, their music, their long hair and their sociosexual behavior. Our teenage generation is already becoming part of a jungle clan. As youth enters this clan world and all their senses are electrically extended and intensified, there is a corresponding amplification of their sexual sensibilities. Nudity and unabashed sexuality are growing in the electric age because as TV tattoos its message directly on our skins, it renders clothing obsolescent and a barrier, and the new tactility makes it natural for kids to constantly touch one another—as reflected by the button sold in the psychedelic shops: IF IT MOVES, FONDLE IT. The electric media, by stimulating all the senses simultaneously, also give a new and richer sensual dimension to everyday sexuality that makes Henry Miller's style of randy rutting old-fashioned and obsolete. Once a society enters the all-involving tribal mode, it is inevitable that our attitudes toward sexuality change. We see, for example, the ease with which young people live guiltlessly with one another, or, as among the hippies, in communal ménages. This is completely tribal. . . .

Playboy: You said a few minutes ago that *all* of contemporary man's traditional values, attitudes and institutions are going to be destroyed and replaced in and by the new electric age. That's a pretty sweeping generalization. Apart from the complex psychosocial metamorphoses you've mentioned, would you explain in more detail some of the specific changes you foresee?

McLuhan: The transformations are taking place everywhere around us. As the old value systems crumble, so do all the institutional clothing and garb-age they fashioned. The cities, corporate extensions of our physical organs, are withering and being translated along with all other such extensions into information systems, as television and the jet—by compressing time and space—make all the world one village and destroy the old city-country dichotomy. New York, Chicago, Los Angeles—all will disappear like the dinosaur. The automobile, too, will soon be as obsolete as the cities it is currently strangling, replaced by new antigravitational technology. The marketing systems and the stock market as we know them today will soon be dead as the dodo, and automation will end the traditional concept of the job, replacing it with a *role,* and giving men the breath of leisure. The electric media will create a world of dropouts from the old fragmented society, with its neatly compartmentalized analytic functions, and cause people to drop *in* to the new integrated global-village community.

All these convulsive changes, as I've already noted, carry with them attendant pain, violence and war—the normal stigmata of the identity quest —but the new society is springing so quickly from the ashes of the old that I believe it will be possible to avoid the transitional anarchy many predict. Automation and cybernation can play an essential role in smoothing the transition to the new society.

Playboy: How?

McLuhan: The computer can be used to direct a network of global thermostats to pattern life in ways that will optimize human awareness. Already, it's technologically feasible to employ the computer to program societies in beneficial ways.

Playboy: How do you program an entire society—beneficially or otherwise?

McLuhan: There's nothing at all difficult about putting computers in the position where they will be able to conduct carefully orchestrated programming of the sensory life of whole populations. I know it sounds rather science-fictional, but if you understood cybernetics you'd realize we could do it today. The computer could program the media to determine the given messages a people should hear in terms of their over-all needs, creating a total media experience absorbed and patterned by all the senses. We could program five hours less of TV in Italy to promote the reading of newspapers during an election, or lay on an additional twenty-five hours of TV in Venezuela to cool down the tribal temperature raised by radio the preceding month. By such orchestrated interplay of all media, whole cultures could now be programmed in order to improve and stabilize their emotional climates, just as we are beginning to learn how to maintain equilibrium among the world's competing economies. . . .

Playboy: Is it really in our hands—or, by seeming to advocate the use of computers to manipulate the future of entire cultures, aren't you actually encouraging man to abdicate control over his destiny?

McLuhan: First of all—and I'm sorry to have to repeat this disclaimer— I'm not advocating *anything;* I'm merely probing and predicting trends. Even if I opposed them or thought them disastrous, I couldn't stop them, so why waste my time lamenting? As Carlyle said of author Margaret Fuller after she remarked, "I accept the Universe": "She'd better." I see no possibility of a world-wide Luddite rebellion that will smash all machinery to bits, so we might as well sit back and see what is happening and what will happen to us in a cybernetic world. Resenting a new technology will not halt its progress.

The point to remember here is that whenever we use or perceive any technological extension of ourselves, we necessarily embrace it. Whenever we watch a TV screen or read a book, we are absorbing these extensions of ourselves into our individual system and experiencing an automatic "closure" or displacement of perception; we can't escape this perpetual embrace of our daily technology unless we escape the technology itself and flee to a hermit's cave. By consistently embracing all these technologies, we inevitably relate ourselves to them as servomechanisms. Thus, in order to make use of them at all, we must serve them as we do gods. The Eskimo is a servomechanism of his kayak, the cowboy of his horse, the businessman of his clock, the cyberneticist—and soon the entire world—of his computer. In other words, to the spoils belongs the victor.

This continuous modification of man by his own technology stimulates him to find continuous means of modifying it; man thus becomes the sex organs of the machine world just as the bee is of the plant world, permitting it to reproduce and constantly evolve to higher forms. The machine world reciprocates man's devotion by rewarding him with goods and services and bounty. Man's relationship with his machinery is thus inherently symbiotic. This has always been the case; it's only in the electric age that man has an opportunity to *recognize* this marriage to his own technology. Electric technology is a qualitative extension of this age-old man-machine relationship; 20th century man's relationship to the computer is not by nature very different from prehistoric man's relationship to his boat or to his wheel—

with the important difference that all previous technologies or extensions of man were partial and fragmentary, whereas the electric is total and inclusive. Now man is beginning to wear his brain outside his skull and his nerves outside his skin; new technology breeds new man. A recent cartoon portrayed a little boy telling his nonplused mother: "I'm going to be a computer when I grow up." Humor is often prophecy.

Playboy: If man can't prevent this transformation of himself by technology —or *into* technology—how can he control and direct the process of change?

McLuhan: The first and most vital step of all, as I said at the outset, is simply to understand media and its revolutionary effects on all psychic and social values and institutions. Understanding is half the battle. The central purpose of all my work is to convey this message, that by understanding media as they extend man, we gain a measure of control over them. And this is a vital task, because the immediate interface between audile-tactile and visual perception is taking place everywhere around us. No civilian can escape this environmental blitzkrieg, for there is, quite literally, no place to hide. But if we diagnose what is happening to us, we can reduce the ferocity of the winds of change and bring the best elements of the old visual culture, during this transitional period, into peaceful coexistence with the new retribalized society.

If we persist, however, in our conventional rearview-mirror approach to these cataclysmic developments, all of Western culture will be destroyed and swept into the dustbin of history. If literate Western man were really interested in preserving the most creative aspects of his civilization, he would not cower in his ivory tower bemoaning change but would plunge himself into the vortex of electric technology and, by understanding it, dictate his new environment—turn ivory tower into control tower. But I can understand his hostile attitude, because I once shared his visual bias.

. . .

Playboy: You've explained why you avoid approving or disapproving of this revolution in your work, but you must have a private opinion. What is it?

McLuhan: I don't like to tell people what I think is good or bad about the social and psychic changes caused by new media, but if you insist on pinning me down about my own subjective reactions as I observe the reprimitivization of our culture, I would have to say that I view such upheavals with total personal dislike and dissatisfaction. I do see the prospect of a rich and creative retribalized society—free of the fragmentation and alienation of the mechanical age—emerging from this traumatic period of culture clash; but I have nothing but distaste for the *process* of change. As a man molded within the literate Western tradition, I do not personally cheer the dissolution of that tradition through the electric involvement of all the senses: I don't enjoy the destruction of neighborhoods by high-rises or revel in the pain of identity quest. No one could be less enthusiastic about these radical changes than myself. I am not, by temperament or conviction, a revolutionary; I would prefer a stable, changeless environment of modest services and human scale. TV and all the electric media are unraveling the entire fabric of our society, and as a man who is forced by circumstances to live within that society, I do not take delight in this disintegration.

You see, I am not a crusader; I imagine I would be most happy living in a secure preliterate environment; I would never attempt to change my world, for better or worse. Thus I derive no joy from observing the traumatic effects of media on man, although I do obtain satisfaction from grasping their modes of operation. Such comprehension is inherently cool, since it is simultaneously involvement and detachment. This posture is essential in studying media. One must begin by becoming extraenvironmental, putting oneself beyond the battle in order to study and understand the configuration of forces. It's vital to adopt a posture of arrogant superiority; instead of scurrying into a corner and wailing about what media are doing to us, one should charge straight ahead and kick them in the electrodes. They respond beautifully to such resolute treatment and soon become servants rather than masters. But without this detached involvement, I could never objectively observe media; it would be like an octopus grappling with the Empire State Building. So I employ the greatest boon of literate culture: the power of man to act without reaction—the sort of specialization by dissociation that has been the driving motive force behind Western civilization.

The Western world is being revolutionized by the electric media as rapidly as the East is being Westernized, and although the society that eventually emerges may be superior to our own, the process of change is agonizing. I must move through this pain-wracked transitional era as a scientist would move through a world of disease; once a surgeon becomes personally involved and disturbed about the condition of his patient, he loses the power to help that patient. Clinical detachment is not some kind of haughty pose I affect—nor does it reflect any lack of compassion on my part; it's simply a survival strategy. The world we are living in is not one I would have created on my own drawing board, but it's the one in which I must live, and in which the students I teach must live. If nothing else, I owe it to them to avoid the luxury of moral indignation or the troglodytic security of the ivory tower and to get down into the junk yard of environmental change and steam-shovel my way through to a comprehension of its contents and its lines of force—in order to understand how and why it is metamorphosing man.

Playboy: Despite your personal distaste for the upheavals induced by the new electric technology, you seem to feel that if we understand and influence its effects on us, a less alienated and fragmented society may emerge from it. Is it thus accurate to say that you are essentially optimistic about the future?

McLuhan: There are grounds for both optimism and pessimism. The extension of man's consciousness induced by the electric media could conceivably usher in the millennium, but it also holds the potential for realizing the Anti-Christ—Yeats' rough beast, its hour come round at last, slouching toward Bethlehem to be born. Cataclysmic environmental changes such as these are, in and of themselves, morally neutral; it is how we perceive them and react to them that will determine their ultimate psychic and social consequences. If we refuse to see them at all, we will become their servants. It's inevitable that the world-pool of electronic information movement will toss us all about like corks on a stormy sea, but if we keep our cool during the descent into the maelstrom, studying the process as it happens to us and what we can do about it, we can come through.

Personally, I have a great faith in the resiliency and adaptability of man, and I tend to look to our tomorrows with a surge of excitement and hope. I feel that we're standing on the threshold of a liberating and exhilarating world in which the human tribe can become truly one family and man's consciousness can be freed from the shackles of mechanical culture and enabled to roam the cosmos. I have a deep and abiding belief in man's potential to grow and learn, to plumb the depths of his own being and to learn the secret songs that orchestrate the universe. We live in a transitional era of profound pain and tragic identity quest, but the agony of our age is the labor pain of rebirth.

I expect to see the coming decades transform the planet into an art form; the new man, linked in a cosmic harmony that transcends time and space, will sensuously caress and mold and pattern every facet of the terrestrial artifact as if it were a work of art, and man himself will become an organic art form. There is a long road ahead, and the stars are only way stations, but we have begun the journey. To be born in this age is a precious gift, and I regret the prospect of my own death only because I will leave so many pages of man's destiny—if you will excuse the Gutenbergian image—tantalizingly unread. But perhaps, as I've tried to demonstrate in my examination of the postliterate culture, the story begins only when the book closes.

KENNETH MELVIN

McLuhan the Medium

It is, alas, impossible any longer to take McLuhanism seriously. At first, the guru's own obscurity of utterance and meaning had a sort of horrid fascination. It was all so bizarre in a nominated expert in communication. Many of us gave it the benefit of grave doubt, waiting for it to shake down into sense. That hope fades under the multiplying evidence that it is paucity of content no less than incoherence of form which reduces McLuhan to the ranks of the pretenders. The more recent demonstrations just about clinch the matter. Nor is this "genius" betrayed by his disciples; the myth has been made by them in a lengthening series of articles and nonbooks to which the great man adds his signature as Rubens did in his picture-factory. Indeed, for any parallel to the descriptions of this "towering intellect" one must go back to the 18th century Encyclopedists or the *uomo universale* of the High Renaissance.

In the TV spectacular based upon the latest joint-book *(The Medium Is the Massage)* the Box became a veritable Cabinet of Cagliostro—or was it an Abrams machine? For a full hour of glorious technicolor the 20-minute minibook was expanded and illumined by every artifice—constant garish lighting, rapid dissolves, Picasso-shock graphics, and kaleidoscopic filters used as visual incense. Amidst this calculated chaos of sensual massage McLuhan Himself came and went like a brooding spirit—or was it the cataleptic trance of the high-priestess-oracle at Delphi? But the authentic charismatic touches were there: the obvious made epigrammatic, the shattered syntax, the disjunctive sentence as the unit of thought, the pronouncement of old axioms as latter-day revelations, the insouciant *non sequitur,* delivered with all the unction of the sadhu amidst the stupid.

Because one can scarcely verbalize such an experience any more than a perfume or a sunset, we are regrettably shut up to some analysis of the

From *Phi Delta Kappan* (June, 1967), pp. 488–91.

lunatic linearism of the version for the faithful, but those of us without inner grace may forego that fine fruit of a decade of scholarly study and settle for the less artful interpretation by George B. Leonard. This particular exegesis may one day rank as the unintentional *coup de grace* to a nonmovement which did not even have sleight-of-mouth to support it.

The misfortune of it all is that this latest example of fashion in idea, like all fads, distracts public attention from the real problems exercising the minds of professional educators who must first make themselves understood and cannot rely upon impenetrable obfuscation. At a time when teachers are asking what has happened to the great simplicities, we are regaled with this sort of thing: (*vide* Leonard, G. B.)

Item: *"His book* Understanding Media *has already changed the world —and he has not finished."*

Someone must be joking. Not even a senior editor of *Look* magazine and "winner of national awards for education writing" can sanify such a statement. If the world has been changed by the work of any educational theorist we in New England are not privy to it: and this is said to be the intellectual center of America. There is surely as much electric circuitry in educational media throughout Greater Boston as anywhere else, and McLuhan himself came to our Bagdad-by-the-Charles in advance-agency for his 1965 film, "The Child of the Future." The millenium has been unaccountably delayed in this part of the "already changed world."

Item: *"The student must get somewhere."*

Indeed he must. And he did when we took our classes to view that historic film "The Child of the Future." Falling back on the deathless line, one student was heard to say, "Let's get the hell out of here." Not to put too fine a point upon it, that McLuhan epic is no more than *disjecta membra* from ill-assorted clips loosely articulated by jointing-fluid and McLuhan's own fragmentary comments. This sort of ill-considered thing furthers the vested interests of the corporate profit-makers so determined to do education good by exploiting the American gullibility for gimmickry; but it leaves in despair those teachers who are trying systematically if unsensationally to reduce the rigidities of classroom situations in favor of humane values and creative involvement for our children. In this particular film it was painfully evident that scarcely an example occurred in which the individual child—as distinct from the activated group—could feel or come to know what all his busy-work meant apart from fact-finding. Nor did McLuhan's commentary at any point disclose any meaning or purpose for the "involvement" which was his leitmotif.

Item: *"The new modes of instantaneous long-distance human communication—radio, telephone, television—are linking the world's people in a vast net of electric circuitry that creates new depth and breadth of personal involvement in events.*"

What kind of involvement? Antic activity with mechanised means, so far from enriching education, is impoverishing it in America. Two-thirds of your top scientists and technical experts now work for military and space projects, draining off some of the pedigree cream of science graduates and leaving peaceful research and development gravely undermanned. Under chronic teacher shortage at every level there are some 200,000 talented high school graduates who cannot afford a college education which might take them into the teaching profession. This nation is short of 140,000 additional classrooms necessary to take up this slack. But there is no career for anyone telling America about this; irony of ironies, there are Schweitzer Chairs for educational entrepreneurs who can divert public attention sufficiently to get dubious means accepted as noble ends for the educational enterprise.

Item: "*A worldwide network of computers will make all of mankind's factual knowledge available to students everywhere in a matter of minutes or seconds.*"

Here again is the reductive fallacy which degrades education to fact-mongering; the academic salesman's spurious enthusiasm for instant education by "data retrieval"; the unhistorical notion that education can and should take Great Leaps, especially when galvanized by solid-state circuitry. Cultural history records a number of "golden ages" in which the illuminati outran their time and place and circumstances; but the Great Leap theory is as illusory as the zealotry it invokes. There are no revolutions in education because it is not now nor ever has been a fully autonomous entity; it may be the principal agency and vehicle of civilization but it is not *responsible* for civilization. Whole societies are. Therefore, if computerized education took over tomorrow, the crucial programming would of necessity be required to maintain the twofold task of maintaining the given civilization—good and bad—in both the idea-system *and* the value-system by which we live. And to the degree that education becomes technologized, mechanized, and uniformalized as primarily a cognitive affair, it either scamps or scorns the richness of the affective life of the spirit of man. This is to favor the bad over the good in our culture; to proliferate media above the message by making them synonymous; to confuse accident and essence in education by arrogating primacy to one over the other.

Item: "*The student of the future will truly be an explorer, a researcher, a huntsman who ranges through the new educational world of electric circuitry and heightened human interaction just as the tribal huntsman ranged the wilds.*"

So the world becomes "a tribal village" to be hunted over—with all the odious connotations of blood sports. But if McLuhan means something nobler than this, how does a "world of electric circuitry" serve the balanced growth and development of the humane personality? Education is nothing if it is not intellectual adventure, but it has always been much more than the exercise of the *mind.* Does nobody any more read Whitehead's philosophy of civilization, or Schweitzer's, or Bertrand Russell's, or Maritain's?

The "student of the future" will wield no magic weaponry which can reduce the straitened sternness of intellectual, emotional, and spiritual discipline inescapable in genuine education as distinct from the acquisition of marketable skills. Even in graduate school where the student may become "an explorer, a researcher," he will still be a growing, developing human personality. With the eye of compassion his teachers will see his essential vulnerability, on the one hand to ephemeral inconsequence, and on the other to inner confusions. Education will always be the slow, patient, self-correcting, self-directing search for the self between the Scylla and the Charybdis.

Item: *"The time is coming, if it is not already here, when children can learn far more, far faster, in the outside world than within schoolhouse walls."*

Here, as in the opening sentence of *Emile,* we stand upon a peak in Darien. That in fact is how McLuhan and his coadjutors see themselves, bent upon "a new pathfinding adventure" designed to reveal their "vision of the shape, the substance, the spirit of things to come." All, all is Maya. This "adventure," this "vision" lead straight into the discredited past. Surely everybody knows that children have always "learned far more far faster" in the world outside the school? Of course children in the hell's kitchens and ghettos do so, as do the hard-rock miner, the combat soldier, the Madison Avenue executive, the policeman on the beat, the journalist doing legwork. But whether the things they learn are truly educative rather than corruptive depends not a little upon what they did or did not learn in schools. This will continue to be true in any flashing-light cybernetic age that may lie in wait for mankind. Open McLuhan's fist and you find not an empty hand but a pin-head sized transistor. Like all the artifacts of man it will make a contribution to education. But because true education has ever been more than information vending, improved communication will not guarantee that knowledge is virtue. McLuhanism is a pretentious foray that demonstrates dramatically what the ancient heresy of methodology can presume under this newest ink-wet banner of cybernetics.

Item: *"The old education gives us a sure-fire prescription for creating dislike of any type of human activity."*

Everybody knows how change-resistant formal education can be: its sins are like the sands for multitude. The great body of educational publication today is preoccupied with their documentation. It is the vogue for American teachers to be fitted with permanent hair shirts for their professional morti-

fication. Rare indeed is the impenitent who speaks out for the "old education"; he is too conscious of the strictures under which labor such rubrics
as the "old religion." But there is a fundamental difference. Education has
always stood with Heraclitus amidst an ever-changing stream, never the
same in two successive generations, let alone centuries. At least since the
17th century and often despite itself, education has liberalized and modern-
ized despite the culture gap. For all its glacially slow evolution the "old
education" in this fluid sense carries forward the real work and thought of
the world of affairs—to say nothing of the achievements of service and the
aspirations of the spirit of man.

Whatever its defaults and defects, it has been formal education of the
non-McLuhan variety which, since the pyramid-builders of ancient Egypt,
has provided the continuum in human enlightenment. Since we bear the
blame for our faults, let us have also the credit for our accomplishments;
and these would not seem to be so contemptible as McLuhan would assert.
Education has not awaited his coming, nor will it greatly benefit thereby,
because these latest despisers of the inheritance are not reemphasizing the
humanities, nor the human science, nor some fresh concept of service in an
age of technological power and arrogance. Not a bit of it. It remains their
stated belief that "the future of education" lies in maximizing technology
and "pervasive electric circuitry." It is here that the new evangel turns out
to be mere hucksterism.

Item: *"Seven-year-olds (the slowest of them) sitting at electronic consoles, finishing off, at their own pace, all they'll ever need in the basic skills
of reading, writing, and the like. . . ."*

If McLuhanism prevails, that may well be all that children *want,* but by
no stretch of even cybernetic imagination can that be all they will *need* in
the world of tomorrow. American education lies naked and exposed to such
perverse dogmas so long as it is prepared to sell its soul for such a mess of
wattage. Its own great telic philosophers are denigrated as "philosophers of
process"; the normative mode of thought, conduct, and values is *de rigeur.*
With this realm of the human spirit the cult of McLuhanism has nothing
whatever to do, yet it receives the highest accolade of this aberrant American culture. There is much to be deplored in British education, much that
goes unmarked by its own practitioners: but it has never seceded from the
primacy of character formation as the educational aim. New Zealand, on
the farthest rim of the English littoral, having learned and adopted so much
from the American universalist tradition, can only be appalled at the dys-
function now so manifest in its avatar of humane values . . . "all they'll ever
need in the basic skills. . . ."

Item: *"Industry and the military, as well as the arts and sciences, are
beginning to consider education their main business."*

This is the real disclosure—the real betrayal of education to functionalism. Like Caractacus, education is to walk in chains behind the military chariot. The form and content ("the arts and the sciences") are now to be dragooned by the utilities ("industry and the military") in the exploitation society. Technology is to subsume education, and under the guise of emancipating the education process McLuhanism would enslave and humiliate it. The machine-media are to interpose their flawless efficiency between teacher and student in the rich relationship of person-to-person. The quantification of information-data is to supplant the eloquent effusion of the fine mind in transaction. The electronic medium in an electronic age is to constitute the electronic message. The triumph of mechanism is to be complete because nothing can live against it. Education is to become a process of having, not being; it is to focus upon a subject, rather than the person as an end in himself. This is the warning given by President Eisenhower ere he left office—"the unwarranted influence by the miltiary-industrial complex" upon the liberties of the people and the independence of the republic through the constraint of education.

As the future of education is planned with all the resource and resources of the great nation, it is fervently to be hoped that no methodological facility will be neglected; but never ought such technology supersede the appropriate goals, nor by its imposed nature limit them. Let it always be required to demonstrate its trustworthiness as an instrument of freedom for teacher and learner, and never be permitted to seize initiative as some prima donna authority. It ought to be considered as another adjunct of the culture, no more and no less important than any other. It is the solemn attainder of McLuhanism to be the latest overreach of the part to become the whole. Let this nation heed the melancholy plaint of one of its finest spirits, Adlai Stevenson:

> While our cars have grown longer, our TV screens broader, our washing machines grander, our kitchens brighter, at the same time our schools have grown more dilapidated, our roads more crowded, our cities more messy, our air more fetid, our water more scarce, and the whole public framework on which private living depends more shabby and worn out.

Do the American people really believe that McLuhanism really touches the heart of this matter? Or that out of this modish eccentricity can come the creative future of education?

Computer Technology and the Future of Education

Current applications of computers and related information-processing techniques run the gamut in our society from the automatic control of factories to the scrutiny of tax returns. I have not seen any recent data, but we are certainly reaching the point at which a high percentage of regular employees in this country are paid by computerized payroll systems. As another example, every kind of complex experiment is beginning to be subject to computer assistance either in terms of the actual experimentation or in terms of extensive computations integral to the analysis of the experiment. These applications range from bubble-chamber data on elementary particles to the crystallography of protein molecules.

As yet, the use of computer technology in administration and management on the one hand, and scientific and engineering applications on the other, far exceed direct applications in education. However, if potentials are properly realized, the character and nature of education during the course of our lifetimes will be radically changed. Perhaps the most important aspect of computerized instructional devices is that the kind of individualized instruction once possible only for a few members of the aristocracy can be made available to all students at all levels of abilities.

Because some may not be familiar with how computers can be used to provide individualized instruction, let me briefly review the mode of operation. In the first place, because of its great speed of operation, a computer can handle simultaneously a large number of students—for instance, 200 or more, and each of the 200 can be at a different point in the curriculum. In the simplest mode of operation the terminal device at which the student sits is something like an electric typewriter. Messages can be typed out by the computer and the student in turn can enter his responses on the keyboard. The first and most important feature to add is the delivery of audio

From *Phi Delta Kappan* (April, 1968), pp. 420–33.

messages under computer control to the student. Not only children, but students of all ages learn by ear as much as by eye, and for tutorial ventures in individualized instruction it is essential that the computer system be able to talk to the student.

A simple example may make this idea more concrete. Practically no one learns mathematics simply by reading a book, except at a relatively advanced level. Hearing lectures and listening to someone else's talk seem to be almost psychologically essential to learning complex subjects, at least as far as ordinary learners are concerned. In addition to the typewriter and the earphones for audio messages, the next desirable feature is that graphical and pictorial displays be available under computer control. Such displays can be provided in a variety of formats. The simplest mode is to have color slides that may be selected by computer control. More flexible, and therefore more desirable, devices are cathode-ray tubes that look very much like television sets. The beauty of cathode-ray tubes is that a graphical display may be shown to the student and then his own response, entered on a keyboard, can be made an integral part of the display itself.

This is not the place to review these matters in detail; but I mean to convey a visual image of a student sitting at a variety of terminal gear— as it is called in the computer world. These terminals are used to provide the student with individualized instruction. He receives information from audio messages, from typewritten messages, and also from visual displays ranging from graphics to complex photographs. In turn, he may respond to the system and give his own answers by using the keyboard on the typewriter. Other devices for student response are also available, but I shall not go into them now.

So, with such devices available, individualized instruction in a wide variety of subject matters may be offered students of all ages. The technology is already available, although it will continue to be improved. There are two main factors standing in our way. One is that currently it is expensive to prepare an individualized curriculum. The second factor, and even more important, is that as yet we have little operational experience in precisely how this should best be done. For some time to come, individualized instruction will have to depend on a basis of practical judgment and pedagogical intuition of the sort now used in constructing textbook materials for ordinary courses. One of the exciting potentialities of computer-assisted instruction is that for the first time we shall be able to get hard data to use as a basis for a more serious scientific investigation and evaluation of any given instructional program.

To give a more concrete sense of the possibilities of individualized instruction, I would like to describe briefly three possible levels of interaction between the student and computer program. Following a current usage, I shall refer to each of the instructional programs as a particular system of instruction. At the simplest level there are *individualized drill-and-practice systems,* which are meant to supplement the regular curriculum taught by the teacher. The introduction of concepts and new ideas is handled in conventional fashion by the teacher. The role of the computer is to provide regular review and practice on basic concepts and skills. In the case of elementary mathematics, for example, each student would receive daily a certain number of exercises, which would be automatically presented, evaluated, and scored by the computer program without any effort by the classroom teacher. Moreover, these exercises can be presented on an individualized basis, with the brighter students receiving exercises that are harder than the average, and the slower students receiving easier problems.

One important aspect of this kind of individualization should be emphasized. In using a computer in this fashion, it is not necessary to decide at the beginning of the school year in which track a student should be placed; for example, a student need not be classified as a slow student for the entire year. Individualized drill-and-practice work is suitable to all the elementary subjects which occupy a good part of the curriculum. Elementary mathematics, elementary science, and the beginning work in foreign language are typical parts of the curriculum which benefit from standardized and regularly presented drill-and-practice exercises. A large computer with 200 terminals can handle as many as 6000 students on a daily basis in this instructional mode. In all likelihood, it will soon be feasible to increase these numbers to a thousand terminals and 30,000 students. Operational details of our 1965–66 drill-and-practice program at Stanford are to be found in the forthcoming book by Suppes, Jerman, and Brian.[1]

At the second and deeper level of interaction between student and computer program there are *tutorial systems,* which take over the main responsibility both for presenting a concept and for developing skill in its use. The intention is to approximate the interaction a patient tutor would have with an individual student. An important aspect of the tutorial programs in reading and elementary mathematics with which we have been concerned at Stanford in the past three years is that every effort is made to avoid an initial experience of failure on the part of the slower children. On the other hand, the program has enough flexibility to avoid boring the brighter children with endlessly repetitive exercises. As soon as the student manifests a clear understanding of a concept on the basis of his handling of a number of exercises, he is moved on to a new concept and new exercises. (A detailed evaluation of the Stanford reading program, which is under the direction of Professor Richard C. Atkinson, may be found in the report by Wilson and Atkinson.[2] A report on the tutorial mathematics program will soon be available. The data show that the computer-based curriculum was particularly beneficial for the slower students.)

At the third and deepest level of interaction there are *dialogue systems* aimed at permitting the student to conduct a genuine dialogue with the computer. The dialogue systems at the present time exist primarily at the conceptual rather than the operational level, and I do want to emphasize that in the case of dialogue systems a number of difficult technical problems must first be solved. One problem is that of recognizing spoken speech. Especially in the case of young children, we would like the child to be able simply to ask the computer program a question. To permit this interaction, we must be able to recognize the spoken speech of the child and also to recognize the meaning of the question he is asking. The problem of recognizing meaning is at least as difficult as that of recognizing the spoken speech. It will be some time before we will be able to do either one of these things with any efficiency and economy.

I would predict that within the next decade many children will use individualized drill-and-practice systems in elementary school; and by the time they reach high school, tutorial systems will be available on a broad basis. Their children may use dialogue systems throughout their school experience.

If these predictions are even approximately correct, they have far-reaching implications for education and society. As has been pointed out repeatedly by many people in many different ways, the role of education in our society is not simply the transmission of knowledge but also the transmission of culture, including the entire range of individual, political, and social values. Some recent studies—for example, the Coleman report—have attempted to show that the schools are not as effective in transmitting this culture as we might hope; but still there is little doubt that the schools play a major role, and the directions they take have serious implications for the character of our society in the future. Now I hope it is evident from the very brief descriptions I have given that the widespread use of computer technology in education has an enormous potential for improving the quality of education, because the possibility of individualizing instruction at ever deeper levels of interaction can be realized in an economically feasible fashion. I take it that this potentiality is evident enough, and I would like to examine some of the problems it raises, problems now beginning to be widely discussed.

Three rather closely related issues are particularly prominent in this discussion. The first centers around the claim that the deep use of technology, especially computer technology, will impose a rigid regime of impersonalized teaching. In considering such a claim, it is important to say at once that indeed this is a possibility. Computer technology could be used this way, and in some instances it probably will. This is no different from saying that there are many kinds of teaching, some good and some bad. The important point to insist upon, however, is that it is certainly not a *necessary* aspect of the use of the technology. In fact, contrary to the expectations sometimes expressed in the popular press, I would claim that one of the computer's most important potentials is in making learning and teaching more personalized, rather than less so. Students will be subject to less regimentation and lockstepping, because computer systems will be able to offer highly individualized instruction. The routine that occupies a good part of the teacher's day can be taken over by the computer.

It is worth noting in this connection that the amount of paper work required of teachers is very much on the increase. The computer seems to offer the only possibility of decreasing the time spent in administrative routine by ordinary teachers. Let us examine briefly one or two aspects of instruction ranging from the elementary school to the college. At the elementary level, no one anticipates that students will spend most of their time at computer consoles. Only 20 to 30 percent of the student's time would be spent in this fashion. Teachers would be able to work with classes reduced in size. Also, they could work more intensely with individual students, because some of the students will be at the console and, more importantly, because routine aspects of teaching will be handled by the computer system.

At the college level, the situation is somewhat different. At most colleges and universities students do not now receive a great deal of individual attention from instructors. I think we can all recognize that the degree of personal attention is certainly not less in a computer program designed to accommodate itself to the individual student's progress than in the lecture course that has more than 200 students in daily attendance. (In our tutorial Russian program at Stanford, under the direction of Joseph Van Campen, all regular classroom instruction has been eliminated. Students receive 50 minutes daily of individualized instruction at a computer terminal consisting of a teletype with Cyrillic keyboard and earphones; the audio tapes are controlled by the computer.)

A second common claim is that the widespread use of computer technology will lead to excessive standardization of education. Again, it is important to admit at once that this is indeed a possibility. The sterility of standardization and what it implies for teaching used to be illustrated by a story about the French educational system. It was claimed that the French minister of education could look at his watch at any time of the school day and say at once what subject was being taught at each grade level throughout the country. The claim was not true, but such a situation could be brought about in the organization of computer-based instruction. It would technically be possible for a state department of education, for example, to require every fifth-grader at 11:03 in the morning to be subtracting one-fifth from three-tenths, or for every senior high school to be reciting the virtues of a democratic society. The danger of the technology is that edicts can be enforced as well as issued, and many persons are rightly concerned at the spectre of the rigid standardization that could be imposed.

On the other hand, there is another meaning of standardization that holds great potential. This is the imposition of educational standards on schools and colleges throughout the land. Let me give one example of what I mean. A couple of years ago I consulted with one of the large city school systems in this country in connection with its mathematics program. The curriculum outline of the mathematics program running from kindergarten to high school was excellent. The curriculum as specified in the outline was about as good as any in the country. The real source of difficulty was the magnitude of the discrepancy between the actual performance of the students and the specified curriculum. At almost every grade level, students were performing far below the standard set in the curriculum guide. I do not mean to suggest that computer technology will, in one fell stroke, provide a solution to the difficult and complicated problems of raising the educational standards that now obtain among the poor and culturally deprived. I do say that the technology will provide us with unparalleled insight into the actual performance of students.

Yet I do not mean to suggest that this problem of standardization is not serious. It is, and it will take much wisdom to avoid its grosser aspects. But the point I would like to emphasize is that the wide use of computers permits the introduction of an almost unlimited diversity of curriculum and teaching. The very opposite of standardization *can* be achieved. I think we would all agree that the ever-increasing use of books from the sixteenth century to the present has deepened the varieties of educational and intellectual experience generally available. There is every reason to believe that the appropriate development of instructional programs for computer systems will increase rather than decrease this variety of intellectual experience. The potential is there.

The real problem is that as yet we do not understand very well how to take advantage of this potential. If we examine the teaching of any subject in the curriculum, ranging from elementary mathematics to ancient history, what is striking is the great similarity between teachers and between textbooks dealing with the same subject, not the vast differences between them. It can even be argued that it is a subtle philosophical question of social policy to determine the extent to which we want to emphasize diversity in our teaching of standard subjects. Do we want a "cool" presentation of American history for some students and a fervent one for others? Do we want to emphasize geometric and perceptual aspects of mathematics more for some students, and symbolic and algebraic aspects more for others? Do we want to make the learning of language more oriented toward the ear for some students and more toward the eye for those who have a poor sense of auditory discrimination? These are issues that have as yet scarcely been explored in educational philosophy or in discussions of educational policy. With the advent of the new technology they will become practical questions of considerable moment.

The third and final issue I wish to discuss is the place of individuality and human freedom in the modern technology. The crudest form of opposition to widespread use of technology in education and in other parts of our society is to claim that we face the real danger of men becoming slaves of machines. I feel strongly that the threat to human individuality and freedom in our society does not come from technology at all, but from another source that was well described by John Stuart Mill more than a hundred years ago. In discussing precisely this matter in his famous essay *On Liberty,* he said,

> The greatest difficulty to be encountered does not lie in the appreciation of means towards an acknowledged end, but in the indifference of persons in general to the end itself. If it were felt that the free development of individuality is one of the leading essentials of well-being; that it is not only a co-ordinate element with all that is designated by the terms civilization, instruction, education, culture, but is itself a necessary part and condition of all those things; there would be no danger that liberty should be undervalued, and the adjustment of the boundaries between it and social control would present no extraordinary difficulty.

Just as books freed serious students from the tyranny of overly simple methods of oral recitation, so computers can free students from the drudgery of doing exactly similar tasks unadjusted and untailored to their individual needs. As in the case of other parts of our society, our new and wondrous technology is there for beneficial use. It is our problem to learn how to use it well. When a child of six begins to learn in school under the direction of a teacher, he hardly has a concept of a free intelligence able to reach objective knowledge of the world. He depends heavily upon every word and gesture of the teacher to guide his own reactions and responses. This intellectual weaning of children is a complicated process that we do not yet manage or understand very well. There are too many adults among us who are not able to express their own feelings or to reach their own judgments. I would claim that the wise use of technology and science, particularly in education, presents a major opportunity and challenge. I do not want to claim that we know very much yet about how to realize the full potential of human beings; but I do not doubt that we can use our modern instruments to reduce the personal tyranny of one individual over another, wherever that tyranny depends upon ignorance.

NOTES

[1]P. Suppes, M. Jerman, and D. Brian, *Computer-assisted Instruction at Stanford: The 1965–66 Arithmetic Drill-and-Practice Program* (New York: Academic Press, 1968, in press).

[2]H. A. Wilson and R. C. Atkinson, *Computer-Based Instruction in Initial Reading: A Progress Report on the Stanford Project* (Technical Report No. 119, August 25, 1967, Institute for Mathematical Studies in the Social Sciences, Stanford University).

DAVID ENGLER

Instructional Technology
and the Curriculum

There is a widespread and unfortunate tendency in education these days to regard instructional technology as being synonymous with such things as computers, teaching machines, and audio-visual devices of all sorts, and to express concern about the possibility that the advent of such machines will mechanize and therefore dehumanize education. The image of the machine, cold and impersonal, manipulating our children as it manipulates rats and pigeons in the laboratory, is a haunting reminder of Huxley, Orwell, and others who have painted for us the frightening picture of the demise of humanism.

This is an unfortunate tendency, because in focusing on the machine as a threat to humanistic education, it is pursuing the scent of the red herring and ignoring the real problems of technology, humanism, and their relationship to each other.

Our thesis here is that the conflict between a humanist curriculum and instructional technology is more apparent than real; that it is, in fact, the product of semantic confusion and fuzzy definitions; that it is based on the assumption that we now have a humanistic curriculum but do not utilize instructional technology, an assumption which on both counts is at best debatable and at worst fundamentally erroneous; that, in fact, we must deal with a problem that is not technological but rather is ecological.

Let's consider first our definitions.

Instructional technology is defined in two rather different ways. First, and most commonly, it is defined as hardware—television, motion pictures, audio-tapes and discs, textbooks, blackboards, and so on; essentially, these are implements and media of communication. Second, and more significantly, it is defined as a process by means of which we apply the research findings of the behavioral sciences to the problems of instruction.

From *Phi Delta Kappan* (March, 1970), pp. 379-81.

Defined either way, instructional technology is value-free. Gutenberg technology, which is widely used but not often recognized as a technology in schools, can produce the Bible, *Mein Kampf,* and *Portnoy's Complaint* with equal indifference. Television can present brilliant insight into the human condition as well as mindless and brutalizing violence with equal clarity. Technology as hardware is neutral. Notwithstanding Marshall McLuhan's preachments to the contrary, the message is the message.

The process of instructional technology is similarly value-free. It can be used to achieve good objectives or bad objectives; it can help to better define objectives and to better measure the achievement of those objectives, but it will work equally well for almost any objective. It is a tool, and like all tools, it is morally and philosophically neutral.

Historically, curriculum, by which we mean the sum total of the content of education, has been largely unaffected by any changes in technology. Motion pictures, radio, phonographs, television, and other widely used hardware have had no significant effect on the curriculum. Where they have been used, it has been to deliver the existing curriculum.

On the other hand, changes in curriculum have rarely required any changes in instructional technology. The vast curriculum reform movement of the past decade led to substantial changes in the goals and the content of many subject matter areas, but virtually all of these reforms relied on the traditional technology. Modern mathematics was taught through the same technology with which traditional mathematics had been taught.

In retrospect, one would be hard put to cite an example of significant curriculum change that was the result of any new technology. This is because decisions about curriculum are largely value judgments, and technology, being value-free, is simply not very meaningful in making such value judgments.

Thus, to raise questions about the conflict between humanism and technology is to tilt at windmills. There can be no curriculum, humanist or otherwise, without some means of delivering instruction to the learner and some strategy that will facilitate learning on his part. There can be no curriculum without an instructional technology. The real question is: Can we devise an instructional technology that will further humanize our curriculum?

To answer this question we must first consider the extent to which our curriculum is now humanistic, as well as the extent to which our prevailing instructional technology facilitates the transmission of that humanistic curriculum from school and society to each individual.

In fact, our society, our times, offer abundant symptoms of a widespread failure of humanism in our educational system. Song My may turn out to be one of the most shattering of these symptoms, but others abound in the crime, racism, alienation, and other sociopathic behavior produced by individuals who are the products of our educational system. If humanism is a significant aspect of our curriculum today, it is not succeeding in humanizing massive numbers of our citizens.

Beyond these social manifestations of the failure of our schools to humanize a significant segment of our population, there is the question of whether or not this failure is the result of an inadequate emphasis on humanism in our curriculum, or an inadequate method of transmitting that humanism to all of our population, or both.

However, to answer the question of whether or not our curriculum is humanistic enough requires one to make value judgments about ideas on which there are many philosophical and ethical differences of opinion among people. That task we shall leave to each individual reader.

The students who picket their university with signs saying, "Do not fold, spindle, or mutilate" bear witness not to the cold impersonality of computers but to the dehumanization that characterizes an educational system which does not value their human individuality. The ghetto dropout bears witness to the same problem. So, in fact, does virtually every youngster who experiences failure in school. Thus, to attempt to transmit a humanistic curriculum by means of a technology that fails to accommodate human individuality is to negate the essence of humanism.

The assumption that our traditional methods of instruction do not constitute a technology seems utterly indefensible. This is so whether one defines technology as a process or as hardware. The most accurate statement one can make about our present methods is that they are an old technology. The basic media of instruction, such as textbooks, chalkboards, and teachers, have been used for many years. Today, teachers are better prepared, textbooks are better written and better designed, and chalkboards have changed color, but their functions and their relationships to learners have not changed essentially in over a hundred years. Moreover, the process by means of which instruction is carried on has not changed in any fundamental respect during this period. It remains teacher-centered, group-oriented, and textbook-based.

It is a technology derived from the impact of an industrial society on the role and methods of education. In its time, it was a technology that contributed enormously to humanizing education by making education accessible to vast numbers of children who had never before had such opportunities. It was a technology designed to implement a curriculum which had as two of its major objectives to raise the level of literacy and to prepare youngsters to function in society as workers and citizens. Its prototype was the Lancasterian model of large-group instruction which developed and spread in Britain and the United States early in the nineteenth century; and while this model has undergone many modifications over the past century and a half, the general configuration of mass-production education remains fundamental to this technology.

The industrial revolution ended in our society many years ago, however, and we are becoming increasingly aware of the fact that we live in a post-industrial society. Our curriculum is changing and will continue to change as our awareness of this reality increases.

What are the factors that lead people to question our present curriculum and its related technology? They include the dwindling social demand for semiliterate and functionally illiterate workers; the concomitant increase in the need for citizens who can cope with the accelerated rate of change that characterizes modern technological society; the emerging realization that there no longer exists a finite body of knowledge constituting at any level what an "educated" individual should know, but that, on the contrary, the so-called knowledge explosion has rendered such a view completely obsolete; the growing recognition that for all citizens education is the *sine qua non* of economic and social adjustment, to say nothing of success; the need for citizens who are capable of bringing critical analysis to bear upon the information aimed at them by government and industry through the powerful and pervasive mass media of communications.

The new curriculum as it develops today and in the years ahead will have to reckon with these factors. It will have to assume responsibility for the successful achievement of its objectives by *every* individual in school. It will have to concentrate on developing the ability to learn instead of imparting a fixed schedule of knowledge. It will have to nurture an independence of mind and related skills of analysis that are all too often missing in the products of our present curriculum.

All of this brings us, at last, to the question of ecology. If we view the ecology of education as the web of relationships between and among learners, teachers, and the environment in which they operate, then it becomes apparent that these relationships are largely defined by the prevailing technology of instruction. Certainly these relationships are not inherent in the individuals or things that are the component parts of education; rather, they are conventions that attach to the traditional goals of education and the methods that are associated with the achievement of those goals.

In the past, many attempts to change education, particularly those attempts to individualize instruction and to develop skills of independent inquiry, have failed because they did not include any mechanism for changing the ecological balance between teachers and learners. Usually, these changes were imposed on the existing ecology in which the teacher leads a group-based lockstep progression through the course of study. This ecology is inevitably characterized by a high degree of active involvement

on the part of the teacher and a comparably high degree of passive involvement on the part of the learner. It accepts as normal a distribution of success
and failure that can be described by a bell-shaped curve; in fact, results
which do not produce a bell-shaped curve often lead teachers to wonder
whether or not their objectives and/or tests are too easy or too difficult.

This ecology more often than not results in a fair amount of boredom in
students because it often attempts to teach them things they already know;
it results in a high degree of frustration in students because it often attempts
to teach them things they are not prepared to learn; finally, it tends to
produce among the students with whom it is successful the habit of conformity, since that is what produces the highest payoff in grades.

To change the ecology so that each individual can receive the attention
and instruction that he needs is obviously no small task. For the institution
of the school and for the teacher in particular to assume responsibility for
the success of each and every child is to go beyond the scope of the resources
presently allocated to education. To transform millions of students who
have been well-trained to pass their tests, get their grades, and move on to
the next subject into millions of independent learners whose most important
rewards come from the pleasures of learning is an undertaking of staggering
dimensions. It should be clear to us by now that our present strategies and
instruments of instruction, the prevailing instructional technology, cannot
provide us with the means for effecting these changes.

Only a new instructional technology can change the existing ecological
balance in education. The state of the art in instructional technology is such
today that many of the tools and techniques needed to effect such change
are available and feasible. We can, for example, by individual, specific
diagnosis and instruction eliminate the practice of teaching youngsters what
they already know or of teaching them what they are not prepared to learn.
We can devise the means and organize the instructional environment to
permit individuals to master the basic skills and acquire the basic information that are necessary ingredients of analytical or problem-solving work in
most subjects. We can leave to the teacher the functions of diagnosis evaluation, decision making, and direct, individual interaction with the learner
on the level of the higher order intellectual, esthetic, and ethical objectives
that are the essential ingredients of a humanistic curriculum.

This technolpgy will require significant changes in how space is utilized
in schools, in how time is allotted for each individual, in how progress and
achievement are measured, in how materials of instruction are designed and
used, in how teachers and learners relate to each other, and, above all, in
how learners relate to the process of learning. Instructional technology in
the form of hardware will obviously be an ingredient of this ecology, just
as it is today; but only instructional technology as process will have the

power to alter the ecology of education so that it is more responsive to individual human differences.

The problem is to get off the pursuit of the red herring of conflict between humanism and technology and get on to the task—huge and long-term though it be—of using technology to further humanize education.

STEPHEN C. MARGARITIS

Teachers and Machines Must Learn to Live Together

Had Mother Nature been more generous in providing us with enough talented teachers, natural teachers, who could reach all students at their unique levels of development, there would be no need to search for supplements. And if these teachers possessed the necessary wisdom and the vision to select knowledge of most value and to share it with youth in the most natural and candid of forms, all technological devices teaching has adopted and will be adopting in the years to come would be of little value. Since this is not the case, people concerned with the education of the young are willing to try anything that promises facilitation and success.

I shall not attempt to add another treatise, pro or con, to the controversy over instructional technology. Because educators have to learn to live with technology, I will reflect on what I regard basic considerations to effective uses of the machine in teaching and learning.

The most important development of technological change, the factor destined to have the greatest impact on man's life, is automation. It has altered the nature of man's labor, has reduced the working hours at an increasing rate, has raised new educational demands for enjoyable leisure time, and has given promise for improvements in education.

The computer is the most recent breakthrough in man's efforts to achieve better communications. It has enormous potential; new dimensions to its use are discovered daily. We are in the process of establishing remote terminals with rapid communication access to central computers. Soon, students will be able, in a matter of seconds, to use the world's best libraries and to receive complex information that would require hundreds of years to develop through conventional channels. Remote terminals may be installed in the home, which would change the patterns of study and work for many people.

This article was written especially for this volume.

Notwithstanding the accelerated change, modern man has been slow in accepting innovations that threaten established practices. Educators are still somewhat reluctant to recognize educational technology and to plan the use of the machine for education. Lack of adequate information, too many misconceptions, and the absence of a systematic approach have rendered impossible any accurate estimates as to the potential of the education media.

Educational technology was invented to facilitate learning, and we must recognize its limitations in advance. In a sense, it is little different from other learning devices or approaches teachers use to teach children and meet their needs. We know by now that no matter what tools we have used, we have not been uniformly successful with all of our students. Technology should be looked at in the same way. Depending on the persons involved, the subject matter being taught, and other related factors, education media can contribute to more effective learning. In my many years of teaching and learning I have found, as did many of my colleagues, that none of the methods man created should be adopted as a panacea or as permanent. Technological devices may not even work well with the same child over a prolonged period of time. Unless proper use is made of them, I suspect that their effectiveness will decrease and disappear altogether when the novelty wears off.

If we were to teach machines and not humans, I would entertain no doubts as to the everlasting, supereffectiveness of the teaching machine. But teaching humans and recognizing them to be as different as nature has made them, there is no single way to satisfy the human element. And if there is to be any justification at all for the teaching business to exist, it is my belief that only humans can teach humans. Let us not confuse the teacher with the teaching tools; the difference is that simple. Teaching machines are merely aids—an extension of the teacher in the classroom. It is my belief that technology is only as capable as those who make it and those who use it; if we use it properly it will help our children learn more efficiently.

Proper teacher training is imperative for the acceptance of technology and its use. Intensive programs must be developed now that will enable future teachers to cope with advancing technical developments. School administrators should cooperate to form inservice programs for the reeducation of practicing teachers. Whether we like it or not, the full range of technological tools will soon be in the schools. It is up to the educators to prepare for them. There is enough evidence already as to their improper use by untrained teachers.

Since new tools should parallel the curriculum, it would be necessary for research specialists to help establish research centers or educational hardware clearinghouses. Teachers need to know what technological devices best correspond to the objectives of their courses in order that they may select the best available media for better effectiveness. Direct communication should be maintained between these clearinghouses and the local resource center every school should have; if there is need for continuous curriculum evaluation and change, the same holds true for the updating of technological tools. It must be the function of the resource center to develop availability plans so the users can find the right equipment in the right places at the right time. Common sense requires that such appropriate administrative rearrangements are of the utmost importance. Technology has failed in many schools mainly because of lack of teacher understanding and lack of administrative commitment. The teacher must not use the media simply because it is fashionable, but rather with wisdom and prudence as a supplement in the presentation of material.

Success, however, requires more than an informed teacher and the right equipment. Administrative rearrangements conducive to intelligent planning and the wise use of the tools are a necessary ingredient. Programming, the location of the equipment, a sense of responsibility of the people involved, and the time element are only a few of the things to be considered. The best intentions can be lost in senseless bureaucratic processes. Effectiveness can be increased with more personal responsibility and trust and with a minimum of frustrating formalities. Some administrators have jealously reserved for themselves all the rights to control education media and, in the process, have abused their responsibilities. Let this not happen again with teachers. There is also the danger of being carried away and forgetting that students are *partners* in learning and that they should share with teachers the responsibility for handling the equipment.

The Changing Role of the Teacher

Lack of professional preparation in the use of technology as well as feelings of insecurity have been responsible for negative attitudes on the part of many teachers. If overdependence on machines is avoided and a balance among a variety of techniques is maintained, teachers stand a chance to expand their talents, perform their jobs better, and utilize their students' time and potentials to a maximum. The computer and the other technological devices can make the teacher more of a teacher than a baby-sitter, as he is sometimes considered. His role can change from a one-way transmitter of information to that of being the manager of an efficient learning environment. He acquires an even more professional role as a listener, a friend, a diagnostician, and a counselor. Within his grasp lies individualized instruction.

Individualized instruction allows the child to progress at a self-determined pace, which is actually an ideal arrangement for both the bright and the slow child. A substantial part of teacher–learner tension could be relieved when the child no longer has to worry about being ridiculed by his classmates for wrong answers or embarrassing remarks. The child is reinforced by the machine's praise and its immediate show of answer results. Since the student is responsible for his progress, his motivation would increase. With no fear of failure, he would be more confident of his abilities to learn and positive ego development would result.

Considerable amounts of time and energy could be saved by setting up laboratories using machines. Individual growth at the child's own speed could be greatly increased, and the teacher could be in several places at the same time. In all probability educational technology would accomplish exactly what the teacher wants it to accomplish.

The Use of the Machine as a Crutch

The threat of becoming overenamoured of the machine is ever-present. It would be a great mistake to become hardware-happy and expect the machine to be a better teacher—better than people. The machine has its place along with other learning experiences, but it should never monopolize the process of learning. Students can certainly learn facts from the machine, but it takes a teacher—a real flesh-and-blood person—to inspire, influence, and encourage a child to learn. The children look to the teacher for many things —recognition, conversation, approval, and/or disapproval—feelings that the machine cannot give with any appreciative degree of sensitivity. The machine cannot offer the emotional human quality a teacher can. Mechanical teaching aids should always be combined with the warmth of a teacher, the personal touch to all significant learning experiences. Dialogue and human interaction are usually more necessary than mechanical devices for most of the children. It is in group interaction that social problems of everyday living are treated, and in-depth studies and opportunities for creativity are in abundance. In group interaction the teacher brings patience, understanding, humor, and compassion with the extra spice only humans carry.

A creative teacher can overcome disadvantages by creating a climate of learning in which none of the available known devices monopolizes learning situations; they should be kept in harmony as promising avenues to the discovery of a purpose in life.

Discussion Questions

1. Why have schools, so far, benefited only modestly from the technological revolution?
2. Has technology already made a lasting impression on education?
3. What does technology profess to be able to do that humans cannot?
4. Can technology help prepare students for a purposeful life?
5. Have educators found it necessary to use technology in preparing children for a technological society? Will every child benefit from the use of technology in education?
6. What type of professional preparation should be required for the training and retraining of teachers in the use of the machines?
7. Has the teacher's role changed because of instructional technology? Will programmed instruction diminish the role of the teacher? What adjustments will teachers have to make?
8. What administrative rearrangements have to be made in order to use educational media most effectively?
9. Will educational technology help equalize educational opportunities in areas in which such conditions do not exist? Will the computer be able to diagnose skills and make worthwhile prescriptions for students in areas of difficulty?
10. What has been the impact of TV on the lives of today's children? Will machines affect children's ability to relate to other people? What is the pupils' reaction to teaching machines?
11. Is technology being used primarily to free the teacher from more mundane tasks so that he is able to spend more time with individual students? How can we prevent teachers from using technological aids as a crutch?
12. When the potential of educational media reaches its maximum, will we need teachers? Will educational hardware replace the teacher?
13. Does educational technology have a dehumanizing effect on children? Does programmed learning provide the necessary motivation for learners? Can a machine stimulate critical thinking?
14. Is technology the answer to individualized instruction? Can a computer be responsive enough to children's needs? How can technology best be used to aid a child to learn and to enjoy learning?
15. Is the effectiveness of educational media worth the expense? Is it wise to spend more money on educational media rather than on more teachers?

Project: In the readings of this section you found authors taking position on a continuum from *pro* to *in-between* to *con*. What is your position, and why?

Selected References

Crosby, Harry H., and George R. Bond, *The McLuhan Explosion: A Casebook on Marshall McLuhan and Understanding Media* (New York: American Book Company, 1968). This is a source of information about McLuhan and his ideas, including pro and con arguments.

Ellul, Jacques, *The Technological Society* (New York: Vintage Books, Random House, Inc., 1964). This is a comprehensive analysis of the effects of technology on our society and on our educational system. The author's approach is pessimistic, and he presents the sharpest and least ambiguous of the arguments that technology is bringing about a loss of freedom and a subversion of human values.

Finkelstein, Sidney, *Sense and Nonsense of McLuhan* (New York: International Publishers Co., Inc., 1968). Finkelstein presents a critical discussion of McLuhan's philosophy and interpretations. He asserts that McLuhan robs the human being of all his creativity and injects it into the media he created, so that the media become the creators and the human beings become the passive recipients, the slaves.

Goodlad, John, *et al., Computers and Information Systems in Education* (New York: Harcourt, Brace & World, Inc., 1966). The authors discuss the traditional responsibilities the educator must continue to assume even in the "Computer Age," as well as the new roles for teachers caused by computers. They suggest that perhaps one of the most valuable results of the introduction of electronic data processing technology into education has been the accompanying need to examine with precision the nature of educational rules, procedures, schedules, objectives, and assumptions.

McLuhan, Marshall, *Understanding Media: The Extensions of Man* (New York: McGraw-Hill Book Company, 1964). Unlike Ellul, McLuhan, for all his abstractness, has found positive, humanistic meaning and the color of life in technological developments man is using. To expand his view of the "new electronic era" of today and the glowing future it upholds, McLuhan draws for support upon the entire history of humanity with its social upheavals and its growth of languages, techniques, inventions, arts, and sciences.

McLuhan, Marshall and Quentin Fiore, *The Medium is the Massage* (New York: Random House, Inc., 1967). The authors contend that societies are being shaped more by the nature of the media through which men communicate than by the content of their communication.

Mumford, Lewis, *The Pentagon of Power: The Myth of the Machine* (New York: Harcourt Brace Jovanovich, Inc., 1964-70). Man and not the machine has been the dominant factor throughout history.

Rosenthal, Raymond, *McLuhan: Pro and Con* (New York: Funk & Wagnalls, 1968). This book is a detailed, lively, often stimulating and revelatory discussion of Marshall McLuhan's ideas.

Silberman, Charles E., *The Myths of Automation* (New York: Harper & Row, Publishers, 1966). Silberman attempts to distinguish between the facts and the myths of automation.

Skinner, B. F., *The Technology of Teaching* (New York: Appleton-Century-Crofts, 1968). Skinner believes that the teaching machine will encourage the student to take an active role in the instructional process. On the other hand, in order to program instruction, the programmer must come rigorously to terms with the subject matter and be precise about the changes he is trying to induce in his student's behavior.

Tickton, Sidney (ed.), *To Improve Learning: An Evaluation of Instructional Technology,* Vol. I, 1970; Vol. II, 1971 (Report to President and U.S. Congress by the Commission on Instructional Technology). (New York: R. R. Bowker Company). Many people contributed their interpretations to an interesting and much needed study.

Toffler, Alvin, *Future Shock* (New York: Random House, Inc., 1970). In our society drastic and fast changes create cultural shock. Man must develop the habit of adapting to change.

Part 3

Student Power: Rights and Responsibilities

Overview

It is utterly impossible to predict the final impact technology will have upon man and society. The ultimate question of whether man will become more human with the aid of obedient machines or will be reduced to being a slave of his own creation will depend largely on the vision and the wisdom of those holding the power.

One of the most interesting and most dreadful phenomena of our times is the expansion and centralization of power at the top level of decision in the areas of the military, economics, and politics.[1] Competition for military superiority between the United States and the Soviet Union and the subsequent U.S. involvement in military action in Korea and Vietnam has elevated our military leaders to the top level of our society's power structure. These military leaders have found their closest allies not among the members of the political directorate, but primarily among the industrialists and financiers whose industries and banks support the military adventures necessitated by U.S. international commitments.

The extended responsibilities of the United States and the complexity of national and international issues has alienated the mass man from his rightful participation in decision making. Middle and lower levels of power

---

[1] C. Wright Mills, *The Power Elite* (New York: Oxford University Press, Inc., 1956).

have had very little to do with decisions of national and international significance such as the Korean War, the Cuban crisis, and the Vietnam War. Throughout the 1960s the ordinary people, primarily the most oppressed, have been awakening from their lethargy and attempting to understand what is happening. Realizing that there are times to be on the move and also times to stay on camp, many people felt they had camped too long and they decided to be on the march again—a march of unpredictable dimensions.

One can find among Americans those who believe that their society failed to provide its members with a sense of direction and purpose in life. Notwithstanding the availability of the most sophisticated technological devices, the schools have failed to provide the young with satisfying and meaningful learning experiences. This failure has resulted in alienation, loss of personal and social identity, confusion, unhappiness, unrest, and confrontation.

Under the current tensions in the school and society, the role of the student has attracted increased attention. Political, social, and economic issues and their resultant crises, both at the national and international levels, have confronted our youths with threats to their futures. As expected, they are rising to seek greater power and a meaningful sharing of decision-making responsibility and authority. We have already seen a number of excessive attempts as they have tried to exert their influence on the policies and practices of the institutions designed to serve their needs. Throughout the country, and for that matter throughout the world, they have employed demonstrations, sit-ins, strikes, and boycotts.

Some observers take the position that faculty and administrators move more slowly than the demands of students necessitate, with the result that they have been unable to avoid conflicts and the creation of unfavorable public images. Whenever and wherever men of wisdom and vision have created a favorable atmosphere for student participation, embarrassment has been prevented.

After a few troubled years of sit-ins, demonstrations against the war, protests against on-campus military recruiting and draft, peace marches, and crusades in the name of minorities, we now know that the American campus will never be the same. The articles in this section try to answer the question of how we can establish orderly channels for registering the legitimate concerns of those whom the schools serve, so that there are alternatives to confrontations and demonstrations.

In the first article of this section, George Bereday examines student unrest from a world perspective. In the Fifties, he says, the adults deplored the quiescence of youth. Now they criticize their exuberance. Bereday suggests that political systems or historical circumstances bare no relevance, and he sets out to identify what is constant and what is regional in student unrest.

Harold Taylor has welcomed student unrest. He puts the American student movement in a world perspective and suggests a redefinition of the students' role. Taylor would like to see the universities take the leadership in giving a sense of direction and unity of purpose to the social order. On the quality of their acts, he says, and on the level of their humanity rests the character of our society and the quality of its purposes.

In "Student Unrest: Blessing Rather Than a Curse," I have alluded to the fact that our society and its institutions had camped too long. The thrust to move again came this time from the students, as a blessing rather than a curse. I do not condone violence, but when it happens I understand it. Violence is not unavoidable; responsible authority must be shared by all members of the college community who are charged to maintain the spirit of place and the climate of learning.

Vine Deloria discusses the attempts colleges have made to introduce sets of courses reflecting the values which minority groups have claimed existed as a positive spiritual force in their communities. He says that Ethnic Studies as a discipline has been marked by the inability of people to distinguish among the variety of interpretations available and the inability to draw up a suitable framework within which guidelines could be structured. Deloria suggests that a new interpretation is needed because the student is at a loss to react to ethnic studies program in a meaningful sense. Exposition of ideas along traditional channels implies an acceptance of the very values which created the history which the ethnic man is trying to escape.

Sidney Hook believes that academic freedom in the United States is currently in great jeopardy; it is threatened by ideological fanatics among students and faculty. He is very critical of student movement and sees changes in educational systems being made only to avoid trouble. Although the sources of jeopardy are many, he adds, the most threatening are the beliefs (1) that the university must become an agency of specific social and political programs and (2) that the techniques of violence and confrontation are legitimate methods of inducing educational change.

Robert Hutchins uses historical and contemporary evidence in describing the changed function of the university. Here Hutchins is at his best. He deplores the changes forced upon the institutions of higher learning by the demands of a technological society. Hutchins calls for a retreat to liberal education, the real mission of the university, and wants to see other institutions assume the responsibility for meeting the technological needs of our society.

A rather balanced account as to appropriate strategies for innovation is presented by David Riesman. In spite of the fact that he has experimented with a new college and has visited a number of other experimental colleges throughout the country, Riesman is more sympathetic to innovations within relatively stable settings. Any viable educational reform, he explains, must be tied to its base of faculty and students, and to the particular cultural context; only a mode of thinking about educational reform might be transferred.

GEORGE Z. F. BEREDAY

Student Revolt:
An International Phenomenon

Everybody knows that the unrest of youth is worldwide. It must, therefore, be subject to some general laws that transcend local conditions. If the young are restless because there is no social justice, they should be quiescent in Communist countries where there presumably is social justice, but they're not. If the young demand their birthright of freedom they should be contented in the West where there presumably is freedom, but they are not. In undeveloped countries students demand jobs and economic security. In developed countries in which jobs are plentiful students are bored by security. In the United States the unrest of youth has been attributed to loosened, relaxed family ties. In Japan family ties are tight and strict; youth riots nonetheless. Something has gone wrong with the relations between generations that transcends national frontiers. Much has been written about it. It will be the purpose of this essay to identify separately what is constant and what is regional in student unrest, based on a lengthy exposure to educational practices in sociological and comparative perspective throughout the world.

Few now choose to remember that during the 1950s the country became concerned about the placidity of its youth. Sons of the generation who had fought off the depression and had won World War II had not, at least in the eyes of their fathers, lived up to the stature of their fathers. Rather than sharing the "unquiet" heritage of their parents the young were reported to be placid, oriented towards security, aspiring to middle-sized income, middle-sized homes, and middle-sized wives. Philip Jacob's study, *Values in College,* though hotly disputed even at the time of publication, seemed to have exemplified the chorus of voices deploring this quietude of the young. Neither the pioneering spirit of the frontier nor the reforming zeal of the New Deal nor the courage needed to win the war seemed to have been bequeathed to the youth of the Fifties.

This article was written especially for this volume.

Now this generation is fifteen years older and their parents are a little older themselves. The new young of the sixties and early seventies who have replaced the quiet ones of the fifties seem to be of a different vintage, or rather enough of them seem to be different, to make present-day adults quiver. Today, although the majority of young people live up to their parents' expectations, prepare for a job and are not troublesome, a sufficiently large percentage of them seem to have changed; youth culture has become newsworthy.

Movements that have acquired news value derive some of their momentum from this fact. Therefore, we must, at first, attempt to discard from our evaluation those elements which seem to be inconsequential. Headlines about youth disturbances serve as a cumulative incentive for young people to display more student unrest, and it became fashionable to riot in the late Sixties. Consequently, riots appeared more frequently and campuses on which there were no disturbances simply did not seem to be in vogue. In a nation such as ours, so susceptible to fads and frills, it is surprising that youth disturbances have not reached more intense peaks of frenzy. At any demonstration there are bound to appear those who are moved by a cause, those who come merely because their friends are moved by a cause, and those who present themselves simply because it is fun or chic to demonstrate. Under the weird coiffures and offbeat clothes by which the more extreme youth are now distinguished, there often hide quite ordinary, sometimes square, sometimes empty human beings. In the last analysis, an observer of youth activities usually yields to his own judgment about what is real or phony.

Yet, with those few qualifications what we witness is hardly phony. The shrill voice of the young, be it legitimate or not, has become a fact of life and a social and political force. The new dimension of youth alienation in the 1960s was the realization that it transcended frontiers and political systems. Of course, some countries have institutionalized youth demonstrations, in some cases for more than a century. In such countries every national holiday, every election, every outrage perpetrated by the powers that be, provokes youth into the streets. But this historical unquietude was in older days at best regional in character. Students may have swarmed the streets of Latin American cities, but they appeared in the streets of Communist towns only when called forth to laud the authorities. Students now appear angry and restless everywhere. There is a reality to their movement and anger that is with us to stay, even if that reality appears spurious in terms of what adults are used to.

Youth unrest is not wholly *weltschmertz* the way Goethe has defined it, nor is it entirely reformist zeal. It is more like an undefined pain within, nonetheless real for want of being defined. Everybody senses this malaise and many adults resent it bitterly, but it is there nagging.

Parts of the restlessness seem to be born out of boredom, the well known ennui of the rich in search not so much of a cause as of titillation. Perhaps the most tragic feature of youth's unrest today is the fact that corrosions of adult life threaten to be followed by corrosions of youth life. Hatreds and myths of yesterday seem to give way only to irritations and fuzziness of today. Discrimination practiced by adults against the young and against each other gives origin to discrimination displayed by the young against the old and against each other.

Youths seem to reach out with ambivalence for ideals. They do not search for God, for they were told God is dead. They do not dream of death on the field of glory, for to them life seems more precious than country. They feel deeply the need for social reforms. But in this, too, the seed does not fall far from the tree. Young reformer groups have no clear program of their own; too many talk grand policies instead of striving directly to reclaim human beings.

One almost longs with Jean-Jacques Rousseau for clean-faced youth that would be cut off from the degenerating influences from which they sprang. Maybe they couldn't successfully build a new world, but they could at least start it or dream of it. Instead, as we have done for centuries, they seem to be content in rocking the boat of the old. Young restlessness is a puzzling phenomenon felt as intensely as it is difficult to define and evaluate. Perhaps it is here to stay, not so much until the adult society changes, but until it is willing to "move over," talk and listen to its young.

When the educational progressives of the 1930s formulated the notion of the active school, they introduced student government on the basis of conviction that in conflicts between the adults and the young the probability that the young are right and the adults wrong is at least half and half. Hard to accept as this simple proposition is, it carries an obvious lesson. In the relation between the adults and the young, understanding is better than authority. Youth can and will speak out. Our century has been principally concerned with making the silent speak. For thousands of years the weak were forced to live without a voice; now one by one they have begun to earn their right to it. The laborers spoke up and the world had to listen. The women raised their voice and the world was never the same again. Now the young demand to be heard. And where they are denied this right, fists and stones are hurled against nightsticks and tear gas.

In such circumstances talk is hardly easy. In adult life dreams of yesterday have faded, and compromises and accommodations with things as they are have been made. Sadder but also wiser for their realization of which things can and which cannot be accomplished, the adults are more jaded and perhaps more faded. The society of adults has learned by experience to make compromises with the realities of life.

Rare are the people who retain a fraction of the ideals they have cherished when they were young. What once were flights of fancy have been replaced by a resigned recognition that experience counts for more. The young have a very difficult time adjusting to this kind of philosophy of the old. The young want to talk about volunteering for work in depressed areas, while their parents discuss the purchase of new automobile rubber tires. The young want to hear the ring of honesty that has eluded the *Catcher in the Rye*. But adults talk in guarded tones that either are, or appear, mendacious. The young search in life for the "hum," the quality of excitement. Adults look for peace and set aside savings for their funeral. The young want to be permitted to make mistakes, to throw out gauntlets to life, and to take their gambles. The adults who have already made most of their mistakes have no courage to try again, but only words of caution to offer.

There is no point in arguing which is the better way. Would the world be better off if the clean-shaven, short-haired, and fully employed Romans won out over the long-haired, unemployed, and unemployable Christians?

Another major sociological reason for the generation gap has to do with age differences. It is common knowledge that industrialization, by freeing men from the necessities of menial labor, has rejuvenated adults artificially and has given them yearning to keep perpetually young. In an older society —let's say a Japanese society—the majestic cycle of time is recognized in a much clearer fashion. The young woman of premarriageable age wears a flowered kimono and a special hair style. When she reaches the age of courtship and marriage, the colors of the kimono change, and so does her hair style. When she reaches thirty, thirty-five, forty, the kimono becomes brown, gray, and in comes a still quieter hair style, and she vanishes from the face of the earth as a woman, only to appear in the form of a mother or a sage counselor, or a symbol of affection and security that women are in every society.

Whereas in older societies experiences counted for most and the older the statesman, the more qualified he was to exercise his tasks, now the change is rapid; knowledge is rapidly increasing, and the latest knowledge, the most fresh training counts most for managerial responsibility. Youth senses that in the management of society there is an artificial slowdown. Experienced, well-deserving men who find themselves in positions of responsibility by the sheer accident of belonging to too old an age group are no longer capable of coping with the tempo. We thus face a built-in conflict between generations.

The adult world knows this. Young people feel it more than know it, but the result in any case is a breakdown in communications. Young people sense that something is wrong with the tempo with which the world is run. Their elders, however, cannot or do not want to make it run faster by surrendering power, and they engage themselves in delaying tactics. Change will come and power will, within twenty or thirty years, pass into the hands of those who are rebelling or sullen on the campuses now. There is a mathematical certainty about that; no one can do anything to stop it. What can be done is to speed up the process by admitting the young sooner into the councils of the old. Older men are much afraid of managerial contact with their future successors, but this is unreasonable. In the Soviet Union, to quote an instance, already several specialties retire workers at 55 or even 50, without any ill effects. Early retirement is much to be preferred to late retirement. It gives time for new exciting patterns of second life to be built up in midstream, before it is too late. Part of the adult adjustment to the rising tide of young ambitions is the difficult but, in the end, joyful lesson of how to switch oars in middle age.

Gerontocracy means too little action too late. In addition, what troubles youth has to do with credibility. On the international front it has to do with the persistence of war, and the continued contradiction of this with the professions of peace that all governments are making. The young are tired of hypocrisies that dominate diplomacies. On the domestic scene most governments practice politics with propaganda rather than honest emphasis. They construct imposing public buildings but do little about the slums; give welfare payments but provide neither jobs nor education for the poor. The young would rather take cynicism than mendacity.

In search of remedies the young instinctively go for places of least resistence. Only this can explain the fact that educational institutions which are most sympathetic to youth were singled out as places of major attack. On the educational scene youth's slogan has become one of change and of rapid adjustment of old training institutions. But the universities and the schools are not unlike the church. They are agents of stability and are poorly prepared to cope with rapid reform. Hence, the educational world is doomed to witness a clash between the conservatism of the teachers and the impatience of the students. The universities in particular were specifically the traditional institutions for the few. As such they place a premium on men who add to knowledge. Hence researchers are more valued than teachers, and teachers more valued than students. It has been the contemporary feature of the university that it has and is greatly expanding in numbers of students. It is easy to foresee the time when it will serve many rather than the few. In a school for the many the traditional emphasis must be reversed. Not adding to knowledge but disseminating knowledge is becoming the first priority. Students demand that more attention be paid to them, that they be taught with greater success and relevance, that practical preparation is more important than the theoretical.

It is only against general clusters of global characteristics such as these that a regional analysis can be set. The more industrialized a country, the more likely is the frustration of youth to appear in the terms suggested above. When students in the universities remain a tiny elite, their support or alienation depends on whether they see themselves as joining the system or as competing with the groups in power. Where sons expect to inherit the positions of their fathers, there is seldom a clash between generations unless the fathers postpone handing over of power for too long. But when the universities produce a new elite, and they usually do because they select on the basis of brain, such elite finds itself in conflict with groups of aristocratic birth or accumulated wealth who are in possession of the country. In such cases youth may act politically or otherwise, spontaneously or at the behest of other agencies unconnected with university life. These regional variations are only a matter of degree. We are facing a scale of student behavior from nonviolent to violent that extends across national frontiers. One can plot a point on the scale for each country, but the whole scale is connected with cross-national rather than regional issues.

HAROLD TAYLOR

The Student Revolution

At Columbia University, on a day of celebration of the university's centenary in 1954, Robert Oppenheimer said:

> The unity of knowledge, the nature of human communities, the order of
> society, the order of ideas, the very notions of society have changed, and will
> not return to what they have been in the past. What is new is not new because
> it has never been before, but because it has changed in quality . . . so that the
> world alters as we walk in it, so that the years of a man's life measure not
> some small growth of rearrangement or moderation of what he learned in
> childhood, but a great upheaval. . . . The global quality of the world is new;
> our knowledge of and sympathy with remote and diverse people, our involve-
> ment with them in practical terms and our commitment to them in terms of
> brotherhood. . . .

The background of any discussion of the role of students in a world
revolution is formed by this shift in the authority of ideas, the shift of the
nation-states to new relations among themselves, a shift away from the
provincial authorities which used to be accepted as valid, and the entrance
of this generation of students and their mentors into a world which does
alter as we walk in it.

We have packed into the history of the last hundred years more than the
world and its history can hold. Through the unavoidable increase in the size
of societies and the detachment of their members from a common purpose,
we are now joined together on a world scale in larger and larger collective
bodies, which at a given time in their growth lost track of what it is that
binds them together. As a consequence, in this century, as it has unlocked
its secrets and unleashed its hidden powers, we have come to an erosion of
the world's confidence in itself and in its ability to deal humanely and

From *Phi Delta Kappan, 51,* (October, 1969), pp. 62-67.

rationally with humanity's problems. In the absence of human compassion the world has become accustomed to running itself by force and violence. The rhetoric of hostility is the norm of the international vocabulary, and the illusory power of coercion has been invoked more often than not to solve the problems which have never before appeared in the present degree of intensity, since the world never before was so completely interconnected.

Confronting each other from day to day, the peoples of the world can now see clearly the reality of the possibility of mutual destruction and the necessity of possible good. We are at a point where the cumulative necessities of history coincide, and we have lost track of the possibilities of achieving a common purpose in humane solutions to practical problems.

The difficulties of achieving those solutions are compounded by the fact that millions more of the world's people have now joined in asserting their claims to be heard where the decisions are made. Where such decisions have been made in the past by white elites, by small groups within nations, by political, military, and economic power held by a few countries and a few persons in those countries all over the world, there are now millions who demand participation in the decision making. Whites and nonwhites achieve confrontations of every kind, in many cases led by students, in order to fulfill a new kind of expectation on the part of those who in former years were victims of oppression. They have now declared their intention no longer to stay in that position. When we look at their actions from a new perspective, the present unrest in the communities of America is identical with that kind of unrest one finds in the communities of the world.

In consequence of the disintegration of the old order and the coming into being of a new structure of world society, we are in an interim period in which the uneducated, the dispossessed, the ignorant, and those who possess intelligence and passion are now asserting their right to achieve ends for themselves which have formerly been denied. In the modern world there are no longer "foreign" problems, there are only problems shared by all societies—deprivation, hunger, poverty, ignorance, social classes, and ideological conflicts—problems which arise from the refusal by established authority to allow those in previous positions of servitude a chance to use political instruments of their own on behalf of the whole community.

It is now possible to say that there is a world student movement, a world revolution led by students who have become the spokesmen for their generation and for all those who in previous years have been held back by the political and social system in which their parents have been captured. This is true partly because of the detachment of the members of the younger generation around the world from direct involvement in the political systems into which they were born, and a refusal to accept the regular educational means through which youth in the past has been inducted into the political and social system. As the students congregate together in the universities of the world, they find assembled in their own internal communities those persons with whom they have like interests—in poetry, politics, the arts, literature, and social action.

In talking with Italian students last winter in Rome, I discovered that some of their early ideas for revolt in the Italian education system came from what they had seen on television and read in their press about what had happened at Berkeley in 1964. In *Obsolete Communism: The Left Wing Alternative,* Daniel Cohn-Bendit pays tribute to the students at Berkeley who first provided the possibility of hope for other students who had never considered the possibility of revolt against their own educational system. In a similar way, the students across this country are aware of the student movements in other parts of the world. The interconnection and the interpenetration of cultures to which I have referred is to be found at its greatest point among the world's students who know about each other.

French student attitudes toward revolution differ from those of most American students; and there is a difference between a student revolution and just plain ordinary revolution. A revolution in the classical sense is an uprising of one sector of a society which sets out to overthrow either by force and violence or by a combination of economic, political, social, cultural, and physical power a system of government and its institutions. This is what the French students set out to do, using as an instrument the universities of France, particularly Nanterre and the Sorbonne.

The Italian students at this moment in time are no longer interested in the reform of the universities in Italy. They refuse, for example, to have student elections, on the ground that they cannot think of any given students who could represent the diversity of their political aims. They do not want to have any representatives with whom the university authorities could negotiate. They reject the parliamentary system along with capitalism and are trying for a political coalition with the labor unions and against the Communist party, which they consider reactionary, since it is part of the establishment and makes deals with the Italian government. The radical students have occupied buildings of the university not in order to have a black studies or an Italian studies or a noncolonial studies project started there, but in order to prevent the country from running its universities. They are using the universities as a base for radicalizing students and anyone else they can reach. That is what a student revolution means when it is designed to overthrow a government.

In the United States, the student revolution is composed of a complexity of parts. Only one very small sector of the American student movement is devoted to the ends sought by the Italian students and by many other European students in their political organizations. The French students are closer to the Italians. Daniel Cohn-Bendit's book indicates that his aim and that of the leadership of the student movement was to bring down the

French government. Cohn-Bendit expresses regret that his supporters in the older generation were not bright enough to occupy two or three more buildings not at that time occupied by the students. Had they done so, Cohn-Bendit thinks the revolution would have been successful and De Gaulle would no longer have been able to continue in office. There is a certain amount of truth in what he has said, although he tends to overestimate the role which he and his friends had in educating the older generation. Cohn-Bendit has now written them off. He is just going to wait until they die out.

Beneath the student revolutionary efforts lay a new philosophy which I suggest is consonant with the philosophy of the present generation of world youth. The philosophy was expressed in the wall slogans of the French students—what could be called a radical subjectivism—the demand that we rethink what life is about, not what official French culture says it is about or what professors say it is about or what we say it is about. "I decree the state of happiness," says one wall slogan. "Forbid all forbidding," says another. "Be realistic, demand the impossible." "Culture is the inversion of life." "Poetry is in the streets." "Re-invent life."

The French students were using demonstration in the streets as a spectacle, to invoke on their own part as well as on the part of others a community of interest and a community of concern. They wanted to change their own lives as much as they wanted to change French society and its political system. The majority of the French students in their revolt were, in Gregory Bateson's term, screaming against an official view of how life should be lived. Through their wall posters, their street slogans, their underground newspapers, and their poetry they proclaimed an attitude toward life.

Their educational demands ran the gamut from free and open political discussion protected from the police on the campuses to open admission of all who wished to attend the university, whether or not they had money or the right qualifications for admission. They wanted the removal of examinations for entrance. They wanted to eliminate the patron system for art students by which in former years the art teacher could determine, with the threat of a failing grade, what style of painting his students must accept.

I would like to say something now about how the American student movement is related to all this. Following the end of World War II in 1945, an enormous influx of new talent came into the American universities. It was brought there by the GI Bill, one of the most important forces in the educational history of the United States. Eight million young men came into the universities, at least 75 percent of whom would never have had the opportunity for further education had it not been for the federal subsidy. That was the beginning of a new phase in higher education in the U.S., since it gave a promise to the youth of that period in history—a promise which has been repeated since then—that all those capable of further education in each generation would be provided with it. In a sense, a commitment to the higher education of youth was made by accident. The GI Bill was politically popular because it dealt with veterans and their needs, and it was in the tradition of American democracy in providing education for all.

The new GI students changed the universities in size, for one thing, producing problems which are still with us. They also changed the attitude of educators toward their students. A colonel in the Air Corps who at the age of 24 had been running his own squadron brought into the classroom a different point of view from the usual high school graduate. After the absorption of these new arrivals into the university system, we moved into the early 1950s and found something journalists called the "silent generation," although it was not silent at all. It was a generation talking to itself, having found conversation impossible with the McCarthyites and the political exhibitionists who masqueraded as political leaders of the time. These students found themselves unable to accept an American foreign policy which on the one hand opposed all countries which were Communist and on the other assumed that some solution could be found which would prevent the use of the atomic bomb against us. These and other issues were discussed by the generation assumed to be silent. They began to hold intercollegiate conferences and began to assemble themselves in larger and larger internal communities. Students would send out notes about a conference on disarmament at Swarthmore and three or four hundred would turn up. Others would write from the University of Wisconsin and say that there is to be a meeting on civil rights at the University of Chicago in three weeks' time, and mysteriously from around the country three or four hundred students would assemble themselves to organize and work on the problems of integration. Theirs was an invisible community. When the student civil rights movement began with the Negro sit-ins of 1958 and 1959, the younger generation of white society in the West, the Midwest, and the North saw before their eyes the members of their own generation who were black beaten by police, set upon by dogs, jabbed by cattle prods, jailed, and in some cases killed.

This was the first time that a younger generation in America had seen itself and its black members presented to itself. Out of that experience came a sense of community between the whites and blacks, between the members of a generation which could identify itself in support of social justice. White students worked with blacks in the South in the development of freedom schools, voter-registration projects, demonstrations for justice and equal rights. When the next stage of the student movement came in 1965, the blacks took their destiny into their own hands, having had their political and social strategies clarified by the relationship they had previously had with the white students. They gained a sense of their own identity and began their own black movement.

In the meantime, the Vietnam war had begun to escalate. Resistance to the war, the black revolution, and the social and political energies which it produced became part of a whole new set of forces within the student movement, symbolized by the actions at Columbia University in the spring of 1968.

Somewhere in the middle of the 1960s, the students and American society together reached the end of an era. At a certain point it became clear that it was no longer possible to stand slack-jawed while the evils multiplied, while we made reports about civil disorders, while we did studies of urban problems, while we issued reports from the Foreign Policy Association about how we must do something about China. We could no longer stand quietly by while history rushed forward. It was the perception of the younger generation that the war and social injustice were no longer tolerable which brought to national consciousness those political forces that made it impossible for President Johnson to continue in the actions he had undertaken. The protest against the war began on the campuses through the student protest movement, as did so much of the social action in support of political candidates who were opposed to the war. Randall Jarrell describes the students of the second world war in his lines:

> We died like aunts or pets or foreigners.
> (When we left high school nothing else had died
> For us to figure we had died like) . . .
> In bombers named for girls, we burned
> The cities we had learned about in school.

In his poem about the ball-turret gunner, Jarrell says:

> From my mother's sleep I fell into the State
> And I hunched in its belly till my wet fur froze. . . .

This generation of students has fallen into the State just in the way Jarrell describes. Their predecessors, the young of the 1940s, who had graduated from high school, did bomb the cities they had learned about in school, without knowing anything about the people exposed to their bombs. Nor do many students know about the people who are now exposed to our bombs in Vietnam. An awareness of the rights of the Vietnamese not to be bombed is in a sense the invention of the students' own educational system, which through social and political action has developed a new body of knowledge in which the students have discovered things of their own about this society and its foreign policy. The student movement is not necessarily revolutionary, although it has revolutionary implications. It has arisen from the civil rights movement, from social protest, from the teach-ins, from the demonstrations, and has invented a new educational instrument, one which creates new forms of education through the work of the students themselves.

The experimental college at San Francisco State, the free university movement, the counter-university, the counter-curriculum, the critical university—all these are variations on a single theme. They are the outcome of social and intellectual experience developed by undergraduates and graduate students who have in their ranks some of the best teachers in America. They do not possess the necessary credentials and are not recognized as teachers. But they are now moving into university life with particular proposals for the curriculum and for institutional change which will have a deep effect on this and on the next generation of high school students who will be coming to the university. The universities are going to have to change not only the curriculum but the way in which they do business with students.

Let me be quite specific. There is no reason why students should not be elected or appointed to boards of regents. I see no reason why students should not run their own political candidates for the state legislature on the educational platform of increasing the budget for the university. Why not open a campaign to elect students to public offices of all kinds through direct political action within the party system? Why should there not be students writing speeches for their own candidates, doing the kind of political work in the community which the students did in New Hampshire for Senator McCarthy and which other students did in Wisconsin and California for Robert Kennedy.

That is one sector of political life in which every student has a stake. In the past we have assumed that the state legislature was responsible to taxpayers who usually didn't want to spend tax money for education. It is time for students to consider themselves taxpayers and to take the same kind of political action about their rights for political representation in the state as do the older groups of taxpayers. The universities must also reconsider the process by which faculty members are appointed, how presidents are selected, how admissions policies are set, how the curriculum is constructed. At Sarah Lawrence College we have had a community of students organizing their own affairs. By a grant of power from the Board of Trustees, students are given responsibility for college policy and a share in making the curriculum. They make reports on the curriculum and on the teaching; they are consulted by the president in faculty appointments. There are no grades, no examinations, no required courses, no faculty ranks, no formal departments. I submit to you that this system works better than any other system of university or college organization in America or anywhere else.

Why?

Because it involves the students in the decisions which affect their own lives. Having involved them, it sets up conditions for the release of creative energy which works through the college system out to the community. It gives students access to new ideas. It develops a loyalty to their own community standards and to those values in which educated men and women can believe.

I suggest that this kind of community is the proper structure for a college or university in the United States, and that our efforts in that community must be to find nonviolent ways of meeting threats and acts of violence. We must look at the actions and demands of black and white students, not merely as current events, but as part of the historical development of a series of political, social, economic, and educational forces which have been at work since the second world war.

What we need today are educational principles consonant with a compassionate view of what democracy means. We must think together as a national community in which students, faculty members, administrators, boards of regents, and the concerned public consider the question of what a college is for. The college is a place where new lives can be created. What is done there must have direct effects on the society outside. Otherwise the college is a community of clerks who spend time with each other in an elite community with no relationship to the going social, political, and economic problems of the society at large. Until we reorganize the internal structure of the university to make the students a central factor in educational planning, we are not reaching the outside community.

It is not that students simply have to be dealt with because they are there, as so many faculty members imply. It is because students are the instruments through which the society is changed. The ideas which work within students' lives on the campus are carried into the society, and the society moves from generation to generation with the help of its students. The students are the foundation of the university and must be considered as such, because they are the instruments and the vehicles of knowledge. If they do not take the knowledge of the university and use it in society, the knowledge lies inert on the library shelves and in the research publications of the faculty.

The task of reform in education and society has no end, but only new beginnings. Reform goes on, planned or unplanned, in one way or another way, usually at a pace many years behind the need. It is advanced by the efforts of those few who cannot be satisfied with what they find and look for better ways. It is advanced by the necessities of historical change which keep pressing upon all institutions and testing their capacity for alteration and survival.

This is the first age in which so many untamed and unmanageable necessities have been pressing all at once. It is the first age in which the historical circumstances have combined to produce a younger generation so fully aware of those circumstances. In other times it was possible to say that that is the way things go in the universities. The students enter and leave, the society changes and moves on, the universities stay at the quiet center, giving the mind its due, keeping the ideals of civilization alive.

It is clear that this is no longer a possible attitude, although the necessity for the quiet center continues to exist, and the protection of the ideals of civilization was never more urgent or necessary. The difference now is that the university is already engaged with the necessities and must act to engage itself with them now, on its own terms. The society will not stand still, even to be studied and observed. It insists on acting.

In this situation of the university the students are once more its greatest allies. If some of them have declared themselves to be its enemies, let them be met by those in the universities who know and can teach that the real enemy of the university is ignorance, force, and violence, and that the way to overcome these is by knowledge, a passion for justice, and a commitment to truth. For it is in the ideal of a community of concerned persons who share a common interest in the life of the mind and the quality of human experience that the genius of the university lies. The rest is a matter of how that community can best be constructed by the best efforts of all concerned. There is nobility and strength in the lovely old words "fraternity," "equality," "liberty and justice for all." The university is the place where these words can become names for the living experience of those within its environs. Unless the reality of that experience is to be found there, it is unlikely to be found in the larger world. Unless students learn through what they do there that equality is a two-edged sword, that fraternity means giving part of oneself away, that liberty is an affectionate state of mind, and that justice in a democracy is a willingness to be faithful in action to agreed-upon principles, all the protest, controversy, radical action, and appeal to the big abstractions of moral enthusiasm will come to nothing but a continual attrition of the very ideals of which the young are in search.

The university should be a place where students help their teachers to teach them, where teachers help their students to learn, where administrators help both to accomplish what they have come together to do. That is why the role of the students must now be redefined, in order to make clear to them and to all others that students *are* the foundation of the university, that when everything else is taken away (as in fact it can be)—the government contracts, the isolated research institutes, the alumni bodies, the services to industry, the traveling faculty, the organization men—what is left are persons working together to learn and to teach.

The education of students, therefore, means nothing less than their personal involvement in the conduct of the affairs of the mind. An equality of position in the polity of the community is a necessary condition of their involvement; otherwise they are playing a game the necessity for whose rules they never learn to understand; the commitment to play is never completely made.

What the world needs above all is a large and increasing supply of incorruptibles, men and women who have learned to act in the interest of mankind, who are capable of noble action as an outcome of premeditated thought, who are capable of clarity of thought as a natural and intuitive result of their experience in thinking and in acting. It is the responsibility of the university so to arrange its affairs that the experience of its students in thinking and acting can teach them what it means to serve mankind and what it means to honor the intellect.

STEPHEN C. MARGARITIS

Student Unrest:
Blessing Rather than a Curse

Under the impact of cataclysmic social and technological changes contemporary man has sharpened his tools of inquiry and has come to question the relevance of the traditional values of paramount authority. The questioning of authority is most noticeable among the "New Left" with its constant attacks against the "Establishment." There is both danger and opportunity in such a situation. People can abandon standards and lose direction, and they may even be exploited as they try to replace traditional authorities. At the same time they may demonstrate remarkable courage and increase their sensitivity to human needs.

The works of the National Student Association and the Student Non-Violent Coordinating Committee, as well as the violent demonstrations from Berkeley to Kent State to Paris, all point to the fact that the establishment has long ceased to be able to satisfy the needs of many of its clients. These clients are now forcing themselves into the social system in an attempt to reform both their educational institutions and the rest of society.

Some readers will probably find themselves in disagreement with my statements. This is to be expected; it is one man's point of view. I am reacting to a situation which has involved me and my students, directly and indirectly, during the last few years. Despite the undesirable excesses of the student movement, institutions have been forced to reevaluate and update themselves, a desirable effect. Many of the things I am going to suggest have already become part of new policies adopted by some colleges and universities.

The causes of student unrest and the ways in which it is manifested seem to be peculiar to each generation. Our generation of students are among the brightest and most socially concerned ever. As a group, they hold a dark view of life. They are searching for quality living and for true meaning in

---

This article was written especially for this volume.

147

existence. They are intensely and vitally concerned over the shortcomings of past generations. Below the surface of the crisis lies man's constant struggle for the "ideal life."

People come to accept the belief that schools are always in need of thoughtful and constructive agitators. For young people to mature and become responsible human beings they must be concerned, committed, and involved. They are idealists; they respond negatively to a society and its institutions whose goals they view as materialistic; they are critical of a society that spends much of its wealth for war and destruction. Most of them are unhappy and even angry about the quality of their education. They are afraid they have no future, and they want their schools and society to revitalize themselves so that they may each enjoy a meaningful life.

In the past colleges and universities throughout the world have been frequently subjected to student unrest for one reason or another. However, the particular form contemporary student movement has taken is phenomenal. The question is, what forces have recently descended upon the students, American students in particular? The American public was taken by surprise at seeing their youth violently expressing disapproval of the established order. Like anything else, the fire of student unrest spread fast and wide to shake the very foundations of the institutions which try to educate them. The causes are many and at times complex. I shall try to discuss only a few, both from without and within the institution.

Societal Causes

1. *Value contradictions*—Youth discovered that the old morality is not always humane or relevant. The implementation of the principles of equality and opportunity in everyday life leaves much to be desired. Prejudice and discrimination still exist against members of minorities. Double standards are practiced by many; and honesty is far from having received universal acceptance—hypocrisy is widespread. Youth revolt against exploitation and the abuse of their individual rights.

2. *The seriousness of poverty*—In this most affluent society of ours wealth is not equally distributed. There are many who are starving or forced to live at the subsistence level. Having nothing to lose, in their despair youth revolt against a system that has left them out.

3. *Dissolution of stable social structures*—Industrialization has altered both the structure of the family and the functions of its members. The old ties of the extended family have disappeared, and the children of many nuclear families find no clear models after which to shape their personal identity and social behavior.

4. *Prolongation of adolescence*—It is a paradox to find that adolescents are dependent longer in spite of the fact that they mature faster and are

regarded as the most informed generation. They claim they need to be given a feeling of personal and social usefulness and relevance.

5. *The evils of dubious foreign policy*—Unprecedented improvements in the means of transportation and communication have made the world a "global village." In trying to solve the world's problems along with the problems at home, we found the task staggering, perhaps impossible. The most serious difficulty is the absence of moral stamina, and our men of decision—knowing nothing better to do—retreated to the old ineffectual diplomatic and military mechanisms. In this respect they have been unable to rise in wisdom and compassion above our friends and foes alike. No wonder that our young have become morally outraged against the draft and against the war. In a state of paranoia some of them have turned to political revolution, convinced that legal channels do not work.

Institutional Causes

1. Students have found many inadequacies in the educational system and have begun to realize how little school has to do with the "real world." Whenever and wherever their demands are not heard they resort to protest and, in extreme cases, to violence.

2. It appears that most of the problems stem from lack of communication. When our institutions of higher learning grow to be large bureaucracies, depersonalization results. Students become numbers and are not looked upon as human beings. All intimacy is lost, and poor (or no) human relations between students and their instructors prevail.

3. Students lack broad involvement in the decision-making process; they claim greater freedoms and responsiblities, and they desire changes in outdated administrative rules.

4. Many students find their courses and the curriculum, in general, dull and irrelevant. They also claim that teaching methods are boring and nonmotivating.

5. An additional cause of unrest connected with college is the fact that certain students are subjected to involuntary college attendance. Family and society pressures are causing some of our young adults to invest time and money in a college education from which very little or no real profit will accrue.

Recommendations

From all indications the student movement appealed primarily to two types of students. The first type seem to be sensitive and aware of needed changes in school and society. They believe that solutions can be worked out within the system in cooperation with their elders. The members of the second group, however, tend to be extremists; they are convinced that the present system is hopeless. For them, significant changes will come by tearing down the establishment completely and they resort to violence.

There is a third group of students who, in spite of the fact that they know things are not going well, have adopted a passive attitude. Not knowing how to act they wait to see.

The Citizen Student

I am not ignorant of the excesses of the student movement and, like many others, have had many a sleepless night doing soul-searching in an attempt to understand what was happening. "All that energy," I was thinking, "why can't it be used constructively? Why let it escape into wastelands?" And I was praying for them to make it less painful and less hurting to those who happened to be in their way.

Let the passions not cloud real issues, the handling of which may decide our very existence. If students are treated as responsible citizens whose reasonable views are valued and respected, violence need not occur. The energy and idealism of youth should be put to good use. There are all kinds of service to society where our young adults can get involved and make real contributions. It takes only a little effort on the part of those in power and not a great deal of wisdom. There is nothing like a common project, and working together we may be able to cope with some of our current problems effectively. Communication and cooperation are key considerations for a better future if more people would take advantage of them.

Environmental pollution is directly related to mental erosion and mental pollution. But how does one begin cleaning the pollution in our heads? The best possible way might be to communicate and share with our children those values that are essential to man's survival, and do it in an open and questioning fashion. We must give second thought to our time-honored reverence for affluence, bigness, and power. Let us honestly face the probability that affluence bores, big systems alienate and frustrate man, and power corrupts. It does not seem possible that man can live without autonomy, intimacy, compassion, faith, love and beauty, and not lose his natural humanity.

Students and the College Community

Student demands upon the educational system should be met with candor and understanding. Better lines of communication need to be established before violence takes over reason. Students, teachers, and administrators should work together and not against one another. We can no longer ignore the voices of youth because they will no longer be pacified by familiar promises. Schools should change from "cold machines" to "caring institutions." Colleges and universities should be places dedicated to the free expression of opinion. They must insure freedom of dissent, while preserving order. Tragedies like Kent State should serve as an awakening to a generation still living on dreams past. Students must be offered alternatives to open confrontation. They must be allowed responsible participation and purposeful involvement. Responsibility cannot be learned in the absence of freedom. *For students to act responsibly, they must be treated responsibly.* Youth must be allowed to learn from their own mistakes. It will give them a chance to develop strategies and effectively resolve their personal difficulties.

Meaningful reforms should start in the individual classroom. We should invite student opinion whenever planning curriculum and learning experiences. Here students must feel that they are worthwhile. They must be treated as individuals with awareness and respect for their unique personalities.

The greatest value a student can receive in college is to become involved with an inspiring faculty member as a partner in learning. Learners are insisting on the right to participate in decisions that will affect their educations. But in order to perform successfully their participation should be responsible and their involvement should be purposeful. Issues should be well defined and should be handled in a sharing fashion in which contributions will be made according to competencies. As novice partners in decision making, students may need the help of those they mistrust. Without some generous orientation the newcomers may feel uncomfortable, become confused and frustrated, and drop out. If they drop out of the college structure they may eventually drop out of the structure of society as well. Given a chance in participatory decisions the students will learn to exercise mental discipline before questioning or acting; they will know that every act has a consequence. Students function better in an open classroom where necessary order and not conformity prevails, where the atmosphere is free, relaxed, and at the same time exciting. They learn more where threats of failure have been replaced by role confirmation, by relevant learning experiences which they have helped to select, and by a search for quality of life.

What's Next?

Student unrest has been more of a blessing than a curse. It has created new awareness of social and academic problems. Youth has forced society and its schools to rethink and reevaluate. There is almost always a bright side which cannot be seen in the midst of darkness and confusion. We must take from the present turmoil that which is constructive and disregard the destructive and purposeless. We must search for points of agreement and work from there; capture the potential energy and use it to promote the interests of the entire college community. Solutions do not come easily, nor is the academic community equipped to effect all the change called for, but being on the move again we may be able to rediscover the "spirit of place" and establish a climate of learning.

It is somewhat of a blessing that student unrest has made its home base on the college campus. The educational system played no minor part in harboring conditions that sparked the dissent. Here, a more objective analysis of basic issues is made by sensitive, concerned, and knowledgeable individuals. As an institution inherently charged with the preparation of citizens to deal wisely with social problems, the college now has a unique opportunity to achieve its goals.

Although the question of student unrest is before us now, the answer may take some time to work out. Institutions of higher learning throughout the country have released forces to innovate and experiment; they will never be the same. In their search for effectiveness, I trust they will be able to maintain their integrity and their proper mission to man and society.

The Rise and Fall of Ethnic Studies

The last five years have witnessed the rising demand by members of minority groups for studies based upon the experiences of their particular group. In response to this demand colleges have made valiant efforts to develop, by whatever means available, sets of courses reflecting the values which minority groups have claimed existed as a positive spiritual force in their communities. The quest has not been without excitement and toil, yet today we still see an incompleteness existing in a field which a short time ago promised to bring a certain amount of order out of the chaos of an intellectual milieu which had been dominated by the majority myths of the western European mind.

Ethnic studies as a discipline has been marked by an inability of people, consumers and producers alike, to distinguish among the variety of interpretations available a suitable framework within which guidelines could be structured so as to stabilize future developments. Consumers and producers is an accurate description of the ethnic studies process since the time span within which ethnic studies has had to develop has allowed little time for reflection or contemplation. Rather the scene has been reminiscent of Henry J. Kaiser's cement ship building process of the last great war. Things are constructed and hopes are high that they will last long enough. And that's about it.

The unfortunate aspect of the development of ethnic studies as an academic discipline is that it came at a time when social maxims were breaking down, but it came so early in the breakdown process that it was fairly doomed from the start to a twilight zone existence of endless circling, never landing and never going any place either. Had anyone had the luxury of time the eventual dissolution of techniques of exposition would have revealed to people the barrenness of the contemporary structure of social

---

This article was written especially for this volume.

thought, thereby freeing the developers of the ethnic discipline from involvement in traditional forms of thought.

Lest the above appear too abstract or vague, we must face a fundamental philosophical question when we speak of ethnic studies development. Alvin Toffler and others have pointed out the destructive nature of future thought shaken continually by what Toffler says is "future shock." But the situation has been more serious than that. Nearly a decade ago Daniel Boorstein outlined the nature of the academic dilemma in *The Image,* a book which examined the type of world created by modern communications in which we receive our knowledge. Marshall McLuhan followed Boorstein half a decade later with his series of books outlining the thesis that the medium was indeed the message.

In the period since the last war, society has undergone a complete transformation in the way that it receives and evaluates its external phenomena. In this transformation value judgments and consequent decisions based upon the judgments have unwittingly reversed themselves. We have become a society which lays helpless before the future, because our most accurate decisions are not really decisions at all but are gut reactions induced by experiences forced upon us by the media. From these experiences we derive our values in the practical sense. Then we go through the additional process of reevaluating the reactions we have against traditional and largely memorized standards of conduct.

We are thus a society without a philosophical base. We stand helpless before a time that bends to accomodate our desire to reenact our most intense experiences and to negate our most fearful moments. And since the process acts in many instances in defiance of our acknowledgement and out of our control, we, in being selective in our intake, negate a large part of the data which we should be receiving. In this process we have broken society into a number of mutually exclusive masses, each with a constituency deriving its understanding from certain political positions which depend for their validity on charismatic enactment by celebrities who are forced to incarnate images of righteousness and ultimate reality.

In this swirl of nontemporal, or more accurately, multitemporal and ahistorical happenings, it has proven impossible for ethnic studies to do more than tag along using traditional techniques of research, compilation, and exposition. The alleged "experiences" are different, therefore, in content only, and not in either point of view or in meaning. What it means to be black, Chicano, or Indian in American society has not yet been developed. What has been developed is a kind of interpretation of what it means to be semi-white in this society. The interpretation is colored by the peculiar characteristics of certain groups which have suffered recent oppression within the society; the oppression is tempered and understood in terms of traditional historical interpretations.

Unfortunately, a full sense of history is badly lacking. It is impossible for people to think in terms of a history that will make sufficient sense to give a validity to the ethnic experience. Once the developing discipline in black, Chicano, or Indian studies goes beyond the historical period of experiencing the white man in whatever form he first presented himself to the particular group, meaning goes by the boards. If there was a valid historical experience for the Indian before the white man that would appear to imply that a valid historical experience *after* the white man is needed. If there was a time in Africa prior to the development of the slave trade, then that experience would seem to imply a time when the white man will no longer oppress and enslave.

Again we can take the concept of space, place, and area and ask similar questions which are vital to any meaningful interpretation of experiences. *Where* do the particular groups exist outside of reservation, barrio, and ghetto? Is Africa, Mexico, or a restored continental America the solution to spatial considerations of ethnic studies? Is it possible for a minority group to create and maintain a sense of country-hood within a nation becoming increasingly more limited in the areas in which it can shift ongoing developments and population centers?

In short, minority groups have discovered history at the precise time when history has ended for the larger majority dominating them politically. Minority groups have discovered space at a time when their white opponents have run out of space. Minority groups have discovered time at a time when time itself is reversible and arbitrarily a function of economics and politics. If the time is not ripe for something, conditions can be developed altering that time and making it suitable for whatever actions are contemplated.

Caught in this situation, the student is at a loss to react to the ethnic studies program in a meaningful sense. Exposition of ideas along traditional channels implies an acceptance of the very values which created the history which he is trying to escape. Content takes on a negative aspect because it has no context within which it can be viewed differently. Incidents of historical importance are casually dismissed as merely another instance of oppression and deceit experienced in everyday life. The student is being driven to accept without question the most nonsensical interpretations of existence because they appear to explain things that in fact have no explanation but merely existence in themselves.

The task of teaching and learning in this whirling mass of facts and values has become virtually impossible to comprehend. The usual solution is to polarize conceivable answers to complex questions so that good guys and bad guys are identified for the students. Interrelationships of forces wholly above and beyond individual influence become merely the alignment on one side of the fence or the other. The very idea of shifting complexes and points of view to account for the rise and crest of developments becomes an arbitrary exercise of will and not a technique of discovery.

In order to escape this epistemological dilemma both students and teachers have a task as formidable as any faced at any period of history. They must in effect create new logics and new systems of explanation based not so much on discovery of great truths but on emotional satisfaction of the moment. Learning must become consumption of diverse and conflicting facts and experiences, all of which carry different energy contents, and of conclusions which can be reached by reflection on the period within which the experience occurred.

When we talk about law it is valid to talk about a system of deprivation set up to oppress certain groups in favor of others. But it is equally valid to consider law as the great civilizing subject which has served to curb racial brutality and discrimination within groups. It is valid to remain within the traditional historical experience of western European man to examine certain historical periods but also to connect those experiences to any other periods as a means of uncovering interpretations of either the compared period or the present time.

Using the traditional Aristotelian logic of either/or, inclusion and exclusion of classes or the newer both/and logics may be the distinguishing marks of education as we shall come to know it. The Aristotelian logic implies the existence of a real world structure and concerns itself primarily with identities, while the newer logic relates to the incorporation of values and facts within situations, thus speaking ultimately of experienced experiences (if it is possible to speak that way), and not of identities which are assumed to be constant for any sequence.

In spite of the contemporary cry for identity we do not really mean identity, for we always presume to structure our experiences according to their usefulness in being distinguished from ourselves. When we cry for identity we are seeking the meaning of events in which we are involved. We seek a summary, a sensible summary, of what we have experienced, or more accurately, what has experienced us. In this sense of the realization of participation we find identity and meaning.

This sense of participation distinguishes students today from all students in the immediate historical past, certainly those students for whom the educational system was designed. Students today are experiencing education and are not being educated, at least in the sense that society has been taught to expect them to be educated. At a deeper level than anyone suspects, students are participating in life processes and have for the first time become consumers of education experience, not simply memorizers of content. The ethnic student, be he at college or primary level, absorbs his experiences at about the same rate and in the same manner whether those experiences be in the classroom or the streets. In doing so he demands a new criterion of truth, and he spots stalking horses and hypocrisies far better than we do.

Until the educational system changes to reflect the world in which we live, we shall not be able to make much headway with minority group students. Much worse, ethnic studies as a discipline will not survive the immediate future because it fails to measure up to traditional measuring devices of effectiveness in transmitting contents of subject area. Educational systems have been the crutch society has used to "make something" of student raw material. But students today want to "be" and not become something. We have always defined education and success and other social values as end products opening the doors of life. Today's students have made them simply timeless, supraspatial, ahistorical alternatives of the present.

All too often, however, students have reduced education to a form of entertainment by developing their capacity to experience to an instinctual level. They demand relevancy in the content of courses that, when examined closely, generally means heightened drama in presentation, simplification of issues with judgmental overtones, and teaching methods comparable to the Mount Sinai's process of spectacular revelation. The reduction to entertainment may mean that the circle is coming to completion; that they feel the subject has deliberately or unwittingly been reduced to a narrow field unrelated to general consumptive practices in which they are engaged.

Education faces a tremendous challenge and a greater opportunity when confronted with ethnic studies as a discipline and minority group students as coarbiters of learning processes. The entire field can be judged according to preselected standards which have always occupied center stage in determining the validity of education itself. Or the field can be correctly considered as the last great opportunity to develop principles of living unfettered by preconceived historical interpretations and cultural imperialism. Academic subjects, to be valid and comprehensible, must be cleansed from their mooring of western European views and sent adrift among the societies of men. Unless we do so the process of education itself will fold and the human mind will revert to the instinctual prowlings of the animal. All indications of the state or our society are that this condition may already be far on the road to absolutizing itself and replacing any conception of civilized man as we have known him.

Conflict and Change
In the Academic Community

Among the current myths that circulate about the American college and university is the view that they have been very conservative institutions, hostile to educational change and cloistered off from the tumults and troubles of the marketplace. On the basis of my own experience as student, teacher, and administrator, covering a time-span of more than a half-century, I testify to the injustice and inaccuracy of such a characterization. Much of that period I have spent, together with colleagues, in prolonged and agonizing reappraisals of the objectives of higher education, particularly liberal arts education, and the refashioning of the curriculum to achieve these objectives. The diversity of our institutions with respect to methods, content, requirements, and standards of instruction is weighty evidence of the experimental nature of American education, and its sensitivity to a wide variety of educational needs. From the multiversity to the denominational college, all are in need of educational improvement. The present ferment within them may provide the occasion for continued improvement but only if we do not assume that every change *is* ipso facto an improvement. Institutions, like human beings, change for better or worse.

At the same time, during the last half-century, the governance of universities and colleges has on the whole been transformed from administrative absolutisms with respect to educational issues to academic communities in which faculties possess preponderant powers if and when they choose to exercise them. The problem of the structure, legal and otherwise, of our colleges and universities is today in debate and in transition, but the proper resolution of this and allied problems seems to me to be clearly dependent upon the prior determination of the educational function or goal of the institution.

From IN DEFENSE OF ACADEMIC FREEDOM, edited by Sidney Hook, pp. 106–19. Copyright © 1971, by The Bobbs-Merrill Company, Inc., reprinted by permission of the publisher.

The history of American higher education, then, shows no hostility to change. The all-important question today is how changes are to be effected —by coercion and/or the threat of coercion or by reflective discussion and debate. Unfortunately, there is a widespread tendency to introduce reforms not in the light of a considered analysis of basic issues but in terms of what seemingly might restore order and prevent further physical disruption of the campus—as if this were the primary criterion of what the best higher education for modern man should be; as if the absence of physical turbulence—the freedom from arson, bombings, violent confrontation—could be anything more than a necessary condition for the *locus* of a liberal educational experience . . .

Before addressing myself to current challenges to the ideals of a liberal education, I wish to take sharp issue with those who confidently assert that today's graduates are better educated in the values and traditions of a liberal arts education than their predecessors. If the perduring quality of the liberally-educated mind is the pursuit of freedom through the arts of intelligence, then by and large we must frankly recognize that liberal arts education has failed dismally. When arson, obscenity, violence and the threat of violence, confrontations, classroom disruptions, hooliganism, and cognate activities are present, the legacy of liberal education is absent. (I find it significant that some apologists for radical student activism contend that, despite the means it employs, this movement is designed to *reinstate* the traditional values of liberal arts education betrayed by its faithless faculty servitors! This reminds me of nothing so much as the contention of advocates of almost all totalitarian philosophies that despite their dictatorial means they are "really" committed to democracy in a "higher" or "truer" sense.)

By a liberal arts education I mean an education whose curriculum has been designed to help students develop those powers and resources—intellectual, emotional, cultural—that will enable them to acquire in a greater or lesser measure:

(1) a perspective on the events of their time with which to meet the challenges of present and future experience;

(2) a constellation of values or a set of meanings or a calling or a developing center around which to organize their lives;

(3) the knowledge, ideals, and techniques necessary for them adequately to perform their duties as free citizens of a free society;

(4) a cultivated sensibility and inner landscape so that they can live a rich and significant personal life, renewed by a continuous process of self-education.

These are generic ideals whose connotations embrace an indeterminate number of special and temporal goals. It should be quite clear that the commitment to a liberal arts education does not entail a single and fixed curriculum for everyone. On the contrary: just as the ideal or pursuit of health is comparable with quite different regimens of hygiene and diet for different individuals, so a liberal arts education will have not only an historically varied content as society becomes more and more complex but will be reached by varied paths reflecting the experience, capacity, needs, and interests of the student.

Today this conception of a liberal arts education, which I regard as a necessary basis for—and sometimes as a proper accompaniment of—all higher professional education, is under attack from many different quarters. I wish to consider some of them.

The first of the many threats to liberal education is the popular view that the curriculum of our colleges should be oriented to meeting the *crises* that periodically arise in society, that threaten to set the world aflame, or to imperil our national survival or the health of our economy. This crisis-oriented approach to education assumes that the course of liberal study can and should be so organized that we can thereby win a war or end it, prevent recessions or inflations, extend civil rights, rebuild our ghettoes, stop the population explosion, prevent environmental pollution—whatever may be the "good cause" which we as citizens rightfully deem to have overwhelming priority at the moment. But in view of the extent to which the colleges and universities of the country have responded to appeals to gear their curricular offerings to special situations and emergencies, the complaint that institutions of higher education have been academic cloisters and ivory towers, uninvolved and unconcerned with the troubled fate of man and society, borders on the grotesque. It is typical of the looseness and irresponsibility of much of the writing about the state of American higher education today. If anything there is a greater need of ivory towers for competent persons who wish to live in them, especially when we recall the great benefits to mankind made possible by those who inhabited ivory towers in the past.

Even practical effects are best achieved by indirection. By any but the most philistine standards of human culture, the larger community has an ever present need for seers, prophets, and lonely men of vision—persons whose findings may seem maddeningly irrelevant to the intellectual and social fashions of the moment. We cannot breed such men, but we should not prevent them from functioning by denigrating them or depriving them of a hospitable environment. They are all too rare under the best of conditions.

It is one thing to aim to develop through curricular means the attitudes and capacities necessary to think and act intelligently in periods of crisis; it is quite another thing to believe that the special knowledge and skills required for the mastery of specific crises can be acquired in advance of their appearance. It is one thing to plan a curriculum of studies with an awareness of the social trends and problems that are shaping the future and that are certain to affect the lives of generations to come; it is simply Utopian in the bad sense of the term, i.e., unrealistic and self-defeating, to imagine that a curriculum must necessarily keep up with all the specific trends and changes that are cried up as important in the great news media—changes that often emerge into and fade out of public consciousness with bewildering suddenness. It is one thing to develop a *readiness of response,* an ability to move promptly and intelligently in grappling with successive problems; it is quite something else to become petrified in a specific posture, however excellent it may have proved with respect to some previous complex of problems.

This particular myth—that colleges and universities can anticipate and help to master, through curricular panaceas, the specific *crises* of the future, not to speak of crises of the present—overlooks the most patent truths about the history of past crises and of the kind of social action necessary to resolve them. It is a myth which has been attributed with some justification to modernists who have invoked Dewey's name but have either not read or not properly understood him.

The opposite of a myth can be just as mythical. Some traditionalists argue, in contradistinction to the above, that the best preparation for social change is the immersion in a fixed curriculum or program of studies. For example, Robert Hutchins writes: "If one neglects history in favor of current affairs, first he will never know history, and second he will not understand current affairs." (Oscar Wilde put this more felicitously a long time ago when he wrote: "He to whom the present is the only thing that is present, knows nothing of the age in which he lives.") We should applaud this recognition of the value of knowledge of history and the plea for its intelligent study. But then Hutchins goes on to add: "The part of the schools is not to expedite current affairs but to initiate students into timeless affairs." One cannot help asking in reply: How can the study of timeless affairs help us to understand historical affairs which by definition are *not* timeless? Surely there is a distinction between the enduring, which is part of historical existence, and the timeless!

An intelligent modernity does not require that we redraw the maps of learning each year or decade or even generation at *every* level. The past— even interpretations of the past—does not change that much. Intelligent revisions and adaptations of the curriculum are always in order, and if better methods and techniques of learning and teaching are available, let us employ them as soon as possible. But not all knowledge becomes obsolescent at once!

There are additional serious threats to the future of the liberal arts education which are allied to this ill-conceived notion that the university be crisis-oriented. These additional threats are more serious, in that they challenge the supremacy of the authority of reason, or better, the authority of intelligence, which gradually has emerged as the *ideal* of the secular university, however much it has been decried by different pressure groups, who in behalf of some private faiths or vested interests have struggled against its recognition. This ideal is intimately related to the conception of the university—in the words of Karl Jaspers—as "the place where truth is sought unconditionally in all forms." It is an ideal which, like the value of intelligence in reflective moral experience, is the only valid absolute, because it is self-critical, aware of its own limitations. The view that American institutions of higher learning stress intelligence and the rational process too much is simply a bizarre notion of the educational underworld for which no rational evidence is advanced. A much more formidable case can be made for the opposite view.

Today the challenge to intelligence takes the form of the renewed cult of raw experience, of glorification of action, passion, and sensual absorption, as if the latter were immediate avenues not only to excitement but to truth and wisdom. Hoary errors in the history of thought have been revived to undergird this view, when those immersed in this cult deign to defend it. "We learn by experience," it is said. "We learn by doing. We learn by going into the fields, streets and factories—by marching, demonstrating, fighting, etc." One might just as well say we learn by living, and that the longer we live the more educated we are. This is absurd on its face. But even if it were not, it is apparent that one does not need a university to acquire this kind of education—if one calls it education.

Life is not a school except as a dubious metaphor. There are many ways by which reality may be experienced or encountered, all legitimate in their context, but the knowing which gives us understanding and truth is a distinctive mode of experience. It is not true that we learn *by* experience. We learn *through* experience, and only when we have the capacity to learn. And what we learn *through* experience is more likely to be valid when we confront experience with a prepared mind. It is the cultivation and development of the prepared mind, and its attendant functions of trained observation and disciplined imagination, which is or should be the objective of all schooling, and especially schooling on the college and university level.

It is true that ultimately we learn by doing. But it is not true that all doing is a form of learning. Here, too, the role of ideas or hypotheses is central. Their presence is what distinguishes the intelligently learned man from the learned ass, from the dogmatic autodidact, and from those long on experience but short in wisdom.

Lest the reader think that I exaggerate the extent to which the cult and glorification of raw experience is cried up today by those who pander to popular life-styles among students, I quote from a college reader, *"Starting Over,"* hot off the press, edited by Frederick Crews and Orville Schell, two professors at the University of California at Berkeley. "We don't rule out the possibility," they tell us in their Preface, "that Lenny Bruce may have more to teach us than Alfred North Whitehead." With characteristic lack of precision, they fail to tell us what, aside from obscenity, Lenny Bruce *can* teach us, more than Alfred North Whitehead—one of the profoundest thinkers of the twentieth century. As for obscenity, whatever its uses, one hardly needs to attend a university to learn it. And although the editors complete their sentence by saying, "We include both of them just in case," surely the bare possibility that one may learn something about anything is hardly an appropriate principle for including subjects for study. For it excludes nothing!

Effective schooling of the prepared mind requires clinical experience that may take the student out of the classroom to amplify the meaning and test the validity of what he or she has learned within it. But it must be intelligently planned, supervised, and carefully assessed. Emphasis on clinical experience, where appropriate, cannot be overstressed. It is analogous to the experimental approach. It is a far cry, however, from current demands that uncontrolled, diverse, helter-skelter forays into "life and experience" be recognized as integral and valid elements of university education. The demand that "action Ph.D's" be awarded, that graduate students receive credit for leading rent strikes, organizing the unemployed, or fighting pollution, and that undergraduates be granted academic recognition *merely* for the experience of traveling or living abroad is a *reductio ad absurdum* of this view. One may as well give them academic awards for sex and marriage!

Another challenge to liberal arts education is implicit in the demand that research, teaching, scholarship—in short, all curricular activity in whole and part—be "relevant." What nonsense is embraced by that term! The cry for relevance extends from the simple demand that the teacher talk sense to the demand that what he teaches, regardless of his subject matter, help achieve the classless society. Strictly speaking, the term "relevant" is relational. We must always ask: "Relevant to what?" Normally, in the life of mind, what is taught, if the teaching is good, is relevant to a *problem.* Problems themselves are relevant to domains of experience. The problem of *who* first propounded the theory of organic evolution, or the labor theory of value, is irrelevant to the problem of its validity. One man's problem may be irrelevant to another man's purpose or interests without affecting its significance in its own field. In a well-ordered university in which the scholarly faculty decides, the existence of certain fields of study is prima facie evidence that the field is deemed to have educational significance, in the light of the objectives of liberal arts study. Any attempt to control the relevance of studies except on educational grounds is an intolerable interference with academic freedom.

Most claims that higher education be "relevant" are either politically motivated or inspired by narrow utilitarian considerations. I shall discuss the political motivations below. The other motivations are open to the easy retort that narrow utilitarian considerations are irrelevant not only to the ideals and delights of a liberal arts education but also to the multiple, indirect, and enlarged social uses of theories which at first are *not* immediately useful. Einstein's special theory of relativity had no earthly use when it was first propounded. But it was highly relevant to a genuine problem— the negative findings of the Michaelson-Morley experiment. The current demands for relevance would have driven Einstein and many others out of the university. Whitehead used to celebrate the perpetual uselessness of the theory of numbers and symbolic logic. They have now found a use, but they always had a sufficient justification in the eyes of those who enjoy the games and beauty of abstraction.

Related to these challenges to liberal arts education is the critical challenge that stresses the importance of immediacy—the demand that the curriculum offer solutions to complex problems that can lead to early, if not overnight, transformations of our society, economy, law, or culture. Radical-activist students are properly aware of the distance between the goals of the American dream and our current achievement—a distance which they have learned about in large part through the despised curricular offerings of the present. They are not properly aware of—indeed, they aggressively ignore—the fact that American society has again and again raised its sights and periodically redefined the goals of the American dream. They have, therefore, systematically ignored the distance covered in removing the obstacles to political and social equality, and, despite the great problems and injustices still remaining, the magnitude of the social gains. Disregarding the fact that American colleges and universities have been the great centers of outspoken criticism and dissent in American life, they have pictured them instead as exploitative agencies of the Establishment. They have caricatured the whole notion of an Establishment (itself a vulgarized Marxist view of "the ruling class") with the charge that the organized working class is part of it. In consequence, they have demanded not only that their instruction be relevant in relation to their purposes but also that it be oriented to reformist, even revolutionary, objectives vaguely defined but completely and explicitly critical of every aspect of American history and culture.

The truth tends to be the first casualty of every war and crusade. One-sided criticism can distort the truth every whit as much as apologetic accolades. On several campuses, *enragés* students have disrupted the classes of professors who have not—in their eyes—taken a sufficiently critical stance towards one or another aspect of American culture. There is no record of interference (which would have been just as deplorable!) with the instruction of teachers openly sympathetic to the Viet Cong or to the totalitarian despotisms of Castro, Mao-tse-tung, or the Kremlin, with their holocausts of victims. It is not surprising, therefore, that these radical activists and their faculty allies have denounced the ideal of "objectivity" as a bourgeois myth. To challenge as a chimera the ideal of objectivity, difficult as it may be to reach, is to renounce the ideal of the truth which is the *raison d'être* of the liberal university. To deny that the concept of objectivity is intelligible is incoherent and self-contradictory, for it would prevent us from distinguishing between historical fiction and historical fact, and make groundless and arbitrary even the radical activist's litany of alleged American crimes.

An unexpectedly formidable challenge to liberal arts education has been nurtured by some *liberals,* so acutely aware of the failures of the liberal tradition to achieve its promise, that *they* have betrayed its perennially valid ideals, sometimes out of simple confusion and sometimes out of cowardice, moral and physical. I refer to the failure to recognize the human experience or the human condition as the basic source and orientation of the curriculum. It is mainly this failure that has caused the growing fragmentation of the curriculum into isolated blocks of studies, into "Black Studies," "Afro-American Studies," "Third World Studies." The black experience, the African experience, the Third World experience, the Jewish experience, the Irish experience, etc., *are* each part of the human experience and as such worthy of inclusion in those areas and subject matters whose understanding is required to achieve a proper liberal education. The revision of the traditional liberal arts courses in history, literature, art and the social studies to do justice to the various ethnic expressions of human experience has long been overdue and is currently being undertaken. That is one thing. But the organization of special blocks of study, often open in effect only to members of minority groups among the study body—groups organized and controlled by members of those same minorities—breaches important assumptions of liberal education as well as the principles of academic freedom. Here I stress only the educational aspect of the question. There *are* no class truths, national truths, or racial truths as distinct from truths, objective truths, *about* classes, nations, and ethnic groupings. The black experience is neither necessary nor sufficient to understand the truth about slavery, any more than the experience of white Southerners is necessary or sufficient to understand the truth about the Reconstruction Period, or experience in Fascist or Communist countries is necessary or sufficient to learn or teach the truths about their terroristic regimes. I find it highly significant that the powerful criticisms of the proposals for *separate* courses of study for black students made by distinguished Negro educators like Kenneth Clark, Sir Arthur Lewis, Bayard Rustin, and others, have provoked no considered replies, but only derisive epithets. Many administrators who have supported the demand for autonomous Black Studies programs have done so not on supportable educational grounds but out of fear that their campuses might be torn apart. Professor Henry Rosovsky has done pioneering work as

Chairman of the Harvard Committee on African and Afro-American studies, in devising a college major in Afro-American studies with the *same standards of academic excellence* that obtained for other majors. He has flatly charged that the action of the Harvard faculty reversing the report of his committee, and in effect giving black undergraduate students "powers hitherto held only by Harvard *senior faculty* and denied to junior faculty, graduate students and non-black undergraduates," was adopted in the face of threats of violence.

To make exceptions to principles of equity as well as valid educational policy in order to compensate for historical injustices is an inverse form of racism just as objectionable to sensitive and intelligent members of minority groups as traditional forms of racism. To lower standards of judgment and excellence, to dilute content and subject matter as a form of intellectual reparations, is to restore and compound the infamies of the double standard. The student is just as much a second-class academic citizen if an institution discriminates in his favor on the basis of his skin color as he is when it discriminates against him on the same basis.

There are dangerous tendencies in the admission policies of some institutions which mistakenly assume that in education democracy requires that all groups in the population be proportionally represented by students and faculty in every course of study. A case can be made for the view that in American democratic society everyone has a human right to the kind and degree of schooling from which he can profit, and which will facilitate the growth of his intellectual and cultural powers to their fullest. But the right to an education no more carries with it the right of everyone to a specific kind of education or to a certain degree of education than the right to medical treatment carries with it the right to one kind of medical treatment, no matter what one is ailing from. Just as no one prescription can adequately meet the medical needs of all people, no one special curriculum or method can adequately meet the educational needs of all students. Quackery both in medicine and education results from this denial. Here as elsewhere individual need, interest, capacity should be the determining considerations. Democracy does not require belief in the moral equality of those who are the same or alike but, rather, belief in the moral equality of the *different*—whether they are physically different, racially different, or intellectually different.

The liberal arts conception of higher education is based upon a belief in the community of educational interest among teacher-scholars, learners, and administrators. This conception is being threatened by something analogous to a "class struggle" view, according to which the university is a factory in which students are processed and exploited by their teachers and administrators. But knowledge is not a commodity of which one can say that the more one has of it the less remains for others. It belongs to the family of values of which it is true to say that they are not diminished but enhanced by being shared. Education is not in the first instance a quest for power, whether student power or faculty power, but instead is a quest for truth and a means of growth, of spiritual enlargement and maturation. Where a community of educational interest prevails in the university, it does not preclude difference, sometimes sharp differences, about a multitude of things. And, so long as the "class struggle" conception of education does not enter to disrupt the rational exchange of views, all of these differences are negotiable in the same way in which we seek to resolve scientific differences. That is why the university can be a conservator of values and attitudes and at the same time an innovator.

All of the challenges to liberal education I have considered come to a head in frank espousals for the politicalization of the university. By the politicalization of the university is meant the direct involvement of the university as a *corporate* institution in the controversial political and social problems of the day. The radical activists of our time speak out of both sides of their mouths on this question, sometimes condemning the university for allegedly already being politically involved, and as guilty of betraying the ideal of noninvolvement, and sometimes—the real burden of their song— condemning the university for being involved on the wrong political side. Not content with having won the right of the individual faculty member to espouse any political cause he may wish without prejudicing his position in the university community, they seek to draw the university *as such,* and *officially,* into the endorsement, teaching, and organization of programs for social reform and/or revolution of the society on whose largesse and support the university ultimately depends. Since the radical activists assert that no program of social reform or commitment can dispense with an ideology, they are proposing that universities cease making a fetish of objectivity and neutrality and become ideological institutions.

This is a recommendation which if acted upon can result only in educational disaster. If the universities attempt to politicalize themselves, and instead of studying, proposing, and critically analyzing programs of social action, seek to implement these programs as parts of an agenda of social action, the unconverted larger community will not only withdraw its support but purge or suppress the universities that are thus self-politicalized. The universities will in this way lose their hard-won relative autonomy and become politicalized with a vengeance, but from an ideological quarter hardly congenial to the radical activists, who will be ruthlessly swept away, together with their liberal allies. Although I am convinced that the consequences of politicalizing the university would be suicidal, I do not wish to base my criticism of the proposal mainly on this very practical ground, but rather upon the values of the liberal arts tradition . . .

Once the university becomes politicalized, the students, too, become politically polarized—if they have not already reached that state. Students and faculty then join forces in ways already familiar to us, not only in the universities of some foreign countries, but on some of our own campuses. Factionalization among extremists leads to a kind of competition among them to implement corporate policies more vigorously and to push the university into the very forefront of the struggle to radicalize society. The consequent effect of ideological commitment on particular departments—especially on the appointment and promotion of faculty personnel—can easily be imagined. The normal frictions and conflicts that operate even when the university is uncommitted and permits all the winds of doctrine to blow freely on the campus become exacerbated to a point where professional competence, which should be the first and main criterion in matters of this kind, is subordinated, under all sorts of pretexts and rationalizations, to ideological considerations. The canons of professional ethics and integrity are celebrated in the holiday rhetoric of convocations and commencements, only to be abandoned in practice.

That politicalization of the university constitutes a threat to academic freedom is acknowledged. Sometimes in an effort to minimize the danger, advocates of politicalization narrow the scope of the "political" to grave issues during periods of crisis. But the definition of grave issues depends on how intensely human beings feel about them, and the world is always in crisis. More often, and especially among students and junior faculty, academic freedom is regarded as a kind of class privilege of professors that can readily be sacrificed or compromised to further larger ideological goals or purposes.

It may sound harsh, but there is convincing evidence that it is true: Academic freedom in the United States today is threatened not so much by fundamentalist churchmen, reactionary businessmen, and political demagogues, as it is by ideological fanatics among students and faculty. It is ironical that they owe their presence in the university and the guarantee they are given of an opportunity to proclaim their ideological wares to the very principles of academic freedom which they violate and undermine. They ignore the truth that genuine tolerance does not require tolerance of the actively intolerant.

The University

In the 1960s, all over the world, the ideal of a university, cherished for almost 1000 years, appeared to be fading, to be replaced by the notion of the university as a nationalized industry. Instead of being thought of as an autonomous community of masters and scholars pursuing the truth, the university was coming to be regarded as the nerve center of the knowledge industry, dedicated to national power, prosperity, and prestige. The president of the largest American university said, "The basic reality for the university is the widespread recognition that new knowledge is the most important factor in economic and social growth."

Is the university to be the servant or the critic of society? Is it to be dependent or independent, a mirror or a beacon? Is it to attempt to meet the nation's immediate and practical needs, or is its primary duty that of meeting the need for the transmission and extension of high culture? Is an intellectual community possible in an age of specialization? Can a nationalized industry pretend to a world outlook? Or can all these apparently contradictory aims be successfully combined in one institution?

Such questions had been asked from time to time since the rise of the nation-state and the beginning of the Industrial Revolution. Somebody was always trying to use the universities for something. Napoleon, for example, wanted to make them a kind of intellectual gendarmerie. He said:

> If my hopes are realized, I shall find in this corps a guaranty against pernicious theories subversive of the social order. . . . These bodies, being the first defenders of the cause of morality and the principles of the state, will give the first alarm, and will always be ready to resist the dangerous theories of those who are trying to single themselves out, and who, from time to time, renew those vain discussions which, among all peoples, have so frequently tormented public opinion.[1]

From *The Learning Society* (New York: Frederick A. Praeger, Publishers, 1968), ch. 8.

The Soviet Union and mainland China have had much the same idea and have added to it the requirement common among industrializing nations, that the university should help supply the programs and personnel necessary to speed the process of industrialization. By the Morrill Act of 1862, the United States, perhaps despairing of obtaining such assistance from established universities, created a whole new set of a new kind that had no other object.

The discovery during World War II that universities could be "useful," particularly in promoting technological advance, swelled the cry that they must change with the times. The universal recognition that technology rested on progress in science and that such progress required a high degree of specialization was forcing the proliferation and fragmentation of instruction and research. The argument was hottest in the developing countries, especially in those that had recently achieved nationhood, because their universities were mostly new and had to fight their way to some conception of their purpose.

The monster, which by definition is an exception to the rule, was becoming the rule. Universities of 50,000 students appeared in many parts of the world, and the University of California was looking forward to 300,000. Though mere growth on this scale and at this rate was disconcerting, it did not necessarily force a fundamental change in purpose and method; for universities could be multiplied and the Oxford and Cambridge principle of small colleges within a large framework was before those who cared to imitate it. The quality of the students, or rather the quality of their preparation, was perhaps more important than their numbers: the rapid expansion of secondary education, and the *ad hoc* character that it had assumed, created a demand that the university adjust itself to a kind of student it had never had before and alter its character, if necessary, to accommodate him.

In many places the university seemed on its way to thorough absorption in the *ad hoc.* It was sometimes said that games were now the only university activity pursued in a liberal spirit, that is, for their own sake. But in some countries, even this was doubtful; for the publicity and the gate receipts often seemed more important than the sport. Certainly the pursuit of knowledge for its own sake, though still referred to, appeared to be a less and less accurate description of anything actually going on in the universities. As Georges Gusdorf has remarked, *Napoleon pas mort.*[2]

The most advanced industrial country, the United States, was pouring money into research through governmental agencies that had a mission and wanted the universities to help them carry it out. The university, if it accepted the money, accepted the mission, which was not the mission of the university, but of the agency. These grants required a kind and degree of specialization hitherto unknown, drew off professors from teaching, and made the agency, rather than the university, the nourishing mother, the Alma Mater, of the professor.

The material base, even the physical location, of the professor was changing. He drew his sustenance now from outside the university and could take it with him whenever he thought he would feel more comfortable elsewhere. In many fields, he could develop into an executive presiding over a large staff who carried on his work while he traveled from meeting to meeting, consulting and negotiating. For him the university could be a place to hang his hat, one to which he owed no obligation and in which he felt no interest. The professor might belong to an intellectual community, but it was not one having a local habitation and a name: it was not a university community as that term had been understood since the Middle Ages.

The conception of a worldwide intellectual community, of the wandering professor, free to go where his work can be done best, of a university without walls, composed of men who meet anywhere that is convenient, whose interest is in their subjects rather than their institutions, is not without appeal. Affluence and technology have introduced a new flexibility and ease into the communication of scholars. A specialist in any subject can assemble material and colleagues from anywhere: the resources of the whole world are open to him. No idea of a university, and no organization of it in practice, can fail to include these new advantages in its scope. The question is whether they can be assimilated to the ancient university ideal.

The Purpose of the University

All formulations of that ideal have involved one proposition in common, and that is the object of the university is to see knowledge, life, the world, or truth whole. The aim of the university is to tame the pretentions and excesses of experts and specialists by drawing them into the academic circle and subjecting them to the criticism of other disciplines. Everything in the university is to be seen in the light of everything else. This is not merely for the sake of society or to preserve the unity of the university. It is also for the sake of the specialists and experts, who, without the light shed by others, may find their own studies going down blind alleys.

The physiologist Emil Du Bois-Reymond pointed this out long ago. Following notes sounded by Bacon and Locke, he said:

> The exclusive study of natural science, like any other exclusive occupation, restricts the circle of ideas. The natural sciences limit the view to what is under our eyes, to what can be carried in our hand, to what gives immediate sense experience with a certitude that appears absolute. . . . In a certain sense, we may regard this characteristic as a most precious advantage, but, when natural science is an exclusive master, we cannot deny that the spirit easily

becomes poor in ideas, the imagination loses its colors, the soul its sensibility, and the consequence is a way of seeing that is narrow, dry, and hard.[3]

The university has been a symbol of human integrity, a trustee for civilization, an intellectual community. Those who like to think of a university as an intellectual community do not do so because the words have a pleasant, friendly ring. The community has a purpose, which is to think together so that everybody may think better than he would alone and so that his own vagaries, which are likely to include an overweening confidence that his subject is the most important in the world, may not carry him away.

The gratifying spectacle of the scholar in Lagos in touch with his fellow specialists in Tokyo, Cairo, Rome, and New York and attending a half dozen international conferences a year is no substitute for the historic role of the university as a center of thought. The members of such a center may take off from time to time to confer with their fellow experts without impairing the vitality of the university; but they must have some continuous attachment to it and dependence on it if it is to remain a center.

Such a center, then, does not exclude specialization or professional study. It does, however, prescribe the kind of professional study it will include and the limits of the specialization it will tolerate. If the sole object in view is to train reasonably successful lawyers, doctors, administrators, engineers, or technicians of any kind, there is no reason for burdening the university with the task. History has repeatedly shown that this can be done on the job or in separate training schools. When Karl Jaspers proposed something new for Europe, a technological faculty in the university, he did not do so because he felt the need for more or more efficient practitioners. On the contrary, he wanted to bring technology within the circle of humane studies. His summary statement was: "The university must face the great problem of modern man: how out of technology there can arise that metaphysical foundation of a new way of life which technology has made possible." Although the British decision to turn the colleges of advanced technology into universities was probably grounded on far more mundane considerations, it may conceivably have the effect Jaspers was seeking. Obviously this effect is not to be expected from a nationalized industry, even the knowledge industry.

The Basis of Autonomy

Nor can a nationalized industry, even the knowledge industry, easily sustain a claim to autonomy. If the university, as we frequently hear, is to reflect the national culture, or if it is to promote national power and prosperity, then there is every reason why the university should be made to follow the orthodox interpretation of the national culture and official prescription for achieving power and prosperity. The university that accepts money from a governmental agency with a mission must try to complete the mission. A university that is an intellectual community cannot accept such grants: it can take no money on conditions that limit its freedom of inquiry or instruction.

So the university has to be clear as to what it is about. Many large American universities appear to be devoted to three unrelated activities: vocational certification, child care, and scientific research. Only the last of these could be the basis of an assertion of academic freedom; and the last, if overpowered by the demand for prespecified results, could add nothing to the argument.

Clark Kerr sardonically said, "A university anywhere can aim no higher than to be . . . as confused as possible for the sake of the preservation of the whole uneasy balance." But this involves great risks, especially the risk that those who attend and support the university may ask someday what it is trying to do, and, on receiving an incomprehensible answer, turn their backs on it.

The Students

All over the world, in the 1960s, students were restless. In large part, their complaints resulted from the confusion ironically recommended by Kerr. They did not know why they had come to the university, what they were supposed to do there, or what the university was.

Most of them were under the impression that the university led on to social status and a good job. But how could social distinction attach to something that everybody seemed destined to have? And perhaps there would not be any jobs, or any of the kind they had been led to expect. They found themselves taught by assistants while the professors roamed the world. They found themselves numbered and computerized. The confused university added to their own confusion.

The ancient ideal of a university obviated these complaints, in principle, if not in practice. According to that ideal, research and teaching were identical; and the students were junior partners in the intellectual enterprise. The ideal could be realized or approximated if the students were capable of independent intellectual work and if the professor joined them with him in his inquiries. The problem of teaching versus research, which plagues all universities today, the problem of the "impersonality" of the university, which is as vexing in Paris as it is in Abidjan, the problem of the role of the student in the university, can never be solved amid the current confusion. These problems become relatively simple if the university is limited to those capable of independent work and interested in doing it.

There is no reason why it should not be limited in this way. Liberal education is for everybody, because everybody has a right to have his mind set free. But not everybody wants to lead the life of the mind. If the university were limited to those professors who wanted to lead the life of the mind and who had the capacity for it, and to those students who were able to associate themselves with the enterprise, the size of the modern universities would be greatly reduced.

The University Versus
Training Schools and Research Institutes

What would happen to those who were not admitted? By hypothesis, they would have had a liberal education and would be prepared to lead human lives. If they wanted to become technicians of any kind, if they wanted to go into business, if they wanted to solve practical problems, if they wanted to enter upon any of the multifarious occupations of life, they could learn to do so on the job or in training schools set up for these purposes.

Those training schools might be located in the vicinity of the university. The teachers and students might avail themselves of its resources. But, since their object would be different from that of the university, they could not be regarded as members of it and could have no part in its management. An intellectual community cannot be built out of people who are not pursuing intellectual interests.

Those scientists or other workers in the knowledge industry who are interested merely in piling up data or in carrying out the missions of government departments or in gratifying the needs of industry might be established in a similar manner in institutes near the university but not a part of it. There is no reason why governments and industries should be forbidden to conduct such investigations as will, in their opinion, meet their needs. There is no reason why investigators who are collecting information should be thwarted in their attempts to do so. There is some reason why specialists should not insist on conducting esoteric researches in isolation —the reason is that they are unlikely to be successful—but, if they are accommodated in institutes of their own, outside the university, they will not confuse that institution. If the university can be an intellectual community, it can fulfill its historic function.

Tendencies in England

The outcome of the struggle going on in England in the 1960s will be instructive. There the government has announced a "binary" or "bilateral" plan for higher education and research. It is reminiscent of the division that must have been in the minds of the framers of the Morrill Act in the United States, a division repeated more recently in Nigeria. According to the British scheme, the universities, which now include the Colleges of Advanced Technology, will continue to be autonomous; but parallel with them will be what is called the "public sector," meeting the demand for "vocational, professional, and industrially-based courses in higher education." Anthony Crosland, Minister of Education and Science, said of these institutions, in 1965: "Why should we not aim at . . . a vocationally oriented nonuniversity sector which is degree-giving and with an appropriate amount of post-graduate work with opportunities for learning comparable with those of the universities, and giving a first class professional training?" Crosland refers to this sector as "under social control, directly responsible to social needs."

The institutions in the public sector will not confer their own degrees: they will recommend their candidates to a Council for National Academic Awards that will formulate the standards. Apparently the institutions in the public sector will not be expected—certainly they will not be required—to engage in much research. Their duty will be to turn out technicians.

The autonomy of the English universities has continued in spite of their financial dependence on the state. The "public sector" is directly controlled by local authorities, who are in turn subject to guidance, or at least to pressure, from the central government. The theory of the binary plan appears clear enough: the universities are to be centers of independent thought and criticism; the institutions in the public sector will be responsive to current needs. If the theory can be carried out, the demand that the universities meet current needs will be assuaged.

The question is whether the theory can be carried out. The division between the universities and the land-grant colleges in the United States has almost entirely disappeared. They are all universities now. Whatever other institutions have asked for, these institutions have obtained. On the other hand, the existence of the land-grant colleges did not assuage the demand that the universities meet current needs. Yale, Harvard, and Princeton do not teach agriculture, but this is almost the only difference the list of their courses discloses between them and those land-grant colleges that are now called universities. What the University of Michigan is doing and what Michigan State University, founded as a land-grant college, purports to do are about the same.

It seems unlikely that the graduates of the institutions in the public sector in England will long be content with "second-class" degrees, that their faculties can or should tolerate being deprived of the chance to carry on research, or that they and their constituencies will acquiesce in a status that will be regarded as less honorable than that of the universities. On the other hand, the pressure to get the universities into the business of meeting current needs is likely to continue, since Britain, like every other country, is convinced that knowledge is power.

If, in spite of these difficulties, the binary plan can be maintained, it will be a tribute to the strength of the university tradition in England and to the public understanding of it. It may, perhaps, be an example to the world.[4]

The Free and Responsible University

How can an autonomous intellectual community be held to its duty? History suggests that all bodies of privileged persons tend to deteriorate, and the Oxford of Edward Gibbon and Adam Smith shows that ancient universities are not an exception to the rule. They do not seem to be able to find within themselves the means of regeneration. The danger in the modern university is greater than ever, because specialization tends to remove the professor from the realm of discussion within the university and makes his field his private property. As Jaspers says: "The conduct of faculty members has been compared with that of the monkeys on the palm trees of the holy grove at Benares: on every palm tree sits a monkey, all seem to be very peaceful and minding their own business. But the moment one monkey tries to climb up the palm tree of another he runs into a heavy barrage of coconuts." Professors must be selected by professors; but departments and selection committees and individual professors seem often moved by fear of competition on the one hand and by affection for their disciples on the other. A university atmosphere, moreover, is not propitious to genius: the academic body is likely to be favorable to accepted doctrine and routine performance. It does not care for fireworks.

Adam Smith proposed to remedy academic indolence and inertia by depriving the universities of their endowments and basing the professors' incomes on student fees. This was at one time the rule in Germany. It put a premium on fireworks, and not necessarily those of genius, but of the television star or vaudeville performer. The remedy actually applied in England was the intervention of the state through royal commissions. Since politics is architectonic, all states have the power to intervene in the affairs of universities. The question is when and how it shall be exercised.

The issue turns on what the state thinks the university is for. A state that regards the university as a means to national power, prosperity, and prestige will—and quite properly, if its premise is accepted—direct the affairs of the university to this end. A state that thinks the primary duty of the university is to look after children will be alert to see to it that no forbidden paths run through the groves of academe. A state that wants a university to be an intellectual community pursuing the truth for its own sake will hold its powers in reserve unless the university, like Oxford in the eighteenth century, flagrantly fails to make the attempt. This has been the general practice of Europe except in such periods as that of Hitler in Germany. Although the vast bulk of all university support in England comes from the public purse, the parliamentary committees that investigate all other public accounts have not been able to get their hands on those of the universities. But the initiative of European ministers of education, like that of governments in England, has on several occasions recalled the universities to their duty.

In those countries in which there are, between the state and the university, intermediate bodies set up to hold the university's property and manage its business affairs, the degree to which they have interfered with academic operations has varied with the tradition of the country. The boards of laymen who nominally control the red-brick universities of England would not think of vetoing a professorial appointment, of deciding on a curriculum, or of determining the scientific value of a research project. They limit themselves to business. Similar boards in the United States, because higher education has traditionally been *ad hoc* in that country, have not shown similar restraint. Where an American state sets up a board of regents to operate its university, the legislature and the board often vie with each other to see which can interfere more in education and research. The boards of trustees of private, endowed universities in the United States, which are the legal owners of its property, have shown a tendency to behave like the directors of an American corporation, regarding the professors as employees and the students as a product to be turned out in accordance with the specifications of the directors. This tendency is both a cause and an effect of the American tradition, which holds that a university is a mirror, and not a beacon.

The vitality of an intellectual community requires that it be free from such interference. But the continued vitality of the community requires that it be subject to criticism. Boards of trustees and regents can be the primary source of such criticism, and, apart from the management of business affairs, it would appear to be their primary duty to supply it.

Administration

Red tape, administrative machinery, and all that goes by the name of bureaucracy are the inevitable accompaniments of large-scale organization. They tend to assume such importance as to give the impression that the organization exists for their sake, rather than the other way around. The tendency is toward dehumanization.

The method of a university is maieutic through and through. A university aiming at the ancient ideal depends on human contact. A university and a factory have nothing in common. Although it cannot escape bureaucracy, a university, if it wishes to remain one, has to minimize it in every possible way. One way is to turn the university into a federation of small colleges, an arrangement that minimizes housekeeping and maximizes human contact while preserving the advantages of the larger community to all its members. This way has the additional advantage of minimizing the administrative functions of those members of the community who have to carry them out.

In that conception of a university which analogizes it to a business corporation, the president or rector and the deans are the bosses or foremen of the labor force and are responsible as well for the inspection and certification of the product, the maintenance of good public relations, and securing adequate financing. They are not chosen because of their commitment to the intellectual life or their ability to lead it. If they had the commitment and the ability, they would not be in a position to lead it, because they have no time. Yet their place in the academic apparatus is such that both inside and outside the university they speak for the corporation.

No man committed to the life of the mind can easily reconcile himself to being an administrator for his whole time or for very long. The system that used to prevail in the Netherlands, where every professor was prepared to sacrifice two years of his life, one as secretary of the faculties and another as rector, or that in Oxford and Cambridge, where the college is so small as not to require much administrative attention, and the vice-chancellorship rotates on a three-year cycle, prevents the development of a panoply of academic bureaucrats who dominate but do not belong to the intellectual community.

The president or rector, if he is to be the embodiment and representative of the intellectual community, has to be chosen by it. The "magnificence" that attaches to his name in many parts of Europe is that of the intellectual community, or of the university ideal.

The Prospects

The theme of this essay has been that in the twenty-first century education may at last come into its own. This chapter can offer little evidence that the university may do so. The tendencies all over the world suggest rather that the university will cease to be an autonomous intellectual community, a center of independent thought and criticism, and will become a nationalized industry. Vast sums of money, hordes of people, and almost all governments are dedicated to the realization of this prospect.

If the prospect is realized, the loss to humanity will be severe. It is like the loss of wisdom, of light. Totalitarian countries, primarily concerned with the perpetuation of an official dogma, may be content with this result.

In the 1960s, there were some slight indications that democratic countries would not be. Centers of independent thought and criticism were springing up outside the university or in very tenuous connection with it. This solution is better than none, but it seems less than satisfactory. It will take generations for these new organizations to acquire the prestige the name of the university carries with it everywhere.

This essay has taken the position that education may come into its own in the twenty-first century because of the practical inutility of continuing the inhuman, antihuman, nonhuman programs of the past. The conscientious critic cannot say the same of the university as a nationalized industry. It can be done, and the results desired can be achieved. The results may be unworthy, even suicidal, but in the closing decades of the twentieth century the desire to achieve them looked unalterable.

This field has produced a lush crop of doubletalk. A contemporary scholar has no difficulty in saying that a university must be a service station for its community and at the same time an international organization; an institution focused on the immediate needs of its immediate environment and at the same time engaged in the study of "universally applicable principles or the development of universally valid scholarship."[5] Nobody wants to come into the open and say that the university ideal is outmoded; its hold on the minds and sentiments of men is too strong for that. Almost every statement about the modern university begins or ends with obeisance to the glories of the autonomous intellectual community. A book on education in Nigeria will talk of the importance of intellectual activity for its own sake and emphasize the necessity of a world view; but when it gets serious it will say of the universities that they are "the people's universities and that their development must be upon lines which decisive public sentiment lays down"; it will leave no doubt that decisive public sentiment demands industrial growth and a parochial Nigerian emphasis. Even Shakespeare's sonnets are to be taught with a view to "the light they shed on contemporary African life and contemporary African dilemmas," a challenge to the teacher if there ever was one.[6]

Clark Kerr, when he has described the university as the central manufacturing plant of the nationalized knowledge industry, asks for the improvement of undergraduate instruction, the unification of the intellectual world, the humanization of administration, and a chance for students who have genuine interest and capacity. He summarizes by saying, "The university may now again need to find out whether it has a brain as well as a body." There are no reasons why an efficient nationalized industry should make any concessions to these aspirations, and there are many reasons why it should not. What Kerr aspires to can be achieved only in an autonomous intellectual community, and this would mean that the university would cease to be a nationalized industry.

It does not seem possible to have it both ways, to preserve the university ideal in a knowledge factory. Unity and clarity of purpose are fundamental. Purpose is a principle of limitation and allocation. It determines what will not be done and how effort and resources will be distributed among those things which are to be done. An institution cannot long pursue cross-purposes; presumably this is what is meant by saying that the university may now again need to find out whether it has a brain. The purpose of the brain is to give meaning, coherence, and unity to the organism and its activities.

NOTES

[1]Georges Gusdorf, *L'Université en Question* (Paris: Payot, 1964), p. 72.

[2]Ibid., p. 74.

[3]Ibid., p. 166.

[4]For discussion of a somewhat similar notion in West Germany, see Ernst Anrich, *Die Idee der deutschen Universität und die Reform der deutschen Universitäten,* 2nd ed. (Darmstadt: Wissenschaftliche Buchgesellschaft, 1962), p. 89.

[5]See Harold R. W. Benjamin, *Higher Education in the American Republics* (New York: McGraw-Hill Book Company, 1965), p. 207.

[6]O. Ikejiani (ed.), *Education in Nigeria* (New York: Frederick A. Praeger, Publisher, 1965), *passim.*

DAVID RIESMAN

Notes on Educational Reform*

Keeping in touch with efforts at educational reform in American universities has become increasingly difficult. Several years ago only a few pacesetter institutions were experimenting with interdisciplinary courses, field study programs, student-initiated courses, and independent study in their undergraduate programs. But today these innovations have spread throughout academia in response to changed faculty attitudes and the newer youth subcultures.[1] . . .

Understandably, educational reform is intertwined with other issues: for instance, with the attack on science as stultifying, "irrelevant," or dangerous to mankind; with programs in black studies or in urban studies which often have the highest priority on a campus, frequently with the aim of doing something about white racism or ghetto poverty. In many colleges the proponents of participatory educational democracy—carrying into (more or less) voluntary associations the national principle of "one man, one vote"—contend that participation per se is a more important reform than any substantive changes in styles of teaching and learning. Correspondingly, whatever else may be happening on a campus, a drastic delegitimation of authority is proceeding, whether this be the authority of experts or professionals, of curricular programs, or of traditions of scholarship and learning. In the place of the older authority there has arisen what Erich Fromm in *Escape from Freedom* and *Man for Himself* described as anonymous authority: the authority of whatever is defined as relevant and consonant with an epoch of rapid social change, in short, with whatever extracurricular preoccupations students and faculty now press upon their institutions. . . .

*I am indebted for helpful suggestions to Michael Maccoby, Edwin Harwood, and Robert Bellah. Support for my research on higher education has come from the Carnegie Corporation and the Ford Foundation.

Excerpted from an article originally written for a Festschrift in honor of Eric Fromm.

Current Themes of Educational Reform

During the academic year 1968–1969, while on leave from Harvard, I had the opportunity to discuss ideas and ideals of educational change and reform with students and faculty at a number of places widely differing from each other: Stanford University (then engaged in a large self-study); the University of California at Davis and at San Diego; the University of North Carolina (where the first two undergraduate years were being examined by a student-faculty committee); the new College of the State University of New York at Old Westbury which had just opened that year; Oakland University in Michigan; and, more briefly, Pitzer College in the Claremont group of colleges. In addition, I perused the student press at a number of colleges and followed the discussions of reform in the educational journals. I have already indicated the similarity of concerns that one meets from coast to coast. Everywhere one encounters the desire for a more egalitarian university. Meritocratic distinctions are under attack and so is the apparatus of grades, course prerequisites, and selective admissions. One often finds encounter groups or sensitivity training sessions praised as the optimal situations for learning, in part on the ground that faculty authority and expertness could be reduced and true mutuality encouraged. While some encounter groups do succeed in opening people up to themselves and others, at times intrusively and at other times with greater care and tact, there may be a general tendency to focus on the intrapsychic in such settings. But one also finds a widespread effort to get students and faculty out into field situations, such as community organizing or experiments in communal living.[2] The range of field settings that is envisaged is likely to be narrow: pockets of poverty, inner-city ghettos, the exotic and the deprived; less often will students involve themselves in the life of a church, a business corporation, or a small town.

In all these areas, the trend is away from what is regarded as alienated learning and toward first-hand experience. An amateur spirit prevails, which has its benign sides but also certain dangers. There is a frequent belief that theoretical work gets in the way of experience: a naive underestimation of the epistemological problems of experience itself. Related to this on many campuses is a rejection of rationalism and of the search for objectivity in scholarship, an attitude which identifies spontaneity with irrationality and regards cognition as necessarily deadening, and the effort to categorize as a sign of necrophilic tendencies. This view finds support in the various drug subcultures on the campus, as well as in the continuing attack on research as a sophisticated support for the status quo, and thus for war. If one asks students of this persuasion why they wish to be in the university at all, apart from the imperatives imposed by the draft, they will sometimes say that this is where their friends are, where they can be away from home, and where they can use the resources of the university as a base for their extramural activities.[3] These ideas of educational reform originated in the elite colleges and among articulate critics, and often had the support of the student press. But they have spread to many campuses in what were once provincial parts of the country, including the "provinces" of large cities, where most students are the first generation in their families to attend college.[4] The vocal students who have been the carriers of educational change are apt to be the more affluent, to be majoring in the humanities or the "softer" social sciences, and to be male and white.[5] These students contend that the educational system oppresses them, though most are not so despairing as the violent activists who see in the university the symbol of "the corrupt society" and seek to stop its operations altogether. Nonetheless, even moderate student reformers and their faculty supporters share with antiuniversity activists an ignorance of the history of American higher education.[6] They are seldom aware of the irony that many in other industrial societies are seeking to incorporate the American practices now under attack in order to strengthen their own systems of higher education. This lack of historical knowledge helps sustain the mythology that American higher education was once uncorrupted by commercialism, careerism, or other worldly constraints.[7]

Many students, however, do read. When I have asked them what books have influenced their ideas of educational change, they mention the writings of John Holt, George Leonard (*Education and Ecstasy*), Herbert Marcuse, Norman O. Brown, A. S. Neill, Edgar Friedenberg, Paul Goodman, and a number of others.[8] The students draw from this body of literature a critique of prevailing educational practice and particularly an attack on the research-oriented university as run for the benefit of the faculty and not of the undergraduates. And their reading leads many to suppose that there are no problems of scarcity, either of talented teachers or of other human resources; the faculty are seen as willfully refusing to teach, and the society is sometimes seen as willfully insisting on dehydrated and irrelevant learning.[9]

Many faculty members, and not only the younger products of the graduate schools, agree with these condemnations. Bored by their own research in many cases, excited by the cultural revolution, eager to identify with what seems to be youthful and energetic, they read into the student movement support for their own educational ideals. Students can also find in Fromm's writings passages which support the way they view matters; consider the following from his contribution to a symposium on Summerhill School:

> What is the student rebellion all about? The phenomenon is somewhat different within each country. In some, it represents socialist demands; in others, a fight for greater student participation in the deliberations and the

decision-making of the university establishment. In these struggles, some groups have rejected violence; in others, various degrees of force have been employed. In some cases, institutional methods have been attacked; in others, particular individuals have been damned. Yet behind all these apparent differences, all the marching, sitting, and shouting students have something in common: *they are all experiencing a deep hunger for life.* They feel that their education is being bureaucratized, and that at best, they are being sufficiently prepared to enable them to earn a good living. But paramountly, they also feel they are not being offered stimulating intellectual food in large enough portions to enhance their sense of aliveness. These students insist that they do not want to be dead in the midst of plenty; they insist that they do not want to study in institutions which, in their yielding to the vested interests of professors, administrators, and governmental forces, pay too little attention to their generation's need for a critical examination of today's conventional wisdom.

The campus rebels, even though sometimes misled through political naiveté and lack of realism, and even though sometimes motivated by destructive drives, at least draw attention to the fact that today's processes of higher education are deemed unsatisfactory by a large number of the young element.

The educational failure of our high schools is even worse. By his very action, each drop-out casts a vote against the education he has been receiving. Who would deny that juvenile delinquency is related to the failure of our educational system to provide stimulation and meaning for our adolescents.[10]

The passage just quoted exhibits only one aspect of Fromm's thought concerning students and education. Furthermore, he might not make the same statement today. Taken as they stand, these remarks seem to me a considerable overgeneralization. It is common for reformers to suppose that protesters largely share their agenda, especially if they say they do. The litany of attack on bureaucratized education and on the vested interests of academia got a good deal of its start among the campus rebels of the Free Speech Movement at Berkeley in 1964–1965. But careful studies of the protesters show that they were more appreciative of their courses and their education and less critical, except for public relations purposes, than the inactive students; what originally led them into action was neither a demand for greater student participation in university affairs nor a search for "stimulating intellectual food," but the civil rights movement in the Bay Area and their desire to use the campus as a platform for it.[11] When, after the Movement began, a new Acting Chancellor (Martin Meyerson) came in who was quite open to change, asking students for suggestions about educational reform, hardly any responded.

Similarly, I regard it as an error to declare that each dropout can be seen principally as a vote against our high schools, although surely many are just that. Such a notion is likely in practice to lead the dedicated and idealistic high school teacher toward the pedagogic equivalent of therapeutic despair because it is a vast overestimation of the role of formal education as against the more compelling influences of the home and the street. The *Coleman Report* on equality of educational opportunity suggests how little of the variance in educational outcomes can be explained in terms of school settings in comparison with home and family and peer settings.[12] Many students and many teachers experience a deep hunger for life and many resist conventional notions of career and consumerism. But many in my observation, in rejecting what they see as mindless and puritanical work for meaningless ends, have relied on a countercultural repertoire which also turns out to be limited. Decency, ingenuity, sensitivity can often be found. But I see a fair amount of psychedelically tuned aliveness which, though sometimes angry, commonly turns sullen and despairing. Indeed, so rapidly do the student movements change their mood and style and so intermittent has been the interest in educational reform (as distinguished from reforms in governance and politics) that it is hard to know what the impact has been on the great majority of uninvolved students, or what the consequences have been for the majority of uninvolved faculty. . . .

In a recent discussion of Harvard with student educational reformers, I suggested that students could actually become more free by learning tangible skills and accomplishments, so that they might be able to do things and not continue to remain dependent. To counter this, one reflective student cited *Summerhill,* saying that it didn't matter if a student sat around for a year or so because eventually he might want to do something, and then he would do it under his own motivation and without pressure. Another student cited Erich Fromm to support his contention that contemporary social science consisted of a series of pigeonholes for compartmentalized disciplines which bear no relation to the problems of the great world.[13]

What is evident to me in many discussions is an idealism about the way learning should go on which can find some support in Fromm's work. It is an idealism that tempts us to believe that we can get rid of all the mixtures of motives with which most of us live, and that then we can find our way to a purity of humane experience unmediated by ordinariness or routine. Any education is worthless which is in any degree compromised by imposed schedules or by the desire to win approval or to get into graduate school; and the fear of having a "corrupt" or impure motive leads to a great watchfulness rather like that of the Puritans. But unlike the Puritans, work is not therapeutic or seen as indicative of election: it is apt to be seen as repressive. Thus, this idealism appears in some students to lead to vacillation between self-contempt for not living up to the ideal and a somewhat passive waiting to be captured by some all-encompassing activity. . . .

Because these students come from families that have arrived, and, indeed, at times from professional and intellectual families, they are apt to say to themselves that they want to "be" rather than to "do." They have a point when they declare that America and perhaps the whole Western world have been undone by an excessive emphasis on performance and achievement, but given the populous world we inhabit, it is an ambivalent and complicated point. To reject competence will not help the Western world survive or become more humane. Sometimes I have asked such students whether they believed that there are any skills at all that their culture is justified in asking them to acquire, or whether in their own development there is any point up to which they believe that they need the counsel of adults in the matter of their own further education. [Frequently,] they don't think there is such a point. . . .

Perhaps as late as 1967, one could still have said that students in the better colleges were seeking to perform well in regular academic terms because they did not really question the curriculum, and because even if they did, they wanted to be able to enter good graduate and professional schools.[14] Students were coming to a growing number of avant-garde colleges with ever more precocious intellectual equipment. In the middle-1960s, college presidents of such institutions saw their task as a struggle to recruit college professors in a market extremely favorable to the latter. Few, if any, observers suspected that major institutions would by the end of the 1960s face financial bankruptcy, and more to the point here, moral delegitimation and loss of authority.

However, when in June, 1970, I attended the annual Institute for incoming college presidents run by the American Council on Education, most of the men and women in attendance were deeply troubled concerning the issue of legitimacy. They were aware that many state legislatures expected them to act like other corporate executives (or, rather, as the latter are in fantasy supposed to act) and to be able to control campus turmoil and to fire dissident or destructive faculty and students. Inside the institution, in contrast, they are supposed to be egalitarian and infinitely accessible, and they are constantly being told that they must maintain "dialogue," or that "better communications" are the answer to all conflicts of interest. Most shrink from the accusation of being authoritarian or high-handed. The distinction Erich Fromm makes in *Man for Himself* between rational and irrational authority is almost impossible for them, as for many other Americans, to make—understandably, of course, when it involves their own conduct. And like most people, perhaps especially Americans, they consider it part of their job to be well liked as well as to be respected. . . .

[Any] viable educational reform must be tied to its base of faculty and students and to the particular cultural context; it is thus (unlike pilot models in industry) not readily transferred to diverse sorts of institutions. What may be transferred is a mode of thinking about educational reform.

I can offer no solution, even a partial one, to the educational problems that beset us. The great social and cultural shifts of our time have unsettled educational institutions as they have unsettled the churches and many individual families. In such a fluid setting my own recommendations tend to be conservative. I am often asked about starting a new experimental college, and having observed a good many such colleges in recent years, my inclination is to say that in the present climate they are apt to attract both faculty and students who are visionaries with competing sectarian visions, and that one needs an extraordinarily firm leader to avoid disaster. As I have just said, I am more sympathetic to innovations within relatively stable settings. I have seen student-led courses which have been useful because of the particular group involved and their dedication; I have seen others turn into therapy sessions or rapidly disintegrate. I have seen some of the most hopeful innovations occur in denominational colleges, such as Immaculate Heart in Los Angeles or Florida Presbyterian in St. Petersburg, though such colleges are certainly not untroubled.

In general it seems to me wrong to tear down given educational structures and curricula, no matter how inadequate, unless one has something better to put in their place. The attack on arbitrary custom and inherited tradition, in education as in other spheres of life, has gained an extraordinary momentum in our time. One approach is to insist that schools and colleges are inherently stultifying, "total institutions," and that young people would be better off without them. Another approach is to set against the existing institutions the vision of new ones, which would be staffed by wholly devoted, wholly empathic teacher-learners, not committed either to the political or the pedagogic status quo. However, proponents of the counter-culture tend to oppose institutions as such, and to believe that free-form education requires no planning, no organization . . .

We are presently moving from a system of mass higher education in which half the age-grade goes beyond high school to some form of college and in which enrollments more than doubled between 1960 and 1970, to a system of near universal higher education up to the fourteenth grade. Our problems would be somewhat less grave if it became general practice after high school to enter on a period of employment or of voluntary service and to rely on adult education rather than on an automatic assumption of post-secondary education for many students who are neither mature enough nor eager enough to profit from college. The majority of these students are pursuing vocational or preprofessional curricula which will lift them socially from blue collar to (often more poorly paid) white collar work;[15] the status of students, their families, and their prospective occupations (along with the draft) all press in the direction of college. . . .

In most colleges it may not be possible to persuade faculty to resume the advising function, especially for students who have not yet decided on a major and hence are not in the province of any one department. But it seems to me important to make the attempt. However, if faculty are to serve successfully as advisers, they will have to learn more than they now know from hearsay about how they and their colleagues perform as teachers. In most colleges the privacy of the classroom protects faculty members from each other's scrutiny. And even if this were not the case, faculty members might be hesitant to be candid in talking with students about other faculty, since this power could so easily be exploited in a vindictive or self-serving way. I am not sure how feasible it is or what the costs would be of breaking down the privacy of the classroom and encouraging mutual visiting and criticism. Certainly, faculty members who wish to be retained or promoted because of the quality of their teaching cannot rightly insist on privacy, yet there have not been enough assessments of the side-effects of visiting to give me confidence that the tact and generosity requisite for such a procedure will be found.

I had the benefit of such a program as a member of the Social Science staff of The College of the University of Chicago, where all members attended each other's lectures and discussed each other's modes of learning and teaching in jointly taught, interdisciplinary courses.[16] We worked with students in small sections, though we did not monopolize the advising function. When I came to Harvard in 1958, I recruited a staff of graduate students and young faculty to work with me in a large undergraduate course whose one requirement for students would be a long term-paper, work on which would facilitate a closer student-faculty relation than is common in universities. In recruiting a staff of ten or a dozen men and women for the course, I have looked for those with an interest in problems of learning and teaching, and with an intense curiosity about self and society; they come from sociology, political science, history, law, clinical and social psychology, comparative literature, and the American Civilization program. While most graduate students have little or no supervision of their initial forays in undergraduate teaching, we encourage visiting of each other's sections and critical discussion of each other's lectures; we meet weekly to discuss books read in the course and the long papers of the students to which we respond with extensive advice and commentary.

In our advising of students in this course—and each section leader became an adviser, as I also did—it was difficult to persuade Harvard undergraduates that, in writing their papers for the course, they could make any original contribution. A great many had had the disheartening experience of finding themselves no longer the brightest stars of their respective high schools, but surrounded with hundreds of outwardly impressive fellow valedictorians. Some came to doubt their own powers; they reacted guardedly to their courses and to each other; their curiosity concerning the world was dimmed by the fear of revealing their inadequacies. We published three volumes of student papers, not necessarily the most elegant, in order to suggest that it was possible for a neophyte to do something original, to describe something new, especially if he could draw on his own access to a particular segment of our society: of school, job or locale.[17]

The political and cultural revolutions on the campus have in the last few years altered what many students bring to such a course and what they expect from it. I would say that whereas our principal problem once was to encourage student self-confidence, a growing problem today is to broaden student curiosity about society. Paradoxically, too much self-confidence inhibits curiosity: some precocious students arrive at college believing that they already know what society is like—and that it is utterly vicious. To spend any energy exploring the details appears to them a delaying tactic at best, at worst a kind of counterinsurgency. Many of these students have been exposed to ideas of liberation from very early on; some have been taught in secondary school by young radicals avoiding the draft or by young anticareerists avoiding what they regard as the rat race of university life. They may not actually have read Nietzsche, Sartre, Camus, Fromm, Fanon, but they have been exposed to the ideas of such writers osmotically in a kind of post-McLuhan way. They arrive at college believing themselves sophisticated; one of the problems we face as teachers is the actual provincialism of young men and women who regard themselves as fully cosmopolitan. Because their emotional and, hence, intellectual interest is so largely focused upon America's underclass, it is difficult to evoke their interest in the full range of human experience. Many say that they want to share "the black experience," assuming that there is only a single experience and that in any case it is only of suffering and debasement on the one side and joyful naturalness on the other. It is hard to get such students to extend their disciplined empathy and curiosity to a wide variety of life in this country (though the tiny minority of active revolutionaries among them talk about contacts with the "working class").[18]. . .

In the present climate, educators like other Americans need to have what I have sometimes called the nerve of failure. I do not mean that failure is romantically desirable or that I am asking people to become heroes or martyrs, but rather that they decide what are the essential issues on which they are prepared to stand firm and if necessary be defeated, and what are the areas where they can compromise and temporize without giving way to the excesses of the cultural revolution. At many points, my own position, immersed in ambiguities, lacks the solace of clarity. My hope is a modest one that what can be discovered will become cumulative, and that even our failures, if we do not deceive ourselves as to why they occurred, may help our successors avoid our errors before they invent their own.

NOTES

[1]Both the sheer magnitude of change and the degree to which it may promote homogeneity are suggested by Harold L. Hodgkinson, *Institutions in Transition: A Study of Change in*

Higher Education, a publication of the Carnegie Commission on Higher Education, 1970; for discussion of change in some pioneering liberal arts colleges, see Morris Keeton and Conrad Hilberry, *Struggle and Promise: A Future for Colleges* (New York: McGraw-Hill Book Company, 1969).

[2]Of course, I am not implying that learning could not occur in field settings! I do my best to encourage my own students to do manageable pieces of empirical work, for instance some enterprise of participant-observation or a small-scale interview study. However, many newly developed programs that boast of putting students out into the field do not provide the kind of preparation that a good anthropology department would. . . .

[3]The term "community" comes up constantly in these discussions: there is the academic community, the black community, the student community, etc. The term carries none of the tentativeness with which Erich Fromm speaks of the formation of Groups in the last chapter of *The Revolution of Hope* (pp. 158–62). There is instead in these discussions a naiveté in assuming that people who share contiguous turf will have anything in common and that they already form a community rather than a series of competing barrios or fractionated sects.

[4]The same is true in the high schools. See Diane Divoky (ed.), *How Old Will You Be in 1984: Expressions of Student Critique from the High School Free Press* (New York: Avon Books, 1969).

[5]Black students on the white campus may come together to demand Black Studies programs and greater "relevance" to the urban scene or to the problems of blacks; but in general, in my observation, they do not favor radical educational reform, but feel more secure with traditional "collegiate" structures both in the curriculum and the extracurriculum; they are often at odds with white radical students who, the blacks feel, can afford to dispense with universities whereas they, as members of a previously deprived group, need all the educational benefits they can get.

I know no coed campus where women have taken the leadership in educational reform, and I believe they suffer as blacks do from some of the current temptations of reformers, since the women need to make full use of their undergraduate years to establish quasi-professional competence if they are not to remain dependent on the chances and mischances of marriage and to have the opportunity to enter careers outside the prevailing range of "women's jobs." *See* David Riesman, "Observations on Contemporary College Students—Especially Women," *Interchange, 1,* pp. 50–63.

[6]There are some notable exceptions. Thus, three years ago Ira Magaziner and Christopher Coles at Brown University compiled a massive dossier on educational reform; impressing many faculty members with their seriousness, they succeeded in many of their aims of loosening the curriculum, abandoning traditional grading, etc.

[7]The best historical work I know is that of Laurence Veysey, *The Emergence of the American University* (Chicago: University of Chicago Press, 1965); Thorstein Veblen's *The Higher Learning in America: A Memorandum on the Conduct of Universities by Businessmen* (New York: Viking Press, 1918) is a caustic account of philistinism and seemly pedantry.

[8]A few mention the writings of Judson Jerome, Professor of Literature at Antioch College; see for instance, "Portrait of Three Experiments," in *Change, 2* (July–August, 1970), pp. 40–54, and other writings in that journal and *Life.* Some students draw from my own writings on education what I would regard as overgeneralized or misapplied conclusions. Thus, they scan Christopher Jencks and David Riesman, *The Academic Revolution* (Garden City, N.Y.: Doubleday & Co., 1968) in order to find ammunition—there is plenty there!—to throw against the graduate schools and the hegemony of academic departments. (Others read the book, also too simplistically, as a complacent defense of the educational status quo.)

[9]There is a more sombre note that occasionally crops up in the discussions I have had with students, especially on the more avant-garde campuses: this is an insistence that the heights of culture are in themselves an offense to the impoverished masses of the so-called Third World, and that the heights should be pulled down in the hope (a vain hope, in my judgment) of filling up the abysses. Sometimes the theme is explicit: if not everyone can share in the joys and illuminations of high culture, then no one should.

[10]See Harold H. Hart (ed.), *Summerhill: For and Against* (New York: Hart Publishing Co., Inc., 1970), pp. 251–52.

[11]There is a large literature. See, e.g., Robert H. Somers, "The Mainsprings of the Rebellion:

A Survey of Berkeley Students in November, 1964," in Seymour Martin Lipset and Sheldon S. Wolin (eds.), *The Berkeley Student Revolt: Facts and Interpretations* (New York: Doubleday-Anchor Books, 1965), pp. 530–58; see also the discussion in Nathan Glazer, *Remembering the Answers* (New York: Basic Books, Inc., Publishers, 1970).

[12]For a full discussion, see Christopher Jencks, "The Coleman Report and the Conventional Wisdom," prepared for *On Equality of Educational Opportunity,* Frederick Mosteller and Daniel P. Moynihan (eds.), to be published by Random House.

[13]Fromm is not always seen as an ally by critical students. An SDS leader at a state university, on being introduced to me, launched into a vehement attack on Fromm's "revisionism" of Karl Marx. This student said that Marx was lulling the bourgeoisie in his early humanistic writings; these were purely propagandistic in intent; Fromm was robbing Marx of his toughness and turning him into a soft bourgeois romantic!

[14]At Harvard College, for example, the "gentleman's C" of the insouciant aristocrat was no longer an admired goal but a deprecated legacy. For a picture of Harvard College in this period, critical of its complacencies while aware of its advances, see McGeorge Bundy, "Were Those the Days?" *Daedalus, 99* (Summer, 1970) pp. 531–67.

[15]The decline of blue-collar work that was assumed to follow upon the rise of automation has been greatly exaggerated. See Robert S. Weiss, David Riesman, and Edwin Harwood, "Work and Automation: Problems and Prospects," in Robert K. Merton and Robert A. Nisbet (eds.), *Contemporary Social Problems,* 3rd ed. (New York: Harcourt, Brace & World, 1971), pp. 545–600.

[16]See for a contemporary discussion, David Riesman, "Some Problems of a Course in 'Culture and Personality,' " *Journal of General Education, 5* (1951), pp. 122–36.

[17]Space forbids discussing the many, undoubtedly overambitious, aims of the course which for many students will be their only exposure to the social sciences. In readings and lectures as well as small group discussions, we focus both on problems of methodology and of substance, illustrating how a great generalizing writer like Tocqueville or Veblen proceeds, and also how a meticulous clinician or participant-observer works.

[18]Michael Lerner, a former Harvard College student, describes such elite student snobberies in "Respectable Bigotry," *The American Scholar, 38* (Autumn, 1969), pp. 606–17.

Discussion Questions

1. What are some of the reasons for student unrest? What are some of the issues students have attacked?
2. What factors are present in our schools that cause students to rebel? Are schools too confining and freedom-lacking?
3. Should social issues play such an important role in student experience at school? Should campuses be the sounding-boards for views related to societal issues?
4. What part do the electronic media play in creating and/or fostering student unrest? Are student demonstrations the product of a general discontent?
5. What types of people become involved in revolts?
6. Is the United States the only country in the world being affected by major student unrest? If not, how do the complaints of students elsewhere compare with those of students here?
7. Students want change, but do they know what changes they want and how to go about them? Do they really know what is best for them in terms of education?
8. What and how much freedom should be allowed to students in determining their own curriculum? Does age and grade level make a difference?
9. What changes need to be made in school and society in order to meet the challenge presented by student unrest?
10. How have faculty and administrators generally reacted to student protests, demonstrations, and violence?
11. What progressive changes have been made in the educational system as a result of student unrest?
12. Has there been any impact made on teacher education because of student unrest, and if so, in what ways?
13. What steps, if any, should the faculty and the administration of our colleges take in order to deal with the problems of student unrest? What can teachers do to achieve better communication with their students?
14. Have students overstepped their boundaries? When students rebel, where does one draw the line in order to protect the rights of others?
15. What is the reaction of the general public to student dissent? What are the conclusions reported by fact-finding commission's investigation of college disorders?

Project: The people of our country have been divided over the issue of student unrest, and the readings of this part of the book testify to that effect. Present a balance sheet of the arguments *for* and *against.* Discuss your own reaction on the implications of the issue along the lines of better school effectiveness.

Selected References

Barzun, Jacques, *The American University: How It Runs, Where It is Going* (New York: Harper & Row, Publishers, 1968). The author has sought to give significant details, and to show their relation to the idea of a university as it might emerge again from the present contradictions. All changes, he says, must commend themselves to those directly affected, the faculty and students.

Califano, Joseph, Jr., *The Student Revolution: A Global Confrontation* (New York: W. W. Norton & Company, Inc., 1970). The author states that students everywhere are experiencing a crisis which is profoundly religious, intellectual, and emotional. For years professors have taught them to be skeptical of every moral doctrine, religious belief and political philosophy. Today we are reaping the harvest of those seeds.

Gaff, Jerry *et al.*, *The Cluster College* (San Francisco: Jossey-Bass, Inc., Publishers, 1970). This book discusses experimental colleges as subdivisions of larger institutions. In reviewing the collected data, two features seem to stand out: first, the economic background of students is above average, and second, their scores on personality tests tend to be similar.

Gleeson, Patrick (ed.), *Essays On The Student Movement* (Columbus, Ohio: Charles E. Merrill Publishing Company, 1970). The views of these essays range from that of Sidney Hook, that the student movement is contrary to the tenets of democracy, to that of Jerry Rubin, that the movement is an exciting energy force for a much-needed social and political revolution.

Hook, Sidney, *Academic Freedom and Academic Anarchy* (New York: Cowles Book Co., Inc., 1969/70). Hook takes the position that the college and university system, in the Sixties, is being transformed not to further the genuine educational growth of students, but primarily to meet the challenge and threats of student unrest.

Jencks, Christopher and David Riesman, *The Academic Revolution* (New York: Doubleday & Company, Inc., 1968–69). This is an all inclusive treatment of problems in higher education.

Kelman, Steven, *Push Comes to Shove: The Escalation of Student Unrest* (Boston: Houghton Mifflin Company, 1970). Three-quarters of the Harvard student body was out on strike at the place they said it couldn't happen. Why?

Keniston, Kenneth, *Young Radicals: Notes on Committed Youth* (New York: Harcourt, Brace & World, Inc., 1968). The author undertook this study with the hope that from this token group of youth we might learn something about our common predicament. He says we should wish radicals success in their search for answers to central issues of our time, and more importantly, we should join in this search. For on its outcome rests not only the future quality of human life, but our very survival.

McGuigan, Gerald *et al., Student Protest* (Toronto: Methuen Publications, 1968). This is an interesting collection of essays on student radicalism and its background. This collection represents, in a way, an open-ended discussion between teachers and students as to the understanding and meaning of the student movement.

Rapoport, Roger and Laurence Kirshbaum, *Is the Library Burning?* (New York: Vintage Books, Random House, Inc., 1969). Here is a report on American students, student unrest, and student power. The observations that fill the pages of this book explain the lost faith of today's student generation.

Reich, Charles, *The Greening of America* (New York: Random House, Inc., 1970). Reich envisions changes caused by youth's acceptance of the "ecstatic community." In such a community everyone is free to do his own thing.

Roszak, Theodore, *The Making of a Counter Culture* (New York: Doubleday and Company, Inc., 1969). The author traces the development of the counter culture and the hip culture, and discusses issues of young dissenters in the late Sixties. He suggests understanding so that better things can happen!

Spender, Stephen, *The Year of the Young Rebels* (New York: Vintage Books, Random House, Inc., 1968/69). The author feels that the young rebels here and abroad are burdened with the problems of physical and spiritual survival in a world haunted by the bombs and the frozen politics of a dying class. He has profound sympathy for the struggles of the young to make a world in which they can not only survive but they can live with honor.

Taylor, Harold, *Students Without Teachers: The Crisis in the University* (New York: McGraw-Hill Book Company, 1969). The universities were entangled in a crisis of their own making, the crisis of neglect—the universities are becoming educationally bankrupt.

———— *How to Change Colleges: Notes on Radical Reform* (New York: Holt, Rinehart & Winston, 1971). Taylor discusses things we do wrong in colleges and universities and offers practical suggestions for radical reform.

Wallerstein, Immanuel and Paul Starr (eds.), *The University Crisis Reader: The Liberal University Under Attack* (New York: Vintage Books, Random House, Inc., 1971). The editors selected original documents to present an over-all outlook on student discontent. These pamphlets, articles and reports, resolutions and manifestoes, and letters and speeches appeared on both sides of the conflict between 1965 and 1970, and discuss issues at the national level and at the university campuses.

Wolin, Sheldon and John Schaar, *The Berkeley Rebellion and Beyond: Essays on Politics and Education in the Technological Society* (New York: The New York Review Book, distributed by Vintage Books, 1970). This is a good book. Half of the essays of this volume center around events on the Berkeley campus of the University of California where the campus troubles began. The other essays survey issues of broader scope.

Part 4

Teacher Militancy

Overview

In recent years the problems of society and those of our schools have been examined and reexamined a thousand times. We now know for certain that something has gone wrong. Had things been different, the education of the culturally different would not have attracted special attention, the use of instructional technology might not have raised controversy, and student unrest could not have happened. That the teacher's role has also been vitally affected shouldn't be difficult to explain.

In this last part of the book, the teacher's role is reexamined in the light of contemporary aggressive teacher attitudes and teacher actions. Only recently have teachers demonstrated increased professional awareness and sought power to make responsible educational decisions. Many teachers are tired of being on the receiving end of decisions, and they are disturbed at being held accountable for low levels of school achievement, when in most cases the fault lies not with teachers, but with administrative decisions. Those who entered the profession after World War II came in great numbers from lower to middle class backgrounds. Choosing teaching as their career they were hoping to increase their status in society, and they joined the profession with no intention of being silent and submissive partners.

Teacher activism was brought about by economic discrepancies, the antagonisms of their professional associations, the collective bargaining policies of trade unions, role conflicts between classroom teachers and administrators, and the influence of mass media. A definite shift in power from public to professional authorities is under way. This phenomenon is best manifested in the actions of the American Federation of Teachers (AFT), the National Education Association (NEA), and their state and local affiliates.

Forty years ago, George S. Counts wrote his essay, "Dare the School Build a New Social Order?" As expected, it disturbed many and excited a few. Counts' ideas are extremely important and of contemporary significance. He states "that the teachers should deliberately reach for power and then make the most of their conquest is my firm conviction" (page 198). He predicted, in a way, the new role our contemporary teachers have undertaken.

Ronald Corwin makes the most penetrating analysis of the issue. He feels that one of the basic causes of militant professionalism among teachers is the constant conflict that exists between teachers' aspirations and ideals and the goals and objectives of a bureaucratic organization. Corwin believes that teachers are attempting to find a more responsible role in education through militancy. He views militant professionalism among teachers as a healthy sign and a positive force in our society, and offers suggestions for the amelioration of the situation.

With profound objectivity, Paul Woodring examines the dimensions of teacher discontent. He traces some of its causes through a brief historical analysis of facts. Woodring asserts that the mistrust of administrators by teachers and the inability of administrators to deal effectively with a new breed of well-qualified professional teachers create problems of discontent.

Over the years people from all walks of life have held mixed feelings about teachers going on strike. Parents, teachers, and students have found themselves divided over the issue. Myron Lieberman takes the position that teachers are justified in taking such an action. He strongly believes that teachers, like all other employees, should enjoy the privilege of withholding services when circumstances call for it.

Helen Bain ascertains that the role of the teacher is no longer confined to the classroom. She expresses the feeling that teachers will not rest until they have attained legal responsibility for that which they are to be held accountable for; this is nothing less than professional autonomy.

Teacher militancy has been characterized by many as unprofessional. In "Teachers Can be Militant and Professional Too," I have expressed my firm conviction that teacher militancy and teacher professionalism go hand-in-hand; I cannot see it in any other way. A militant teacher is more professional because he is unhappy being associated with an institution which apparently has failed to fulfill its mission and to which he has made a lifetime investment. He is more professional because he maintains active interest; he is alert and questions the way the school operates; he takes risks and goes into action with a new-found dedication.

AFT president David Selden discusses teaching militancy in an historical perspective in an attempt to explain what happened during the sixties to change hundreds of thousands of formerly quiescent teachers into vocal activists. He believes that militancy as a localized phenomenon has seen its day; it remains to be seen how soon the devices of statewide and nationwide militancy can be developed. Selden adds that as long as there are oversized classes, too-heavy teaching loads, and deficits in supportive services, there will be militant teachers.

GEORGE S. COUNTS

Teachers Should Reach for Power

If we may now assume that the child will be imposed upon in some fashion by the various elements in his environment, the real question is not whether imposition will take place, but rather from what source it will come. If we were to answer this question in terms of the past, there could, I think, be but one answer: on all genuinely crucial matters the school follows the wishes of the groups or classes that actually rule society; on minor matters the school is sometimes allowed a certain measure of freedom. But the future may be unlike the past. Or perhaps I should say that teachers, if they could increase sufficiently their stock of courage, intelligence, and vision, might become a social force of some magnitude. About this eventuality I am not over sanguine, but a society lacking leadership as ours does, might even accept the guidance of teachers. Through powerful organizations they might at least reach the public conscience and come to exercise a larger measure of control over the schools than hitherto. They would then have to assume some responsibility for the more fundamental forms of imposition which, according to my argument, cannot be avoided.

That the teachers should deliberately reach for power and then make the most of their conquest is my firm conviction. To the extent that they are permitted to fashion the curriculum and the procedures of the school they will definitely and positively influence the social attitudes, ideals, and behavior of the coming generation. In doing this they should resort to no subterfuge or false modesty. They should say neither that they are merely teaching the truth nor that they are unwilling to wield power in their own right. The first position is false and the second is a confession of incompetence. It is my observation that the men and women who have affected the course of human events are those who have not hesitated to use the power that has come to them. Representing as they do, not the interests of the moment or of any special class, but rather the common and abiding interests of the people, teachers are under heavy social obligation to protect and further those interests. In this they occupy a relatively unique position in society. Also since the profession should embrace scientists and scholars of the highest rank, as well as teachers working at all levels of the educational system, it has at its disposal, as no other group, the knowledge and wisdom of the ages. It is scarcely thinkable that these men and women would ever act as selfishly or bungle as badly as have the so-called "practical" men of our generation—the politicians, the financiers, the industrialists. If all of these facts are taken into account, instead of shunning power, the profession should rather seek power and then strive to use that power fully and wisely and in the interests of the great masses of the people.

The point should be emphasized that teachers possess no magic secret to power. While their work should give them a certain moral advantage, they must expect to encounter the usual obstacles blocking the road to leadership. They should not be deceived by the pious humbug with which public men commonly flatter the members of the profession. To expect ruling groups or classes to give precedence to teachers on important matters, because of age or sex or sentiment, is to refuse to face realities. It was one of the proverbs of the agrarian order that a spring never rises higher than its source. So the power that teachers exercise in the schools can be no greater than the power they wield in society. Moreover, while organization is necessary, teachers should not think of their problem primarily in terms of organizing and presenting a united front to the world, the flesh, and the devil. In order to be effective they must throw off completely the slave psychology that has dominated the mind of the pedagogue more or less since the days of ancient Greece. They must be prepared to stand on their own feet and win for their ideas the support of the masses of the people. Education as a force for social regeneration must march hand in hand with the living and creative forces of the social order. In their own lives teachers must bridge the gap between school and society and play some part in the fashioning of those great common purposes which should bind the two together.

This brings us to the question of the kind of imposition in which teachers should engage, if they had the power. Our obligations, I think, grow out of the social situation. We live in troublous times; we live in an age of profound change; we live in an age of revolution. Indeed it is highly doubtful whether man ever lived in a more eventful period than the present. In order to match our epoch we would probably have to go back to the fall of the ancient empires or even to that unrecorded age when men first abandoned the natural arts of hunting and fishing and trapping and began to experiment with agriculture and the settled life. Today we are witnessing the rise of a civilization quite without precedent in human history—a civilization founded on science, technology, and machinery, possessing the most extraordinary power, and rapidly making of the entire world a single great society. Because of forces already released, whether in the field of economics, politics, morals, religion, or art, the old molds are being broken. And the peoples of the earth are everywhere seething with strange ideas and passions. If life were peaceful and quiet and undisturbed by great issues, we might with some show of wisdom center our attention on the nature of the child. But with the world as it is, we cannot afford for a single instant to remove our eyes from the social scene or shift our attention from the peculiar needs of the age. . . .

RONALD G. CORWIN

The Anatomy of
Militant Professionalism

Teacher Power

In this time of change and experimentation it is perhaps natural that teachers are becoming more powerful. For this is, by definition, a time when no particular group has a monopoly on the answers. And in practice it has become necessary to delegate decisions, implicitly if not officially, because administrators cannot maintain firm centralized control over a system that does not work effectively. The failures of the system cannot help but reflect on the authority of those who run it, and teachers are not likely to submit enthusiastically to the authority of an administrative system that has failed to come to grips with their occupation's problems.

Added to this general situation is the fact that in this era of job opportunity and a supply-demand ratio favorable to teachers, the proportion of teachers in the work force is also expanding at a rate four times faster than the general population explosion. The projected growth, together with the continuing trend toward concentration in metropolitan areas, is likely to serve only to strengthen their influence.

But probably the most important basis of the teacher's sense of power is the growth of specialization within teaching. Not only has a segment of teachers made a substantial gain in their educational level, but also, there is likely to be marked increase in the specialized use of teaching techniques for distinct populations, and perhaps separate career lines for teaching various classes and types of students are beginning to appear as well. All of this gives teachers leverage in knowledge and skill over the administrators, who nevertheless are still responsible for evaluating them. The time may be rapidly approaching when it will be difficult, if not impossible, for

From MILITANT PROFESSIONALISM: A STUDY OF ORGANIZATIONAL CONFLICT IN HIGH SCHOOLS by Ronald G. Corwin, pp. 325-32, 349-54. Copyright © 1970 by Meredith Corporation. Reprinted by permission of Appleton-Century-Crofts, Educational Division, Meredith Corporation.

201

administrators to assume the exclusive responsibility for evaluating teachers.

And if teachers have gained more access to power, they also have found more reasons for exercising it. Disproportionate numbers of lower class people are being attracted to the profession precisely as a way to improve their social status, and they are finding that their own positions depend as much on the fortunes of their occupation as a whole as upon their individual efforts: the relative lack of opportunity for individual mobility within the occupation only encourages their efforts to achieve collective mobility.

It is important, too, that at a time when teachers are beginning to develop a sense of competence which would justify greater control over some decisions, they are bearing the brunt of much criticism for poor quality education, particularly in the inner-city schools, for which many of them feel they really are not responsible. The fact that many of the changes being proposed are aimed at altering the teachers' classroom behavior seems to suggest that they somehow are responsible for the problems; and many of them seem to be saying that if they are to be held responsible, they have the right to exercise more control over the situation.

But a number of crucial questions remain unanswered here. For example, does the reading achievement of students reflect the quality of classroom teaching, or does it more accurately reflect the quality of the administration responsible for deploying adequate resources and making the necessary adjustments in procedure? Or perhaps it reflects the unrealistic goals and inadequate procedures of the system itself. A persistent problem is that though the system of organization may be at fault, it is unlikely that teachers and administrators who benefit from the system will be willing to change their own roles—and often these are precisely the roles that need to be changed.

Erosion of Traditional Modes of Administration

The corollary of teacher power is the impending change in the roles of administrators. Their traditional jurisdictions, which already are being undermined by the growing influence of the federal government and of local militant groups, are being challenged by the demands of teachers as well. Just as it is now recognized that the logical distinction between "policy decisions" and "administrative decisions" has not really provided an effective division of labor between administrators and school boards so the presumed division between "administrative" and "teaching" responsibilities will be no real barrier against the encroachment of teachers on traditional administrative prerogatives. It is probably significant in this connection that this study of staff conflicts has demonstrated that the most frequent type of dispute in public schools—one in every four—concerned authority problems between teachers and administrators. Teachers are demanding a greater role in the decision-making process.

The tension between teachers and administrators is also accentuated by the fact that they are often separated by more than a generation of experience. Most administrators were trained during an era when the problems of classroom teaching could be reduced (or so it was thought) to the psychology of individuals, and when the central administrative problems seemed to revolve around efficient internal management. The current generation of teachers, by contrast, has been reared in a sociological era characterized by rapid social change and group conflict, and during which administration has become largely a matter of managing increasingly complex balances of forces from both outside and inside the schools.

But in final analysis the professional status teachers are demanding is in many crucial respects incompatible with traditional principles of administration—principles originally fashioned in a unified, small-town America, premised on teacher compliance and justified by the legal fact and fiction that administrators are, and can be, responsible for literally every facet of what is sometimes referred to as "their" system. Centralized authority and system-wide uniformity are difficult to reconcile with decentralized decision-making authority—the central component of professionalism. If classroom teachers are to professionalize, therefore, they must gain more control, perhaps the primary control, over key matters.

Limited evidence that professionalization is a militant process came from this study; the incidence of most types of conflict in a school (with one important exception which will be noted) increased with the faculty's average level of what we took to be indicators of their professionalism. But what is perhaps even more important is the fact that this association was most prominent in the more bureaucratized schools (compared with the least bureaucratic). In other words, it is in precisely the most highly organized schools that support for professional concepts seems most likely to produce conflict. But these general propositions now need to be qualified in light of the evidence.

Some Qualifications

Despite all of the discussion about teacher militancy, probably only a minority of teachers are militant, and an even smaller minority are what might be termed militant professionals. However, it is equally apparent that, given the growing concentration of the population, small proportions can be numerically large enough to be important. The numerical minority of militant professionals identified in most of the schools in this study is far from being a marginal group. On the contrary, they constitute a core of the leadership and have the backing of the majority of teachers. Compared to their colleagues they are better educated and more respected and better integrated into their peer groups, and they have more support from their peers. Also, although it is often thought that the youngest, least "mature" teachers are the ringleaders, it is the middle-aged, well-established men in this sample who most frequently actually become involved in conflict (even though it is true that the youngest teachers express the most belligerent attitudes). This seems to indicate that opposition to professionalization, in effect, means opposing the most influential segment of teachers.

In this connection, the evidence also suggests that there are no clear answers to the great debate over the relative degree of militancy of the AFT and the NEA. The AFT officers in this sample are more professionally oriented and express more militant attitudes in some respects, and they become involved in more disputes over authority. But over all, the NEA officers have become involved in more of almost every other type of conflict (although this sample was from the Mid-West, which does not necessarily include the most militant AFT chapters). What is more important than this debate is the fact that there seems to be a group of informal leaders who have not been officers in either organization, but who are by far more militant than either group's official leaders. In sum, militancy is spearheaded by a small group of largely unidentified but influential teachers.

There is a second point that sometimes remains obscure in these discussions: The issue of whether teaching is in fact a "profession" (in some ultimate sense of that term) is in many respects less important than the fact that a large portion of teachers believe that they are entitled to more authority than they now have; for example, 70 percent of the sample agree with the statement that they should have "the ultimate authority over major educational decisions."

Participating in militant causes may restore some of the sense of influence not provided within the system itself. It is in this connection that one finding from the study has its real significance: Both job satisfaction of individual teachers and morale of school faculties increase with rates of conflict within the staff.

However, as another qualification one must add that it would be a mistake to assume that militancy comes about as a reaction to any presumed loss of control on the part of teachers. It is sometimes assumed that they have lost influence as schools have become less personal and more bureaucratized. Perhaps there are elements of this, but the data suggest that teachers in the larger, more hierarchical schools actually have more decision-making authority over their classrooms than teachers in less bureaucratic schools. And these are also the schools where the most conflict occurs.

The preceding comments suggest still another qualification which will be of interest to those who hope to pacify teachers' desires for authority by giving them only minor concessions. Increases in teachers' decision-making authority seem to lead to more rather than to less conflict. Apparently, a little authority does not "go a long way" toward pacifying professional employees. On the contrary, expectations in this area seem to be increasing faster than achievements. Success feeds aspiration; and involvement in the decision-making process, even in a minor way, can involve teachers in a wider range of issues than would otherwise have been the case. Some possible reasons will be explored later in this discussion.

But this statement is, in turn, qualified further by still other evidence. For it is true that some of the most severe conflicts in the study occur less frequently in schools where teachers report having more authority. In other words, an opportunity to participate in decision making seems to be more conducive to disputing in general, but it may prevent grievances from accumulating and erupting into major outbreaks. The establishment of regularized communication procedures could have the same effect.

Also, an earlier generalization must be qualified in that professionalization does not necessarily lead to conflict—if the environment is already compatible or if accommodations have been made. Professionalization, for example, is not necessarily associated with conflict in the less bureaucratic schools, and there are some signs that schools are making at least some minor adaptations to professionalization. The more professionally oriented faculties in the sample report having more decision-making authority over classroom matters even though, in other respects, the schools are not adjusting to professionalism as rapidly as might have been expected.* Also, the data suggest that even more conflict might have been found were it not for the fact that the most professionally oriented teachers are randomly distributed among schools instead of being concentrated in a few, whereas the most employee-oriented people are concentrated in the most bureaucratic schools to which they are most compatible.

The corollary to the previous point, of course, is that bureaucratization in itself does not necessarily lead to conflict either. The problem occurs when there are attempts to apply mechanisms such as close supervision, standardization, special rules, and centralized decision making to faculties intent upon increasing their professional status. It was found that in the least professionally oriented faculties the rates of conflict were lower when they were more bureaucratized. The effectiveness of administrative practices, therefore, obviously is not inherent in the practices themselves, but

---

*The over-all index of bureaucratization is not negatively related in any significant way to the degree of support given for professional roles, as might have been expected if bureaucratic schools were debureaucratizing to any appreciable extent.

depends largely on the setting to which they are applied. While this point is perhaps obvious, it seems safe to assume that most administrators probably have not systematically tailored their practices to the changing conceptions of their faculties.

As still a further reservation, it should be recognized that professionalization produces not only conflict with the administration but also conflict and segmentation among the teachers themselves. Tension rises between the militant teachers who are professionally motivated and those who are militant for other reasons. It is essential to keep this distinction in mind when interpreting the meaning of militancy. While the most professionally oriented faculties in the sample have higher conflict rates than those which are less professional, the reverse is not necessarily true—that is, the most conflictful faculties do not necessarily strongly subscribe to professional principles. Other sources of tension include the organization itself (that is, complexity in the authority structure), general conditions within the society (such as the adolescent revolt and variations in militancy based on differences between the sexes), and the civil rights movement in the big cities. The civil rights movement in particular seems to be on a collision course with teacher militancy. Questions can be raised about the degree of support that teacher organizations have given desegregation plans and experimental projects leading to more community control and about what this means for the prospects of professionalization.

This leads to still another qualification which, while obvious, nevertheless sometimes eludes the discussion. Militancy can take a variety of forms and degrees of intensity. While the term is most frequently used in connection with work stoppages, strikes represent only the most visible signs of a much more prevalent phenomenon—a posture of challenge to authority. Authority can be challenged in a variety of ways. In particular, the most professionally oriented militants in the sample are involved in very different forms of conflict than their less professional counterparts who also become involved in disputes. With one exception. they did shy away from what were labeled here as the "major incidents"—that is, the sustained, heated conflicts involving large numbers of persons. This might at first seem to suggest that the more professionally oriented teachers are not the ones actively leading the recent rash of strikes, except that the data do not warrant such a conclusion. It seems more reasonable to assume that the role that professionally oriented teachers play in strikes will depend heavily on the circumstances. For, in contrast to the general pattern, in the most bureaucratic schools professionalization is associated with even the frequency of major incidents.

Perhaps the lesson here is that administrators will have to put up with many forms of friction if they want to maintain professional faculties, but supporting the professionally oriented teachers may be a more effective way of controlling the outbreak of at least the major incidents than attempting to suppress them by imposing more bureaucratic controls—which is probably a more typical reaction.

In any event, the behavior of teachers can be explained better in terms of principles of social power than exclusively in terms of either idealism or economic considerations. For one thing, teachers no longer have to rely exclusively on cultivating the public's benevolence. Many people believe this to be unfortunate, and perhaps it is only natural to formulate the philosophical questions about whether this or that practice is "right" or "wrong," according to one's personal values (and, of course, his own personal interests), but the questions that need answers right now concern what is going to happen.

Perhaps at this point it is too early to expect teachers to be concerned about justifying their every move or staying within the limits of legitimate behavior; given the fact that they are challenging the legitimacy of the present system, and must act defensively against it, one could hardly expect them to stay within the bounds of propriety. Within all professions (and not just teaching) there is a generic tension between idealism and self-interest. Professionalization is motivated partly by material gain as critics frequently claim, but what is distinctive about professionalization is that it represents a shift from self-interest, or what Hofstadter calls "interest politics," toward the "politics of status."[1]

But if the immediate objective of teachers is power, they eventually must return to the question of how to legitimate that power once it has been achieved. And in order to legitimate professional status, the occupation eventually must demonstrate its ability to protect its clients' welfare. Therefore, it is obviously to the profession's advantage to combine self-interest with idealism. Teachers, for example, maintain that they cannot do their best for students under poor working conditions and without sufficient authority, and that high salaries are needed to attract qualified people. It is no accident that these assertions are difficult to prove or disprove and that there is no clear-cut answer to the question of the "real" motives of teachers. But, of course, all professions seek to use ideals in the service of self-interest, and to mobilize self-interest so that it better serves professional ideals. Physicians do not often strike, for example, but they restrict the number of people who can enter the profession and restrain economic competition among themselves. The situation is not unique to teachers.

The evidence on this point is not very convincing, but it appears that among the most militant teachers those who are most professionally oriented are at least more concerned about the welfare of their students than their less professionally oriented, but equally militant, colleagues. At the same time, it appears that teachers are more ready than administrators to define certain children as being unable to learn.

It also should be noted in this connection that professionals obviously are not the only ones who have ideologies. There are competing contentions advanced by administrators and laymen which are equally difficult to prove, such as the notions that "employees must be supervised," that there is a special class of "decision makers" in schools, and that school boards' sovereignty must remain inviolable in a democracy. In these ideological disputes, of course, each side seeks to define the public interest to suit its own purpose. . . .

Our premise is that although some relaxation of traditional forms of bureaucratic control has already taken place, the prevalence of conflict in some schools is evidence enough that the adaptations in school systems are not keeping pace with the demands of professional employees. If the sources of tension are structural, we have argued, then the potential solutions to organizational problems must be found at that level. Therefore, conflict analysis can help suggest some needed new approaches to organizing schools.

There is always a danger that concern over the problem of containing conflict will only obscure its more positive functions. However, conflict should not be romantically glorified either, and in any event answers to this question can reveal a great deal about the conflict process.

At least three approaches to reducing conflict can be inferred from conditions under which there was only a minimum of conflict in this study— recruitment procedures, manipulation of the informal structure, and structural changes.

Recruitment

The first recourse is through the recruiting process. Professionally oriented and employee oriented teachers already are distributed among the different schools in such a way as to reduce the amount of conflict below its full potential. Professionally oriented teachers were distributed randomly in different types of schools, rather than being concentrated in the more bureaucratic ones where the greatest incompatibility with the professional role exists, and the more employee-oriented teachers were found in the more bureaucratic schools, thus maximizing the compatibility between teachers who uphold this role and their context.

Administrators of the most bureaucratic schools might wish to increase the amount of match between role conception and school structure by hiring only employee-oriented teachers. The evidence suggests that even in generally professionally oriented schools the rate of conflict declines with the average employee orientation. However, because a person's employee orientation is not closely associated with his professional orientation (in fact tends to be negatively related), simply hiring people who are good employees provides no assurance that they will be of high professional caliber. To the extent that people who want more decision-making authority for themselves are excluded, it will also mean excluding the people who place most emphasis on knowledge and who are strongly oriented toward colleagues and to a lesser extent toward students. Also, because the more militant people are concentrated disproportionately in certain disciplines and are typically males rather than females, this tactic might soon become impractical.

Informal Structure

Administrators and teachers might be able jointly to arrange an informal interpersonal setting that would help minimize conflict. The data are not clear on this point, but it appears that professionally oriented faculties are more likely to become militant in schools where the faculty is less sociable (that is, does not frequently associate for lunch). However, obviously, there is no simple answer. In older faculties conflicts seem to increase with frequency of lunching, while in younger ones it seems to decline with lunching; and most conflict rates seem to increase in proportion to the frequency with which the faculty see one another socially outside of the school.

Structural Change

As a third approach, administrators and teachers might want to attempt to manipulate the way in which the school itself is organized. At present the almost universal administrative response to conflict seems to be to tighten bureaucratic controls. Yet, it appears that efforts to maintain close surveillance of employees in some types of organizations only aggravate conflict. In this sense, the efforts of administrators to control employees are as responsible for conflict as the actions of employees themselves.

There are at least three alternatives to tighter control—altering the authority system, establishing different evaluation standards, and experimenting with administrative style.

First, the process of decision making in public schools can be appreciably altered. This will probably happen anyway once the demands of teachers for more authority are officially recognized and accepted by the public. However, most forms of conflict will not automatically diminish as teachers gain more authority. On the contrary, our data suggest the opposite; most forms of conflict increase with a faculty's decision-making authority. Nevertheless, the fact that major incidents declined in direct proportion to a faculty's decision-making authority does suggest that participation in decision-making channels at least forestalls the more extreme forms of conflict.

Furthermore, were teachers given greater recognition, it would bring the lines of responsibility, power, and authority into closer harmony. In many instances teachers now have the power; the problem is that channels have not been provided for its exercise within the structure of the school system itself. And, while teachers do not necessarily have the answers, they share much of the responsibility for the present problems of education along with administrators and school boards. In a complex, technical society the best that can be expected is that mechanisms will be established for including the diverse viewpoints of many groups and for their compromise.

Of course, many school boards and administrators are now talking about "allowing teachers to participate more in the decision-making process." However, teachers undoubtedly want more than merely the opportunity to become involved with some stages of decision making at the discretion of the administration. They want final authority over certain types of decisions.

> The problem with so-called "democratic administration" is that the participation of subordinates usually continues to be at the discretion of the administration. As an uncertain privilege, the opportunity to participate can be withdrawn or withheld in practice. Lefton, Dinitz, and their associates, for example, found that when wards in a hospital were operated according to so-called "democratic" principles of administration, the actual result was far from democratic; moreover, professionals working in this situation, where only an illusion of democracy was perpetuated, were more frustrated and negative than those working on boards that were admittedly less democratic.[2]

Hence, to regard the problem simply as one of "creating good administration" is to ignore the very condition that professionalization is designed to remedy—that is, the fact that teachers' authority still depends on the discretion of the administration. When the problem is viewed as one of organization, it becomes apparent that the teacher's professional authority will continue to be in jeopardy until it is supported by the structure of the organization itself.

Yet the same authority structure that provides teachers with a measure of status will make them reluctant to accept the many changes proposed by the administration, just as administrators will be suspicious of teacher-initiated proposals for change. Conflict analysis can help to assess the relative investments of different groups in various aspects of the existing system and perhaps find acceptable status substitutes when a proposed change threatens someone's position.

The resolution of teacher-administrator conflicts strongly depends upon whether power in schools is necessarily a fixed commodity, in which case the expansion in the power of teachers would require a corresponding reduction in the power of administrators. It is possible, however, that it is not fixed but can be enlarged in such a way that both teachers and administrators can gain power concurrently. This, in turn, depends, in general, upon whether new divisions of labor emerge, especially new roles for administrators now threatened by the encroachment of teacher authority. Many of the problems persist because administrators continue to view themselves as curriculum and instructional leaders, which necessarily thrusts them into the teacher's classroom.

Other problems develop, on the other hand, because teachers are powerless to cope with community and national problems from their particular vantage point. If administrators shifted their attention from their traditional concerns with internal problems and attempted to provide more leadership in areas that involve the school with the community—problems involving race, poverty, and financial support—they could expand their sphere of influence even while teachers expand theirs.

If, on the other hand, administrators continue to react defensively to outside challenges, other agencies will capture, and indeed already have, the leadership over these problems. For example, school administrators have not as yet exercised substantial leadership with respect to the poverty program, the Job Corps, and even the Teacher Corps. It is significant that it was the Department of Defense that proposed a new exploratory program for educating the semiliterate people in this country. Until school administrators begin to exercise more leadership with respect to problems now being attacked by the Urban Coalition and the NAACP and other community organizations, they will not be able to stake out new areas of authority.

Second, evaluation standards can be manipulated in such a way that conflict will be channeled into more constructive directions. Certainly, as teachers assume more authority, the traditional standards and rewards are likely to become inappropriate. Many administrators now lack a coherent philosophy for evaluating professional employees and for guiding their own conduct with respect to conflicts that develop because of incompatibilities in professional and employee roles. The dilemma that has to be faced is that the teachers who are the most loyal employees, and the ones who make the administrator's job easier, are not necessarily the ones who will contribute the most to the long-range development of education, and certainly are not the only types worthy of support.

If recognition were provided for the more militant teachers in the system, it might provide for a system of checks and balances and prevent excesses of control or unwarranted dominance by specific groups and force compromises to be made. It does not seem likely that the militant professionals will receive much recognition under existing circumstances, while they endure much blame if they do take matters into their own hands when their professional standards are in jeopardy. What is to be the fate of a teacher guilty of "insubordination" while attempting to protect his students from a textbook or a curriculum guide he believes to be ineffective? And what should an administrator do with a teacher who rebels because his responsibilities exceed his authority? How is an otherwise competent teacher who leaves the building early to be treated?

At present, teachers are promoted or rewarded with salary increases largely on the basis of how long they have been in the system, how little trouble they have caused, and how closely they follow the curriculum guide and other directives. The person who attempts to defend his standards runs the risk of being penalized. Perhaps what is needed is a system that reverses this procedure—that is, a system in which the person who does not take risks is penalized and in which people are directly rewarded only for successfully participating in innovations. Also, perhaps it would help if evaluations were reviewed by groups outside the school system—for example, professional groups, universities, and regional committees, which have less vested interest in a particular school.

Third, more effort could be made to find more precise ways of combining administrative styles with appropriate organizational climates. Certainly bureaucratic procedures should not be entirely abandoned, or even indiscriminately modified. In some situations bureaucratic procedures might be used even more effectively than at present; and in some cases it might be sufficient simply to clarify existing communication and policy procedures and to give subordinates more access to them. Our data show that in the less professionally oriented schools conflict declines if there is tighter control. But different strategies are needed for more professionally oriented faculties.

What, then, are the alternatives to the hierarchical model? One alternative is a coalition form of government consisting of permanent steering committees composed of representatives of different types of teachers, the administration, and interested community groups. Teacher-school board negotiation teams represent the microcosm of such an arrangement. As teachers demonstrate that they are able to apply power upon a statewide and nationwide basis, they may achieve control over the certification and even the accreditation standards, and hence be in a better position to demand this form of participation. In some matters these committees would serve in an advisory capacity to the local school board, and in certain areas they might actually determine policy. Such committees would provide a stable system of checks and balances and channels for compromising competing vested interests. More important, they would institutionalize much of the concern and imagination now often dissipated on minor disputes and unexpressed frustrations.

Another alternative is a fully institutionalized dual system of administrative and professional authority based on a division of policy-making responsibility among teachers, administrators, and school board. For example, teachers might exercise final authority over textbook selection or the hiring of other teachers, while administrators would continue to control scheduling and salaries. As teachers make their demands felt to participate in the budget-making process, some such division of responsibility seems likely to develop. However, this division of labor would be more fruitful if ways could be devised to evaluate the long-range effectiveness of administrators and teachers. Evaluating teachers on the basis of changes they have brought about in students' achievement levels is at present not particularly relevant because teachers do not have the authority to change the system in such a way as to improve achievement levels. However, this standard might be more appropriate after teachers have achieved the necessary authority to experiment, alter the system, and make changes in resource allocation.

Perhaps it is remarkable that the principle of hierarchy has withstood so well the new complexities that have arisen and for which it was in no way designed. But, in practice, it *is* being modified by the intrusion of expertise and greater independence and greater lenience being shown by some administrators toward their subordinates. The hierarchy has imposed arbitrary limits on the amount of mutual exchange that can develop between the various levels. If the chain-of-command principles were modified, it would leave room for more open relationships between the echelons. If individual teachers or groups of teachers were able to approach relevant administrators at any level of hierarchy, and if they were brought into administrative decisions early in the process, they would be more likely to make contributions and to be more supportive of the decisions eventually made.

To summarize, then, conflict is not likely to be curbed simply by screening out belligerent people: its roots go deep into the organizational climate and structural variables. Conflict is so firmly implanted in complex organizations that, though it can be regulated, it seems futile to try to eradicate it. It may, in fact, not even be desirable to eliminate some forms of conflict which often perform important and beneficial functions.

NOTES

[1] Hofstadter, Richard. "The Pseudo-Conservative Revolt." In Daniel Bell (ed.), *The Radical Right* (Garden City, N.Y.: Doubleday and Company, Inc., 1964), pp. 75–96.

[2] Corwin, Ronald G., "Professional Persons in Public Organizations," *Educational Administration Quarterly*, Autumn, 1965, p. 16.

PAUL WOODRING

On the Causes of Teacher Discontent

What Do the Teachers Want?

Teacher strikes, threats of strikes, and refusals to sign contracts have plagued American schools to an unprecedented degree this school year. What do these strikes mean? What do they portend for the future of the teaching profession? Why are teachers now more willing than ever before to face public disapproval and risk their jobs by engaging in activities which, in many states and cities, are of doubtful legality? What do the teachers want?

The obvious answer to the last question is "more money." Demands for salary increases have ranged from $300 a year in Kentucky to $4,550 for teachers at the top of the bracket in New York City. But money is not the complete answer. Behind the strikes are more subtle causes of long standing which have contributed notably to the lowering of teacher morale.

Though salaries still are too low, because they are not fully commensurate with the social significance of the teaching profession, teachers are better off financially today than they were in previous years and decades when strikes were much less frequent. The average salary of all classroom teachers in the United States, which was about $1400 in 1929 and $3000 in 1950, stood at $6821 during the school year 1966–67 and will be a little higher this year. The rise has been more rapid than that in either the cost of living or the wages of all industrial workers. According to National Education Association figures, the purchasing power of teachers increased by 39.5 percent from 1956 to 1966. Their pay in current dollars increased by 63.7 percent during the same decade.

These increases, however, started from a very low base. A generation ago teachers' salaries were lower than those of industrial workers whose jobs required only an elementary education. Moreover, today's teachers have, on the average, made a much more substantial investment in their own education, both in terms of time and money, than did the teachers of 1929. They can reasonably demand higher salaries on the basis of their increased preparation. Perhaps teachers' salaries will always be below the income of the fee-taking professions whose incomes are not dependent upon either legislative action or popular referendums. Modest salaries seem to be an inevitable characteristic of a socialized profession that requires 2,000,000 members and hence must take a large slice of the tax dollar. But it is also true that substantial raises in salaries would, over the years, attract better qualified people to the profession and raise the quality of education. And a prosperous nation—one that can send men to the moon—can well afford to provide first class education for all its children.

Trouble at the Top

Today, though the salaries of beginning teachers still are somewhat below those of college graduates entering other professions, the largest discrepancies are found at the top of the scale. The income of mature teachers of exceptional competence still falls substantially below that of equally competent people in many other vocations. Even the most talented elementary and secondary teachers in the nation rarely receive more than $12,000 per year.

In part, this low ceiling for men and women of exceptional talent is the result of the persistent refusal of teachers' organizations, including both the NEA and the American Federation of Teachers, to accept any kind of merit pay scale that would provide higher salaries for those most competent. Many legislators, school board members, and taxpayers, who might be willing to provide salaries running as high as $20,000 for truly outstanding teachers, can never be persuaded to provide such salaries for all those who have the master's degree plus fifteen years of experience if no consideration is given to the quality of their work.

Teachers are reluctant to accept pay differentials based upon merit because they fear that under such a system the access to higher salary levels would be based upon ratings made by supervisors or principals, and they do not trust these administrators to judge their work competently and fairly. They contend that under a merit pay plan, the higher salaries would go to those who conform to the principal's wishes rather than to those whose teaching is outstanding.

This mistrust of administrators, which is closely related to the larger problem of teacher morale, is a major problem in American schools. Because teachers are prone to look upon administrators as employers or bosses rather than as professional colleagues, a growing number of them are transferring their allegiance from the NEA, which admits administrators to the professional fold, to the AFT, which excludes administrators.

The reasons for the mistrust are complicated. It is true, as administrators contend, that some teachers—like some members of any other vocation—have an almost paranoid antipathy toward anyone in a position of authority over them, however competent he may be. It is also true that some teachers seem eager to lead revolts against the administration. But the number of such individuals is not large enough to account for the widespread hostility that exists between teachers and school administrators. Most teachers are reasonable people who will accept intelligent leadership. Administrators themselves must accept a substantial part of the blame. Many still have a great deal to learn about human relations within a group of qualified professionals.

This problem is by no means universal. In some of the smaller school systems, teachers and administrators work closely together as members of a common profession. In these systems strikes are rare because the teachers can make their voices heard and are convinced that their administrators are doing all they can to improve working conditions, salaries, and educational quality. But, in a great many of the larger school systems, communications between teachers and administrators have either broken down or were never established. There are many teachers from New York to California who, even in 1967, fear their principals, who look upon them as petty tyrants or at best bureaucrats, who reject their professional leadership, and who would never dream of turning to them for advice or assistance. They fear the day when the principal will come tiptoeing into the room during a class period to make critical notes that will become a part of the teacher's permanent file.

Younger Teachers Have Case, Too

The younger and less experienced teachers do, of course, need supervision and assistance, but "snoopervision"—the occasional stealthy visit of a supervisor or principal who drops in unannounced—is not supervision. It does nothing to help the insecure young teacher; it does much to break down his confidence. Yet this sort of thing, which was standard practice a generation ago, still is all too common in a great many schools.

The relationship between teachers and administrators developed at a time when many teachers were lacking in higher education and professional training and a considerable number were temporary members of the profession who planned to move on to some other work or to marriage after a year or two. In dealing with these neophytes, principals considered it necessary to make elaborate rules and even to require them to punch timeclocks, because they could not be trusted to get to work on time. The curriculum and the choices of textbooks were made by administrators or by someone in the state office of education rather than by the teachers as a faculty.

Teachers were required to account for their every movement and to submit daily lesson plans for the principal's approval.

Today the majority of both elementary and secondary teachers are well educated individuals, holding advance degrees, who are making lifetime careers of teaching. A steadily growing proportion of them are men. Many are better qualified than their administrators to make curriculum decisions, to plan their own lessons, and to decide what books should be used and how the school day should be organized. But they have not been afforded the independence that should go with mature professional status in a learned profession. In a great many schools, administrators still treat their teachers as irresponsible children who must be told what to do and how to do it.

In learning how to deal with the new breed of well qualified professional teachers, school principals might learn something by watching the operation of a good college. In such a college the dean would never dream of trying to tell his senior professors what to teach, how to teach it, or what books to assign for student use. He assumes, quite properly, that his professors know more about such things than he does. His job is to exert intellectual leadership on matters of broad policy, to coordinate the work of the various faculty members, and to provide the necessary organizational structure. The faculty makes academic policy and a faculty committee establishes standards for the promotion of faculty members. Today, many public-school teachers are as well qualified as college professors to make such professional decisions. Their assigned role should be appropriate to their level of professional competence.

Once the proper relationship between teachers and administrators has been established, both should look upon themselves as members of the same profession, working together toward a common goal—the education of children. Consequently, it is appropriate for them to belong to the same professional organizations. On this issue the NEA may stand on firmer ground than the AFT, whose policy of excluding administrators makes cooperation more difficult. But so long as administrators continue to look upon teachers as subordinates and employees rather than as professional colleagues, the teachers will continue to look upon administrators as employers and as their natural opponents. When frustrated, they will organize against their employers, making use of all the techniques available to employee groups, including strikes.

MYRON LIEBERMAN

Teachers' Strikes:
Acceptable Strategy?

Teachers can hardly be considered a militant group. In fact, of all occupational groups, teachers are among the least likely to strike. A recent study by the Bureau of Labor Statistics reveals that there were only ninety-one strikes by public school teachers from 1940 to 1962. These strikes resulted in loss of 251,660 man-days during this twenty-two year period. By contrast, several strikes in private employment have resulted in more man-days of idleness than all the strikes by public school teachers from 1940 to 1962; a single strike at General Motors during 1945–46 resulted in loss of 22,200,000 man-days.

In the light of this record, the widespread outbreak of teacher strikes and threatened strikes during the past year, and especially since the November, 1964, elections, takes on special significance. In Kentucky, New Jersey, Georgia, and Oklahoma, areas hardly characterized by militant teachers' organizations, strikes actually occurred, albeit sometimes under euphemistic labels such as "professional holiday." In Pawtucket, Rhode Island, where a six-day strike took place in October, a second strike was narrowly averted in November. In East St. Louis, four-day strikes took place in September and again in October. Even in France, Germany, Spain, and Japan, teachers in American schools have been considering strikes to improve conditions of employment.

Typically, teachers resort to strikes only in the most extreme situations, when their case is likely to be a strong one. Nevertheless, public opinion, which is usually hostile to teachers' strikes, is not the major reason why teachers so seldom resort to strikes. More importantly, most teachers believe that strikes are "unprofessional" and that public employees do not and

From *Phi Delta Kappan* (January, 1965), pp. 237–40. Reprinted by permission of the author and the publisher.

should not have the right to strike. These beliefs are increasingly difficult to defend either as ideology or as practical policy.

Teacher thinking seems to be that doctors, lawyers, and dentists do not strike because (or hence) such action would be "unprofessional." It is unclear whether teachers think the mere fact that these groups do not strike is adequate evidence that strikes are unprofessional or whether teachers believe that the same reasons which supposedly induced the professions to adopt a no-strike policy also apply to education. Either way, the reasoning is weak.

Doctors, lawyers, and dentists are fee-takers. They do not have a common employer. Thus they do not have common grievances or demands that can be achieved by means of a simultaneous concerted withdrawal of services from a single employer or group of employers. In short, to the extent that these groups do not strike, the reason has nothing to do with the notion that a strike is inherently unprofessional.

Actually, doctors do strike when they have a common employer, i.e., when their employment situation is analogous to that of the teachers. Recent doctors' strikes in Saskatchewan and Belgium bring this out clearly. In these situations, government-financed medical plans made the government the common employer of the doctors. When the latter were dissatisfied with the conditions of employment offered by the government, they showed fewer qualms about striking than our "professional" teachers do.

Practically, we must distinguish between (1) whether teachers' strikes are "unprofessional," regardless of the circumstances, and (2) whether a specific strike in particular circumstances should be so adjudged. Clearly, the former position has no professional justification. Professional codes of ethics not only permit but obligate professional workers to withdraw their services under certain conditions. For example, doctors are not supposed to serve where they cannot take responsibility for the outcome. Lawyers are supposed to withdraw from the service of clients who insist upon unethical means to achieve favorable verdicts. Even with a person's eternal salvation at stake, a priest does not perform services for an excommunicate, i.e., a person who has not met the conditions set by the clergy itself. The professional groups concerned have made a collective decision that persons must meet certain conditions in order to receive professional services. Whether the professional is employed individually or whether his employer is an individual or a community is irrelevant; he is still obligated to withdraw his services under certain conditions. Teacher strikes are usually discussed in the context of teacher welfare, but nothing is more clear than this: If teachers followed the actual policy and practice of the acknowledged professions, teacher strikes would occur much more frequently than they do.

The teacher's status as a public employee raises more complicated issues. Most persons assume that strikes by all public employees, including teachers, are illegal. However, by 1962 only eleven states had passed statutes making such strikes illegal. In four of the thirty-nine other states, the state supreme court had ruled that strikes by public employees were illegal. Teachers were involved in only two of these cases (Connecticut and Rhode Island). However, in the absence of a statute, the issue is in doubt and there is precedent for a different view. A state district court in Minnesota stated that the view that public employees cannot strike is:

> to indulge in the expression of a personal belief and then ascribe to it a legality on some tenuous theory of sovereignty or supremacy of government. . . . The right to strike is rooted in the freedom of man, and he may not be denied that right except by clear, unequivocal language embodied in a constitution, statute, ordinance, rule, or contract.

The decision in this case was upheld by the Minnesota Supreme Court (*Board of Education* v. *Public School Employees Union,* 45 N.W. [2d] 797 [Minn. 1951]). Shortly thereafter, the Minnesota legislature passed legislation prohibiting strikes by public employees. However, the important point is that the state supreme court did not accept the view that strikes by public employees are illegal, even in the absence of any statute to this effect. This raises the issue of whether teacher strikes should be prohibited by statute and also whether the prohibitory statutes already passed are in the public interest.

Is there any compelling reason why public employees generally or teachers specifically, should not have bargaining powers comparable to those in private employment? If public employees are restricted in ways that do not apply to employees in private employment, conditions of private employment will be superior to those in public employment. Such disparity may be in the short-run interest of private employers who fear the competitive implications of government as a model employer, of citizens who fear higher taxes, and of public officials who prefer to deal with weak organizations of public employees—or none at all. But if public schools are to employ substantial numbers of talented citizens, we avoid restrictions on teachers that cripple their efforts to maintain a competitive position, unless such restrictions are clearly required to protect the public welfare and safety. It is difficult to argue that a flat prohibition of teachers' strikes is so required.

A common argument is that public services are essential and therefore must not be interrupted. Thus any interruption of a public service is deemed a threat to the welfare and security of the public. One can readily agree that strikes in certain areas of public service, such as the armed forces or the police, should be prohibited without implying that we should prohibit strikes in all areas of public employment. For example, the public welfare or safety is hardly threatened by strikes of gardeners in public parks. Inconsistently, employees of a privately owned utility can strike, whereas employees of a publicly owned utility, providing the same service, cannot strike. And there is not much logic in permitting teamsters to close a school by not delivering coal to it but not permitting teachers to close it by refusing to teach.

Should teacher strikes be prohibited "for the sake of the children"? No teacher strike recorded has ever lasted long enough to result in irreparable educational harm to children. We do not even know how long such a strike would have to be, but it would have to continue a long time indeed to justify this argument. Schools are closed for summer, Christmas, Easter, and Thanksgiving vacations, for football games, basketball tournaments, harvesting, teachers' conventions, inclement weather, presidential visits, and for a host of other reasons without anyone getting excited over the harm done to the children. But if schools are closed for one day as a result of a teachers' strike, suddenly the time lost constitutes irreparable damage to those innocent victims, the children. Actually, students can (and do) learn as much or more when we reduce the amount of time they normally spend in class or in school. The amount of time many students spend in school is more a reflection of the custodial than the educational function of our schools.

Do teachers' strikes set a bad example of lawlessness? In most jurisdictions, this assumes a legal result which is in doubt. However, even in jurisdictions where a strike is illegal, there is no convincing evidence that teacher strikes have had any lasting impact on students because of the illegality factor.

In the private sector, public authorities cannot prevent strikes even when they clearly threaten the national welfare or safety. The President can delay such strikes but he is not legally authorized to prevent them altogether. It is hypocritical to argue that teachers must not be permitted to strike because such strikes would endanger public safety or welfare while simultaneously supporting the right of other groups to strike in situations that constitute a far more serious threat to public safety or welfare. Granted that certain services must never be subject to strikes, only a preoccupation with labels instead of social realities justifies the conclusion that all public services belong in this category. The public–private dichotomy is not a logical basis for deciding what groups should be permitted to strike. Some strikes in the "private" sector constitute an extremely serious and immediate threat to public welfare and safety; some strikes by public employees constitute no such threat whatsoever. Like all strikes, those by teachers inconvenience some people but they do not endanger the public welfare or safety.

Some people are unable to take a realistic attitude toward teachers' strikes because of their tendency to associate strikes by public employees with overthrow of the government by force. This may be a hangover from the situation in other countries where strikes are intended to overthrow a government or bring about radical social change. Needless to say, nothing could be further from the minds of American teachers on strike. They are not plotting overthrow of the government or radical social change. Typically, they are seeking to achieve quite limited objectives.

The October strike in Pawtucket, the third since 1946 in that community, was widely regarded as a victory for the teachers, and in a way it was. But the victory was hardly a financial one—the teachers got $150 more this year and the prospect of a somewhat larger raise next year. In fact, the major teacher objectives were nonfinancial. For example, as part of the agreement reached in the governor's office after a six-day strike, members of the school board agreed to cease discrimination against married women teachers. It is difficult to understand the logic of those who remain silent during decades of such discrimination but immediately condemn the teachers for striking to eliminate it. Perhaps it would make more sense to ask why it took so long to remove the discrimination.

One point is crucial: Laws prohibiting strikes by public employees do not necessarily prevent such strikes from occurring. In some situations, such laws, especially where coupled with heavy penalties, actually breed strikes. First, they so weaken the power of the employees that public employers perpetuate extremely inequitable conditions of employment, to the point where the employees strike anyway in desperation. Secondly, penalties against strikes by public employees may be so severe that public officials are afraid to impose them. Realizing this, public employees may be encouraged to strike. This is not idle speculation. New York State has experienced many strikes by public employees, including public school teachers, despite the Condon–Wadlin Act, which prescribed heavy penalties for public employees who went on strike. The very severity of the penalties played into the hands of the strikers, who were well aware of the fact that public officials could not realistically impose them.

Ironically, those who deplore the illegality of teacher strikes are often the same persons who support policies that make strikes inevitable regardless of their illegality. The teachers' strike that is an example of lawless behavior is often also an example of the futility of legislation that prohibits strikes but renders them inevitable by ignoring their basic causes. One such cause is that school boards are not legally obligated to negotiate in good faith or even meet with the duly chosen representatives of the teachers. Thus school boards and administrators can—and frequently do—make major changes in conditions of teacher employment without conferring or bargaining with the teachers. For instance, school boards unilaterally lengthen the school day or increase the number of days in the school year without making any corresponding change in teacher compensation. Economic autocracy may have been abolished in our factories, but it still prevails in our schools.

Some school boards have refused to bargain collectively with teachers on the dubious grounds that such bargaining would constitute an unlawful delegation of their statutory powers. A few state courts and advisory opinions by attorneys general have also taken this position. Logically, the position is indefensible. Collective bargaining would not require either teachers or school boards to accept a proposal made by the other side. It would require only that the parties negotiate in good faith. Some recent decisions and statutes authorize public officials to bargain collectively, but permissive legislation or judicial authorization will be as inadequate in public education as it was in private employment. The need is for legislation that protects the teacher's right to join teachers' organizations; provides for exclusive representation by the majority organization of teachers; requires school boards to bargain in good faith with the representatives of the majority organization; establishes an impartial agency to make bargaining unit determinations, conduct representation elections, and investigate unfair practices such as refusals to bargain; and provides fact-finding, mediation, conciliation, and arbitration services as requested by the parties concerned or by legislative mandate. A few states have already moved in this direction.

Some teachers' strikes are hardly more than protests against the antiquated procedures and restrictions that must be followed in raising school revenues. Such revenues are frequently raised through taxes specifically subject to voter approval. These taxes often transform powerful interest groups into "anti-education" lobbies because of the disproportionate share of educational cost they bear. Because these groups, such as real estate lobbies, are often stronger politically than the teachers, it becomes extremely difficult to increase school revenues. Property taxes, by far the largest local source of school revenues, are frequently limited by ceilings going back to depression years and by unrealistic assessments.

The post-election teachers' strike in Louisville illustrates the problems that result. The ceiling in Louisville, set by the state legislature in 1935, limits the school operating tax to $1.50 per $100 of assessed valuation unless the voters approve a higher rate by referendum. This ceiling was reached in 1950. Voters rejected an increase in 1955, 1956, 1963, and 1964. Kentucky law requires assessment at "fair market value," but assessments are only a third of this. At the same time, the legal and political difficulties of achieving full assessment are insurmountable, at least in the short run. Thus despite the fact that the present Louisville tax is among the lowest in the country for cities of its size, conventional approaches to school revenues there were unable to prevent a deterioration in the economic position of its teachers, a dangerous curtailment of school maintenance, the elimination of kindergartens, and widespread cutbacks in remedial and other educational programs. The over-all deterioration, despite the need to strengthen public education and despite increasing ability to support it, illustrates the factors that led to many recent teachers' strikes. It also illustrates the dangers in restricting the bargaining power of teachers. When they are too weak to protect their own welfare, they are usually too weak to protect the public's as well.

Low ceilings, low assessments, the need for voter approval when school taxes are the only direct outlet for voter resentment, the opposition of powerful interest groups which may or may not bear a disproportionate burden of school taxes, reliance upon local revenues when the states and federal government have preempted the most productive, easily administered taxes—these factors are only part of the problem. School boards in many states and communities are "dependent." That is, they have no independent taxing powers of their own but can only spend the funds granted by another city agency. When the teachers ask the school board for higher salaries, the board can say, "We don't have the money or the authority to raise it." At the same time, the municipal authority which does have taxing power refuses to meet with the teachers, since it is not their legal employer. In New York City, Pawtucket, and many other communities where teachers' strikes occurred recently, the teachers were caught between a school board without taxing authority and a taxing authority under no legal obligation to recognize the teachers in any way. The public may be the ultimate employer of teachers, but unless some person or agency representing the public has both the responsibility and the authority to reach binding agreements on school budgets, serious trouble is likely.

Teachers are apt to criticize the public for tolerating the conditions that lead to strikes. They would be wiser to criticize their own organizations for failing to develop and implement feasible procedures for raising school revenues and for negotiating conditions of employment in education. For example, the National Education Association, whose membership includes about half of all the teachers and school administrators in the country, has no consistent policy concerning strikes. A resolution adopted at its 1964 convention states that "the seeking of consensus and mutual agreement on a professional basis should preclude the arbitrary exercise of unilateral authority by boards of education and the use of the strike by teachers." Obviously, this resolution does not assert that the NEA is opposed to teachers' strikes, regardless of the circumstances. Neither does it state the conditions under which the NEA would approve a teachers' strike. In effect, it says only that strikes shouldn't happen if people are reasonable.

In the more distant past as well as in recent months, the NEA has supported some teachers' strikes. However, it has been careful to avoid applying the term "strike" to a walkout by one of its affiliated associations. When such an association walks out, it is "employing sanctions" or taking a "professional holiday" or "teachers' recess"—but never striking. The NEA's attempts to distinguish the walkouts of its affiliated associations from strikes is ludicrous but not laughable, because of the confusion it causes. For example, the NEA maintains that a concerted refusal by a local or state association to sign contracts for a forthcoming year is not a strike, although such action is so regarded in every other field and in the Bureau of Labor Statistics. "No contract, no work" is not a no-strike policy. Undoubtedly, the NEA's inability to develop consistent policies concerning strikes, as well as other aspects of employee relations in education, is due partly to the strong employer component in its 900,000 membership. Whether realistic policies will emerge from its confused groping over the present crisis is an open question.

Historically and at present, the 100,000-member American Federation of Teachers has shown more sophistication than the NEA concerning strikes and related matters. AFT policy recognizes that teachers' strikes may be justified in some circumstances, and the federation is far ahead of the NEA in advocating collective bargaining between teachers and school boards. Nevertheless, the AFT's approach to employer-employee relations in education is also clearly inadequate. Like the NEA, the AFT suicidally supports the establishment of fiscally independent school boards. In so doing, the AFT is missing a tremendous opportunity to promote collective bargaining between teachers and fiscal authorities having access to sources of revenue far broader than those available to school boards—or likely ever to be granted to them in the future.

To achieve collective bargaining at local levels, state legislation is necessary. It is doubtful whether the state federations in the AFT can achieve such legislation. In fact, both organizations are poorly prepared in many ways for the massive shift already under way to state and federal determinations of educational policy. This shift will have a profound impact upon all aspects of employer-employee relations in education, an impact for which neither the NEA nor the AFT is ready at this time.

To sum up: Teachers' strikes should be considered in the broad context of employee relations in education. The recent outbreak of such strikes reflects the growing crisis in these relations. This crisis will continue until we develop new approaches to school revenues and to the determination of conditions of employment in education. These approaches should take into account the fact that an ultimate right to strike may be legally qualified by so many procedures and difficulties that the right may be virtually useless for practical purposes.

Clearly, the increasing interdependence of our society is leading to more procedural restrictions upon the right to strike in both public and private employment. Such restrictions should be evaluated on their merits, not according to some vague philosophical concept concerning strikes. Some procedural restrictions on teachers' strikes (as distinguished from flat prohibitions of them) are desirable. However, simplistic punitive anti-strike legislation is a much greater danger at present than indefensible strikes by teachers. The public interest in continuous educational service will be best served by avoiding such legislation and by the development of realistic, equitable procedures for resolving whatever issues may arise between teachers and their employers.

The Militant Teacher:
Crusader and Leader

Teachers have the most important job in the world. They work with the minds of young people—at this point in time, young people are impressively idealistic, articulate, and dedicated to social justice for all. Nothing is more stimulating, satisfying, and rewarding than this service to society. It is tragically ironic, therefore, that teachers so often are frustrated in their efforts by inadequate teaching and learning facilities. However, teachers are determined to overcome the climate of inaction and retrenchment pervading many school districts. They are asserting themselves by moving to the forefront in identifying problems in the schools and establishing priorities for overcoming them. THE MILITANT TEACHER image has emerged as a dynamic and potent force within the community, state, and nation, and is a far cry from the old-fashioned image of the school marm.

Teachers constitute the greatest resource of educational expertise in this country; their knowledge and experience should be used in education planning and development. They want to and should be directly involved in the formation of policies and programs that affect their performance in the classroom. Today teachers will not sit quietly by, aware of inequities and inadequacies in the system. They know they could be more effective in the classroom if they were allowed to use creativity and ingenuity in substituting relative innovations for some of the old-fashioned teaching methods.

They know that when people think of schools, they think of teachers. Consequently, failure of our public schools is often attributed to the teachers. But it is not the teachers who are failing the children, it is society. No one is more aware than teachers of the grim crisis existing in our schools today. They are aware also that it is society that has failed to provide the money, status, legal support, and organizational base to insure educational progress adequate for today's needs. The teachers know the situation has

This article was written especially for this volume.

227

to be remedied, and they are working through their professional education associations to improve education.

The clamor for teacher accountability is getting louder, but it is a fact that classroom teachers have either too little control or no control over the factors which might render accountability either feasible or fair. To overcome this injustice, teachers are stepping up their efforts in seeking self-government for their profession.

Precedence for such autonomy has long been established by such other professional groups as doctors, lawyers, and certified public accountants. The professional standards and policies regulating their respective professional groups are not confused with the administrative or legal functions of the institutions within which they may operate. Similarly, the idea of self-government for teaching involves not control of the educational system, but only the governance of the profession.

In pursuit of this goal, the National Education Association, by mandate of its membership, which includes the majority of the nation's two million teachers, has launched a phase-by-phase program to obtain in every state a law which would give teachers control of the teaching profession. This program represents a major political effort on the part of educators in every state.

The teaching profession must be assured the legal rights necessary for it to assume responsibility and accountability for its own destiny. At a minimum, any program must include the following points:

1. Authority to issue, suspend, revoke, or reinstate the legal licensure of educational personnel,
2. Authority to establish and administer standards of professional practice and ethics for all educational personnel,
3. Authority to accredit teacher preparation institutions,
4. Authority to govern inservice and continuing education for teachers.

Obviously, if these goals are to be achieved, new legal machinery is needed. No state now has a comprehensive, balanced, on-going program in which teachers bear the *legal* responsibility. Instead, crucial decisions about the profession are commonly made at the state level by lay boards of attorneys, labor leaders, businessmen, housewives, and other noneducation personnel. Teachers are kept in a perennial advisory posture, even in matters that concern them most directly.

At the heart of the increased efforts in the NEA long-range political action program is a recently issued "Model Teacher Standards and Licensure Act." Using this document as a flexible guide, the NEA and its state affiliates in eight pilot states are seeking legislation under which the teaching profession would have the authority to determine standards for the preparation, licensing, and certain aspects of the performance of teachers.

Closely allied with the quest for professional autonomy is the quest for professional negotiation laws. Half of the states have such statutes now. Legislation has been introduced at the federal level making provision for professional negotiation. Such procedures lessen the need to strike and improve communications with school boards by providing an orderly, constructive way to achieve fair contracts. School boards which deny teachers negotiation agreements have only themselves to blame if teachers are forced to take drastic action.

Teachers are becoming more prominent and more effective in politics. Because major decisions are made in the political arena, teachers are identifying and rallying support for issues and candidates favorable to education. They are ringing doorbells, organizing voter-registration campaigns, raising funds, conducting polls, and even running for office. Through the political system, teachers are working to insure that every child in the country receives a quality education.

The lack of funds has caused school closings, and in some instances the teachers have had to strike to call attention to deplorable conditions. At the same time, teachers have recognized the unconscionable burden being placed on local taxpayers to support the schools. Through the NEA they are seeking federal funding for one-third of the cost of the nation's public schools. This funding would relieve the overburdened local governments, which now are paying nearly 50 percent of the cost of education, while the federal government pays less than 7 percent. The teachers of America feel that support of education at the federal level has been on the back burner too long. They feel that education should be moved to the front burner and have publicly called for creation of a separate Department of Education at Cabinet level.

They backed up this action in the spring of 1971 with a massive letter-writing campaign which resulted in a quarter of a million letters being sent directly to the White House, advising the President of the urgent need for such a Cabinet-level post for education. Subsequent legislation, introduced by Senator Abraham A. Ribicoff with more than 20 cosponsors, is being supported with equal enthusiasm by mail and other lobbying efforts. The teachers are assuming the responsibility and using their own resources to demonstrate their conviction that education of the nation's 50 million children is deserving of Cabinet-level status and top priority attention.

The role of the teacher is no longer confined to the classroom. The teacher's voice is being heard where the decisions are being made, be it in a citizen's group, a local school committee, a local or state school board, the governor's office, the state capital, a government agency, the White House, or the U.S. Capitol. It is fortunate for the future of this country that the teachers have had the wisdom and courage as reasoning activists to crusade for the cause of improved education. They have dared to be militant, and the children of the future will benefit.

Teachers have learned that they have more than the *right* to get involved; they have the *responsibility* to get involved. They represent the largest single professional segment in our entire society. They realize that if they do not participate fully in the democratic process, the country is deprived of a voice it ought to hear if that democratic process is to function effectively. This role is magnified all the more because of their special relationship with most of the public as parents and with the whole future generation as students.

STEPHEN C. MARGARITIS

Teachers Can Be
Militant and Professional Too

Until a few years past most educational decisions were made by persons other than teachers. Teacher influence and teacher participation were superficial and limited. Only recently have teachers sought power in decision making for the solution of educational policy matters. Teacher activism, or better still, teacher militancy was brought about by economic inequities, the antagonisms of competing professional organizations, the collective bargaining policies of trade unions, role conflicts between teachers and administrators, and the influence of mass media.

A definite shift in power is under way from public to professional authorities over education. This shift is best evidenced in the actions of the American Federation of Teachers (AFT), the National Education Association (NEA), and their state and local affiliates. Teachers' militant behavior has been intensively reinforced by the unrest permeating society in general.

I find it unnecessary to define a militant teacher and a professional teacher. I do, however, feel it necessary to make a distinction between the so-called *professional teacher* and the *militant professional teacher*. Defining the latter would be sufficient to demonstrate the difference. A militant professional teacher is an angry professional teacher who would risk any reasonable action to help make wrong things right for his profession and to guard it against further abuses. This is the kind of professional I am going to talk about, and my statements will reflect my philosophy on the new exciting role of contemporary teachers.

New professional awareness has generated among teachers a strong desire to exert direct influence over educational decisions which determine their teaching effectiveness. While those holding the power of the purse play the game of over-supply of teachers, teacher organizations are presented with a unique opportunity to assume greater control over the qualifications

---

This article was written especially for this volume.

of their practitioners. This last battle is perhaps the key to gaining real professionalism.

We can no longer afford the teacher's traditional apathy toward the criteria and standards of good teaching. It is time for teacher colleges and public authorities to welcome the teacher as a new partner who is vitally concerned and best qualified to guard the profession. Teacher organizations should assume greater responsibility for:

1. The recruitment and preparation of teachers,
2. The selection and admission to the profession,
3. The placement and continuous professional growth of teachers and administrators,
4. The protection from those who fail to meet the standards, and
5. The education of the public as to the importance and understanding of educational services.

For the teacher organizations to meet this challenge, I would call on both the AFT and NEA to increase their efforts toward the achievement of a merger. They must find ways to accommodate their differences and start building upon the common blocks of strength and concern. A unity should emerge of the best of philosophies, policies, and practices of the two organizations. A merger would be the fastest and surest way to enable them to assume professional control. It is only a short step to take in their call for militant actions.

Why Have Teachers Committed Themselves to Action?

Teachers have been alienated by large schools and lack of public support. The more alienated the teachers, the more they feel that they do not have an active part in school affairs and that the future is beyond their control. Their professional autonomy is limited. Many of them are not allowed to pick materials or direct their classrooms in ways they see fit. In the absence of adequate financing, they lack instructional materials, work in over-crowded classrooms, and lack special services and clerical assistance. Their salaries are not at a par with other individuals having the same qualifications. Lack of parental cooperation and understanding, and lack of empathy between students, teachers, and administrators results in frustration. Social status in the community leaves much to be desired.

Teachers are only asking for rights which should have been taken for granted, as they have been for other professions. The newest generation of teachers is better educated. Their better preparation and increased knowledge has caused them to become more conscientious about their work and to accept as their moral responsibility the need to improve conditions.

Teachers have chosen direct action as an appropriate means of curing professional ills. They have learned that economic and political power of organized groups can promote change and reform. They are convinced that the main thrust for improvement in public schools must come from the teachers themselves. Teacher organizations now recognize the expediency of political activism and its resultant power as important tools in the fight for change. They are resorting to direct means in airing their grievances and they are getting results. Already they have made tremendous gains in the areas of salaries and working conditions.

It seems that teachers are just beginning to realize their long-overdue power. The traditional paternalistic attitude of the school board can no longer be tolerated. Being more professionally minded, teachers are demanding a partnership in determining those aspects which will directly affect their teaching effectiveness. They want, in fact, to be *equal* partners in the process of educational planning, and they are demanding more authority and responsibility because of increased professional competency. Using newly found muscle, they are willing to fight for more autonomy and to bring about important curriculum and method changes.

In my view, the truly professional teacher is the militant teacher. Being militant means giving up some comfort and taking a risk. It is in his aggressive behavior that the militant is different from the ordinary teacher. He has committed himself to resort to any policy that will bring about necessary change. He is professional because he is aware and active in current situations of his profession. Under such circumstances, dedication and commitment to the teaching profession receive a new meaning—the true meaning. True dedication and true commitment, in my estimation, must inevitably lead to militancy.

Suggestions

In my previous comments I have referred to the merger of the teacher organizations in the fight to qualify themselves for complete professional status and assume the necessary professional control. Through better organization teachers could become more intelligently militant. It should be remembered, however, that education should not suffer in its quest for recognition and power.

There must be a redefinition of the roles of teachers and administrators so that what is expected from each group may be clearly understood. For both teachers and administrators to function well there must be more interplay as well as good rapport between them. Our schools can use more administrators who actually teach; and they need more teachers who understand administrative duties. It is important to encourage, improve, and maintain this type of communication. A dialogue approach would create new understanding and break down barriers which, so far, have prevented true and fruitful discussions. Teachers and administrators must work together with mutual respect, more trust, and with as little pressure as possible.

The power should be evenly distributed among administrators, teachers, students, and the public. A team approach should be adopted in meeting the role expectations set by the educational community, and the rights and responsibilities should be shared according to competencies.

No administrator will deny that staff morale affects staff proficiency. It seems reasonable then, to assert that happy and contented teachers are much more effective. Teachers should feel free to speak their minds, the same as any other responsible citizens. Problems of great concern to them must be pursued with fortitude, patience, and understanding.

The educational professions should develop and enforce their own standards. To accomplish these tasks they would have to build powerful organizations and convince the public that what teachers want is what children actually need. They should make every effort to alert people to the fact that schools need better and more resources.

Collective bargaining has proven to be a successful tool in obtaining better quality education for children along with better salaries and working conditions for teachers. Whenever school demands fall on deaf ears, the dedicated, committed, professional, militant educators should withhold services to create pressure for quick settlement. But a strike should occur only as an extreme measure.

There is ample evidence that the current militancy of teachers will increase in the years to come, and it will bring teachers broader participation in decision making. However, more power and "new authority" for teachers will result in added responsibilities and greater challenges for the education of youth.

DAVID SELDEN

The Past, Present, and Future of Teacher Militancy

"Teacher militancy" is one of those intriguing terms which stick in one's consciousness because of some unresolved, vaguely troublesome, inherent conflict. There is an internal inconsistency in the phrase: teachers epitomize the middle class; they are the defenders—the purveyors—of rationality, orderly process, and nonviolence; militant persons are from the lower class; they are angry, wild, and violent.

The caricatures of teachers in literature—Ichabod Crane, Mr. Chips, Miss Dove, the Hoosier Schoolmaster, and a gallery of others—project a series of long-suffering, wise, trust-in-God individuals who could not be envisioned defying a school board or a superintendent under any but the most unusual and extreme circumstances. When entire faculties picket, shout slogans, and strike, the caricatures are shattered and the observing public shakes its collective head in bewilderment. What happened during the 1960s to change hundreds of thousands of formerly quiescent teachers into vocal activists?

The greening of the teaching profession in the sixties and seventies followed quite naturally and logically from the depression of the thirties and the economic and social changes of the post-war (World War II) period. The catalytic agent was the teachers' union—The American Federation of Teachers. A summary of AFT history helps explain what happened and why it happened.

The AFT was chartered by the American Federation of Labor in 1916. The National Education Association at the time was primarily an organization of college professors and state and local school administrators, dedicated to the improvement of educational techniques. Even the state associations, to which most teachers belonged, were cast in the Horace Mann mold and dominated by the superprofessionals. In those days, teach-

---

This article was written especially for this volume.

ers were nowhere. They were expected to be "good" and follow the directions of their betters.

The nonunion associations were hampered by the vital defect of including educational managers and workers in the same organization. Any inclinations to teacher militancy were bound to generate internal conflicts, with the management forces almost always being able to suppress incipient revolts. Although the AFT was not troubled by such internal restrictions, it nevertheless did not fulfill its potential as a vehicle for teacher militancy until the 1960s. For nearly the first half-century of its existence it was, for the most part, an organization of protest with a strong affinity for lost causes.

Militancy without power is merely angry impotence. Organizational power is dependent on membership, commitment, and leadership, on being able to attract enough determined people to the group to create the possibility of success if the "right" strategic and tactical choices are made. For many years the AFT could not attract enough members to provide a basis for power; hence lawsuits and intellectual alarums and excuses tended to take the place of more militant action. Teachers, lulled by sentimental appeals to "professionalism" and "dedication," and viewing themselves as solid residents of the middle class, were not impelled to risk either the mystique or the reality of their status by joining a union.

The depression of the thirties was the seminal period for teacher militancy. It was a time of reality for many Americans who had been dazzled by the golden promises of the first quarter of the century. Unionism, long considered faintly un-American, came to be accepted in law and in the minds of millions of workers. The teachers were slow to react, but while teaching was certainly better than unemployment, as an income and status producer it was revealed to have serious shortcomings. The AFT began to grow.

The first really large-scale militant teacher action occured in Chicago in 1936. Throughout the union and even in some nonunion educational circles this "walk" of the Chicago teachers in defiance of the school board became a legend. In retrospect, stripped of its romantic clothing, the incident seems remarkably naive and circumspect.

Like most other school systems, Chicago experienced much financial difficulty as the depression deepened. The city began paying employees in "script"—its own paper money—and finally, during the 1935–36 school year, it decided to lop off a month's pay. The teachers, led by an AFT committee, assembled *on a Saturday morning* and marched a few blocks to where the Board of Education was in executive session. The teacher leaders forced their way into the meeting, with the ultimate result that the teachers were paid.

So impressive was this action that the five Chicago locals merged to become AFT Local #1, the Chicago Teachers Union; and John Fewkes, the young physical education teacher who led the walk, became president of the new local. Fewkes remained president for the next 30 years, except for periods when he held the title of Vice-President to get around a constitutional limit on the number of consecutive terms a president could serve. He was finally engulfed in the new wave of militancy which centered around the collective bargaining movement, but his action and that of thousands of other union teachers on the fabled walk was a source of inspiration for the new militants who came later, even if there was little immediate observable increase in militant action.

Although the way was prepared by the growth of unionism in general during the thirties and the general rethinking of social and economic beliefs brought on by depression, the immediate causes of the teacher militancy of the sixties were the inflation following World War II, the vast and disturbing societal changes of the post-war period, and the frustrations teachers experienced in the stodgy, status quo, nonunion associations.

Teachers' salaries were not frozen or controlled during the war period but they remained close to depression levels. When consumer prices began to rise sharply, as rationing and other wartime controls were relaxed after V-J Day, teachers found themselves even farther behind. In conjunction with the decline in real pay, teachers in the big cities found that they were "teaching more and enjoying it less." Staff increases did not keep up with increased enrollments resulting from the wartime baby boom. More important, the American social compact was dissolving. The old constraints of church, family, trust in democracy, and knowing and staying in one's place were rapidly breaking down. The new social turbulence had direct impact on classroom life, making the job of the order-preserving teacher much harder.

And when teachers turned to their traditional organizations they failed to find an adequate response. In the few years immediately following World War II, there were many spontaneous teacher workstoppages, but this sporadic militancy failed to coalesce into a movement because neither the NEA and its state affiliates nor the AFT condoned the strike as an organizational tool. Though the positions of the two organizations were similiar, there were important differences. The associations eschewed advocacy of the strike, because of their traditional prissy-professional attitude and because the strike brings teachers into direct conflict with superintendents and other administrators. The union was cautious about fomenting strikes because it feared it would not be able to win them.

The fear of government reprisals has always been a serious deterrent to teacher militancy. In private industry, the right to strike was won only after long, heart-breaking, and often bloody struggle. During the nineteenth century strikes were considered illegal conspiracies and attempts to deprive factory owners of their property without due process of law. Even after the main battle had been won in the private sector and the Norris-La Guardia

Act, outlawing the use of court injunctions in such disputes, had been passed in 1932, public employees were still enjoined from striking, on the ground that such action violated the sovereignty of the government.

Given the history of the private sector, the public attitude against strikes by government employees, and the assurances by lawyers that reprisals would be automatic and severe, teachers had little faith in their ability to carry off a strike successfully. Hence, even though the union had no moral objections to teacher work stoppages, it would not openly advocate strikes as normal union activity, even under appropriate circumstances.

There were large-scale union teacher strikes in Providence and Pawtucket, Rhode Island, in the postwar decade, but the thrust of the emerging militant movement centered in New York. The national AFT, while involved in the Rhode Island strikes, was chary of becoming too strongly identified with what were widely regarded as likely losers. While the union national office reacted in pretty much the same way when teachers in New York City began to march, the Empire City is too big to be ignored. What happens in New York is bound to cause nationwide ripples, if not shock waves. So it was New York City teachers who led the way to teacher militancy.

The first outcropping of teacher militancy in New York City was in 1950 and 1951. High school coaches, loosely organized in an association within an independent organization called the High School Teachers Association, decided to halt all after-school athletic activities in an effort to win higher pay for themselves. This controversy was widened so that the HSTA itself, and later a dozen or more organizations, including the miniscule AFT local, participated in informal negotiations that resulted in a spectacular three-year salary increase for all teachers. Throughout the extracurricular work stoppage, there was no serious consideration given to calling a system-wide teacher strike, but many teachers had learned a lesson: militant action pays.

For the next few years the High School Teachers Association tried to repeat the success of the original extracurricular stoppage, but the result of this activity was the discontinuance of after-school activities altogether by the Board of Education. The AFT local, then known as the Teachers Guild, tried to compete by calling a slowdown—euphemistically entitled "The Minimum Service Program." Most teachers did not even try to carry out the rules for the slowdown, and those who did found it extremely difficult, if not impossible, to curtail their professional effort when confronted with the reality of their classes. As a device for militancy, neither the slowdown nor the peripheral, partial work stoppage proved effective in the long run.

A decade after the high school extracurricular stoppage of 1950–51, high school teachers again tangled with New York's educational establishment, and again it was not a frontal assault. This time it was a strike in the night schools. The night high school strike lasted more than a month in the dead of winter, and it ended in a modest victory, but the strike itself was more significant than the terms of the settlement. The strike brought together new, militant leaders from the growing, but still small, union and from the old-line, but larger, HSTA. This new leadership group coalesced during the next year to form the United Federation of Teachers, and the old Teachers Guild surrendered its AFT charter to the new organization. The UFT became the engine of teacher militancy as we have come to know it.

Almost from the start, teacher militancy as a movement, as distinguished from the spontaneous random outbursts which preceeded the New York breakthrough, began undergoing the process of institutionalization which became typical of the seventies. The strike, with its accompanying picketing, histrionics, and rallies, was the manifestation of the new mood, but it was collective bargaining that gave militancy meaning, rationality, and form. The first New York City school strike occurred November 7, 1960. To a large extent it was a result of manipulation by the leaders of the new UFT, who had become convinced of the strike's efficacy as an organizing device.

The UFT founding agreement included a series of demands for salary and other benefits backed up by the declaration that if satisfactory negotiations on these demands did not occur there would be a teacher strike. A strike date was set for mid-May, 1960. Most of the leaders of the UFT believed that New York City teachers were not yet ready for an outright city-wide work stoppage. Three days before the strike date, after Sunday afternoon negotiations in which Mayor Robert F. Wagner participated, a settlement was reached. The strike was called off, even though the teacher leaders were far from confident that the terms of the settlement would be carried out.

In the fall, the failure of the Board of Education to comply with the May agreement became all too evident and the union set a new strike date. November 7 was chosen because it was the day before the 1960 national election. The union leaders felt that the Democratic administration of the city would not take punitive action against the teachers at such a crucial time. Furthermore, since Veterans Day, like Election Day, was a holiday in New York City and occurred that same week, teachers could be out a week while missing only three days of school.

Approximately 10,000 of the city's 40,000 active teachers responded to the strike call, although the Board of Education, by excluding temporary teachers from the count, made it appear that many fewer were on strike. At the end of the day, a rally was held, and spirits were high, but many observers realized that getting a quarter of the teachers to engage in a work stoppage on the day before election day was more a lark than a solid strike. Hence, the union leadership agreed to allow three prominent labor leaders —David Dubinsky, President of the International Ladies Garment Workers Union; Jacob Potofsky, President of Amalgamated Clothing Workers;

and Harry Van Arsdale, President of the New York City Central Labor Council—to negotiate while the teachers would report back to work. Many striking teachers were filled with bitterness and frustration by the ending of the strike after only one day, but most teachers felt that an important forward step had been taken, and that the course of wisdom was to not go too far at that time.

A year later, the first collective bargaining representation election among any sizeable group of school teachers in the United States was held in New York, and the union was an easy victor over a hastily put-together coalition affiliated with the National Education Association. During the campaign the union had emphasized its ability to "get things done" through the use of teacher "action." The NEA group had run on its more dignified, "professional" approach. In addition to other issues and considerations which had a bearing on the election result, the teachers had voted for militancy. Within a few weeks that decision was put to the test.

The UFT, now the officially recognized exclusive bargaining agent of all New York City teachers, set out in January, 1962, to negotiate a contract which would be comparable to those in private industry. Such comprehensive contracts were extremely rare in the public sector. The usual relationship was one of negotiations once a year at budget time for a salary increase or a fringe benefit only. These negotiations seldom resulted in more than sketchy memoranda of agreement when there was any written agreement at all. Although the chief negotiator for the school board agreed with the union's total agreement approach, the inevitability of a showdown conflict became apparent when the UFT presented its demands. There were more than a hundred demands.

The showdown came in April. Once again the teachers "hit the bricks," and before the first day was over the Board of Education had obtained a court injunction which directed the union leaders to order the teachers back to work. The immediate future of teacher militancy hung in the balance. It was saved by an unusual train of circumstances.

The UFT executive board, admonished by its lawyer of the dire consequences which would follow disobedience of the injunction, voted, after a debate which continued until 3:00 in the morning, to call off the strike. However, a week before the strike, one of the union negotiators had hatched a scheme to make an additional thirteen million dollars available for the negotiations. The idea had been rejected by city officials, but it had then been relayed to the governor's office. At the very moment the UFT was throwing in its hand, telegrams from the governor were on their way to summon all interested parties to a meeting.

The summit meeting was held amid great confusion. Hundreds of New York City teachers walked the sidewalks in front of their schools, while hundreds of others, getting their instructions from early morning radio, had reported for work. There was no doubt that the teachers were angry. However, their anger turned to jubilation later in the day. Knowledge of the union's capitulation came too late to call off the governor's meeting. When the union and the public officials met they took only a short while to discover that the union's thirteen million dollar claim was valid.

Although the strike was settled, the contract still was a long way from completion. It was not until October 12, six months after the strike, that the contract was actually signed. The chief delay during this period was over the strong no-strike pledge demanded by the Board of Education. The contract was finally approved by the UFT delegate assembly with the no-strike pledge, but at the same time the delegate assembly adopted a declaration of policy: henceforth New York City teachers would work only in accordance with the terms and conditions of a collective bargaining contract. In other words, "no contract, no work."

The institutionalizing of teacher militancy was further advanced by the adoption of the no contract, no work principle. The final step was taken one year later, when the UFT signed its first two-year contract. The present contract runs for three years. Thus negotiations occur only at stated times and only once every two or three years. Strikes occur only at the beginning of the school year. Militancy has been put on a time schedule.

Can militancy be caged and still survive? Whatever the eventual outcome, the orderly and "responsible" use of militancy by the UFT proved to be an appealing package for teachers in other cities. It soon became apparent that collective bargaining backed up by strike deadlines was not just a New York phenomenon. Teachers throughout northeastern United States soon started marching along the trail New York City teachers had blazed, and the NEA and its affiliated organizations were forced to compete.

Throughout the 1960s the policies of the association, under the stimulus of AFT union rivalry, became increasingly militant. But although the associations adopted the techniques of the union they had great difficulty in establishing their credibility as true militants. The association traditionally depended upon superintendents and principals to herd teachers more or less gently into association membership. If the association followed policies that displeased the administrators, the source of members and dues money would be turned off. On the other hand, if the association did not compete with the union it would also lose members. So the officials of the association tried to have the game without the name.

They used the term "professional negotiations" as a substitute for collective bargaining, and they developed an elaborate policy of sanctions as a substitute for the strike. They approached the problem of negotiations by designating three different levels of agreements among which teachers would presumably choose. The purpose of all this pussyfooting, of course, was to reassure administrators that association teachers were really not marching on them, and at the same time convince teachers that they had more to gain the "professional" way than by outright unionism.

The change in the attitude of the association towards collective bargaining and the use of the strike progressed step by step through the 1960s. The long-standing opposition to the strike weapon by the associations was finally abandoned in 1968. In the fall of 1969 and again in 1970 and 1971, there were far more strikes by associations than there were by AFT locals.

The conversion of the associations to teacher militancy and collective bargaining was not quite total. In many states, particularly in the South and West, the associations still are going along on a business-as-usual basis, but as soon as the AFT appears on the scene things begin to change. What has happened in the states of the Northeast will come to the southern states, too, sooner or later.

The greatest single deterrent to teacher militancy has always been fear. For a time, when unions and associations were striking local school boards without any dire consequences, it appeared that the old fears of official reprisal were simply bogeymen stories. Even the state antistrike acts proved unenforceable. But as teacher strikes became more commonplace, school boards lost their inhibitions. Teachers began to go to jail, and striking organizations began to pay heavy fines. Even without a specific statute school boards can file for common law injunctions against teacher strikes just as employers used to do in private industry. If a teacher violates a court injunction he is guilty of contempt of court. Some states place limits on fines and jail sentences which can be levied on a single contempt of court citation. Others do not, but even if there is a limitation, each day of a strike can be viewed by a court as a separate violation.

A frightening example of what can happen if teachers defy a determined school board and a reactionary court occurred in Newark, New Jersey, in 1970 and again in 1971. More than 200 teachers were sentenced to jail, four of them with terms of over one year. Individual fines came to nearly $100,000 and the union itself was fined $270,000. It seems doubtful that militancy can survive in the face of such an onslaught.

The AFT has mounted a campaign to restrict the power of courts to grant injunctions in teacher disputes. Getting legislative action is slow work, however. By 1971, two states had passed limited right-to-strike laws, but in most instances legislative action seemed a long way off. Peculiarly, the NEA has not mounted a similar campaign. As a matter of fact neither the national nor any of its state branches (so far as is known) have anything at all to say about the abuse of the injunctive power by judges.

In the meantime, there have been indications of other developments which may have a further restrictive impact on the strength of teacher militancy. As the decade of the seventies began, more and more persons concerned with the future of education were recognizing the fact that little progress could be made so long as school systems depended upon local and state sources of revenue. Furthermore, courts were coming to recognize what most educators have known all along: inequalities in the wealth of school districts create serious inequities in educational services. The children who need education most generally live in the areas with the greatest financial problems. Hence, for fiscal reasons and for reasons of social justice, the day of the local school district as a sanctuary for well-to-do whites was seen to be drawing to an end. Instead, the nation was moving rapidly towards state financing of education. With statewide financing, statewide collective bargaining would be necessary.

Teacher militancy in the sixties was largely a localized phenomenon. Teachers in Skokie, Illinois, could be up in arms and seemingly ready to lynch the superintendent, while in next door Evanston, teachers were contentedly going about their appointed rounds. Only occasionally was there a statewide uprising of teachers; and in every instance successful statewide manifestations of militancy were carried out with the complicity of, if not actual management by, school administrators. For instance, there was a two day work stoppage in Utah in the early 1960s which was a highly successful attempt to coerce the legislature. The administrators simply "let it happen." There were similar managed stoppages in Oklahoma and Kentucky during the sixties. The only genuine grass roots, statewide teacher work stoppage was in Florida in 1969. Very few administrators participated in the strike; many of them masterminded strike-breaking activities. After a month the teachers went back to work with less than they had before they went out. Hundreds lost their jobs. The Florida strike was called by the Florida Education Association. Following the strike, the classroom teachers division within the FEA was disbanded. The Florida strike was a heavy set-back for statewide militant action.

The AFT has never talked about a statewide strike for the simple reason there is no state where the AFT is in the majority. So, with the NEA shying away from statewide action and the AFT unable to mount a statewide stoppage, the shift from local to statewide bargaining is likely to act as a deterrent to teacher militancy, unless the often talked about NEA–AFT merger actually occurs. So long as the two organizations are competing, neither has the strength to call a statewide strike except in states where such action is extremely unlikely to occur for other reasons. In Illinois, for instance, it is doubtful that the Illinois Education Association could call a successful statewide strike, but neither could the AFT. If the two organizations ever got together, however, they quite obviously could shut down the state if the need arose.

Peering ahead into the seventies, what is the future of teacher militancy? It is obvious that the angry, formless thrust of teacher militancy which characterized the early sixties is gone for a long time to come, driven out by the increasing institutionalization of teacher–management relations, and by the increasing complexities of the problems confronting the schools. Militancy as a localized phenomenon has seen its day; it remains to be seen how soon the devices of statewide and nationwide militancy can be developed.

The universe for teachers is shifting, as it is for everyone else. And just as the militancy of the thirties was not adequate to meet the challenge of the sixties, so the militancy of the sixties will not be adequate to meet the challenge of the seventies and beyond. But as long as there are oversized classes, too heavy teaching loads, and deficits in supportive services, there will be militant teachers.

Discussion Questions

1. Who is a militant person and what is militancy? What criteria are used to determine teacher professionalism?

2. Is teacher militancy a reflection of growing militancy within society in general?

3. What specific issues have arisen in the past few years to make people in the teaching profession increasingly militant?

4. Do teachers give up some rights in order to become educators? Should teachers use force in support of their rights? Should teachers strike? Is it possible for teachers to be militant and professional at the same time?

5. What are the targets of teacher militancy? What are some of the demands raised by militant teachers?

6. Will present economic conditions increase or decrease teacher militancy?

7. Who suffers, if any, when teachers go on strike? Have students been affected by teacher militancy? Doesn't teacher militancy set a bad example for students to emulate?

8. How has the community at large reacted to the militant spirit of teachers?

9. Will teacher militancy improve the education of the young?

10. Will teacher militancy affect the reputation of the teaching profession? In what ways?

11. How have school administrators handled teacher militancy? Can't teachers and administrators get together?

12. What progress, if any, has been made on account of teachers' greater participation in policy-making decisions? How can the new power of militancy be effectively channeled and perpetuated?

13. What future implications could one predict as the natural outcome of teacher militancy?

14. What are the nature of and the similarities and differences between the professional teacher organizations? Should teacher organizations exclude administrators?

15. How can the community become more sensitive to the problems of the teacher and the school in general? Would a political solution be the answer to school problems?

Project: Considering the issues of the culturally different, technology and education, and student unrest, do you foresee any better solutions to the problems of schooling with increased teacher participation in decision-making? Whatever the answer, present your arguments in a professional manner.

Selected References

Andree, Robert, *Collective Negotiations; A Guide to School Board–Teacher Relations* (Lexington, Mass.: Heath Lexington Books, 1971). This work is the product of many minds. It represents more than 250 collective professional years as teachers, school board members, state and national leaders in teacher organizations and practical administrators. The book is basic to the formulation of thinking on collective bargaining by many educational groups.

Blum, Albert A. (ed.), *Teacher Unions and Associations: A Comparative Study* (Urbana, Illinois: University of Illinois Press, 1969). This volume was designed to give some insight into the problem of teacher militancy. Experts were solicited to look at teacher unions and associations in a number of countries so that we could better understand the organizations teachers are developing as they make their demands.

Cole, Stephen, *The Unionization of Teachers; A Case Study of the U F T* (New York: Frederick A. Praeger Publishers, 1969). This is a case study of the New York United Federation of Teachers with an interesting sociological interpretation.

Doherty, Robert and Walter Oberer, *Teachers, School Boards, and Collective Bargaining; A Changing of the Guard* (Ithaca, New York: State School of Industrial and Labor Relations, 1967). These authors hoped that their volume might serve as a faint beacon for those concerned with providing a more appropriate structure for teacher-school board relations in a time of somewhat chaotic, but creative, flux.

Elam, Stanley M., Myron Lieberman, and Michael Moskow (eds.), *Readings on Collective Negotiations in Public Education* (Chicago: Rand McNally & Company, 1967). The selections are directed to the collective negotiations in the sixties. Here the editors hope to produce a more sophisticated and knowledgeable approach to the important issues involved.

Gilroy, Thomas, *et al.*, *Educator's Guide to Collective Negotiations* (Columbus, Ohio: Charles E. Merrill Publishing Company, 1969). This volume outlines some of the background and framework with which collective negotiations are most often associated. It is nonpartisan and helpful to all those who are involved.

Lieberman, Myron and Michael Moskow, *Collective Negotiations for Teachers; An Approach to School Administration* (Chicago: Rand McNally & Company, 1966). This book is a status study of collective negotiations in education. To what extent do teachers and school boards actually engage in collective negotiations?

Lutz, Frank and Joseph Azzarelli, *Struggle for Power in Education* (New York: Center for Applied Research in Education, 1966). The book studies the new distribution of power which is in the making in American public school systems.

Moskow, Michael H., *Teachers and Unions; The Applicability of Collective Bargaining to Public Education* (Philadelphia: University of Pennsylvania Press,

1966). This is the first major study of a significant development since the rash of teacher organizing drives, strikes, and withdrawals from service began with the successful unionization of the New York City teachers in 1961.

Shils, Edward B. and C. Taylor Whittier, *Teachers, Administrators and Collective Bargaining* (New York: Thomas Y. Crowell Co., 1968). This book is the result of the collaboration of a school superintendent and a chief negotiator who settled negotiation agreements for the Philadelphia School District in 1965.

Stinnett, Timothy, *Turmoil in Teaching: A History of the Organizational Struggle for America's Teachers* (New York: The Macmillan Company, 1968). This is a historical account and interpretation of teacher movement.

Stinnett, Timothy, Jack Kleinmann, and Martha Ware, *Professional Negotiation in Public Education* (New York: The Macmillan Company, 1966). This book provides basic information on all aspects of the professional negotiation process.

Zitron, Celia L., *The New York City Teachers Union, 1916–1964; A Story of Educational and Social Commitment* (New York: Humanities Press, 1968). The author provides an all-inclusive treatment of a case in teacher unionism with social and political backgrounds and interpretations.

About the Authors

Ashton-Warner, Sylvia Sylvia Ashton-Warner was born in Stratford, New Zealand, where she was educated at the Wairarana College and later at the Auckland Training College. She married a teacher and for seventeen years was an infant mistress in Maori schools. After the death of her husband Miss Ashton-Warner travelled widely. She recently accepted a post at the Simon Fraser University, British Columbia, where she is teaching and training teachers. Her publications include *Spinster, Incense to Idols, Teacher, Bell Call, Greenstone, Myself, Three,* and *Spearpoint.*

Bain, Helen Helen Bain was born in Nashville, Tennessee, in 1924. She received her B.A. from George Peabody College for Teachers, Nashville, and her M.A. from the University of Michigan, Ann Arbor, Michigan. She is a speech and English teacher in Nashville, and a past president of the National Education Association (1970–71). She campaigned for the NEA presidency on a platform which urged greater political activity for teachers. As a member of the NEA Executive Committee since 1965, Bain is well acquainted with the problems, needs, and trends of education today. She has been involved in civic, welfare, and political affairs for many years. She is one of the founders of the National Council of Urban Education Associations, of which she was president in 1963–64. By appointment of President Johnson, Bain was chairman of the Advisory Committee for Title III, Elementary and Secondary Education Act. In addition she has served on several other committees and delegations to international conferences on education and has contributed a number of articles to professional journals.

Bereday, George Z. F. George Bereday was born in Warsaw, Poland, on July 15, 1920. He received his B.Sc. from the University of London in 1944, his B.A. and M.A. from Oxford in 1950 and 1953 respectively, and his Ph.D. from Harvard in 1953. He teaches at Teachers College, Columbia University, where since 1959 he has been Professor of Comparative Education. He has studied and taught in such diverse places as Moscow, Poland, Tokyo, Singapore, Finland, and Hawaii. He was director of Japanese-American Teacher Program, Ford Foundation and Institute of International Education from 1964 to 1968 and was a member of the U.S. delegation to the 4th U.S.–Japan Cultural Conference in 1969. Bereday has published *Comparative Method in Education, The Making of Citizens,* and *Essays on World Education,* and numerous articles in such journals as *Harvard Educational Review, Teachers College Record,* and *Educational Forum.*

Bruner, Jerome S. Jerome S. Bruner was born on October 1, 1915, in New York City. He received his B.A. from Duke University in 1937, and his M.A. and Ph.D. from Harvard University in 1939 and 1941 respectively. He became Associate Director of Public Opinion Research at Princeton in 1942. In 1945 returned to Harvard to teach educational psychology. He has received a Guggenheim fellowship from Cambridge University and a fellowship from the American Psychological Association. During the Eisenhower administration, he served on a White House panel on educational research and development. In 1959 he served as chairman of the Woods Hole Conference sponsored by the National Academy of Science. Bruner has been Director of the Center for Cognitive Studies at Harvard since 1961. He received the Distinguished Science Contribution award from the

National Academy of Science in 1962, and in 1965 he was appointed Bacon professor at the University of Aix-en-Provence in France. He has written a number of books on education, the most important being *The Process of Education* and *Toward a Theory of Instruction.*

Corwin, Ronald Ronald Corwin was born in Waterloo, Iowa, on January 14, 1932. He received his B.A. from Iowa State Teachers College in 1954, and his M.A. and Ph.D. from the University of Minnesota in 1958 and 1960. He joined the faculty of the University of Minnesota in 1959, where he stayed until 1961. Since 1961 he has been associated with Ohio State University. He has served as research coordinator, Bureau of Research, U.S. Office of Education, 1966–67; research associate and principal investigator, University of Minnesota, 1961; visiting lecturer, Teachers College, Columbia University, 1965; consultant, U.S. Office of Education, 1967 to present. Corwin authored *A Sociology of Education,* "The Professional Employee," and "Educational and Complex Organization."

Counts, George S. George Counts was born on Dec. 9, 1889, near Baldwin City, Kansas. He received his B.A. from Baker University, Baldwin City, Kansas, in 1911; Ph.D. from the University of Chicago in 1916; and LL.D. from Baker University in 1935. Counts served at Delaware College, Newark before becoming professor of Educational Sociology at Harris Teachers College, St. Louis, Missouri, 1918–19. He has been professor of Secondary Education, University of Washington, 1919–20; at Yale, 1920–26; at University of Chicago, 1926–27; at Teachers College, Columbia, 1927–56, where he is professor emeritus. He was also visiting professor at University of Pittsburgh, 1959; Michigan State University, 1960; and Southern Illinois University, Carbondale, 1962–1971. Counts was the editor of The Social Frontier, 1934–37; member of the Educational Policies Commission of NEA, 1936–42; president of the American Federation of Teachers, 1939–42; member of the Executive Committee of the National Commission on Education and Defense, 1940–42; National Committee of Civil Liberties Union since 1940; Commission on Motion Pictures in Education, 1944–48; chairman of the American Labor Party, New York State, 1942–44; chairman of the New York Liberal Party, 1955–59; member of the U.S. Education Mission to Japan, 1946; member of the Commission on International Exchange of Persons, 1948–50. Counts was the recipient of the Annual Educator's Award, B'nai B'rith, 1953; Teachers College medal for distinguished service, 1954; award for distinguished service in school administration, American Association of School Administrators, 1968; Phi Delta Kappa award, 1967; and John Dewey Society award, 1967. Counts authored several books (sixteen books, 1917–42) such as *Education and the Promise of America, Education and American Civilization, The Challenge of Soviet Education,* and *Education and Human Freedom in the Age of Technology.*

Deloria, Vine, Jr. Vine Deloria, Jr. received his B.S. from Iowa State University in 1958, B.D. from the Lutheran School of Theology in 1963, and J.D. from the University of Colorado in 1970. He is now a member of the faculty of Western Washington State College, College of Ethnic Studies. He has served as Executive Director for the National Congress of American Indians and has been active in many organizations dealing with Indian affairs and with poverty in the United

States. Deloria received the Anis Field-Wolf award in 1968. Among his publications is the best seller *Custer Died for Your Sins.*

Engler, David David Engler received his B.S. from New York University and his M.S. from Teachers College, Columbia University. He did additional graduate work at the University of Paris. For eight years he taught elementary, junior, and senior high schools in New York. Since 1959 he has been with McGraw-Hill, where he is now Group Vice President for Instructional Technology. His executive responsibilities include Educational Development Laboratories, Inc., Film Division, Instructional Systems Division, and Spitz Laboratories, Inc. He is a member of Advisory Panel, National Science Foundation, Computer Innovation in Educational Section and Education Systems Committee, National Academy of Engineering. Engler has contributed numerous articles to periodical literature.

Friedenberg, Edgar Edgar Friedenberg was born on March 18, 1921, in New York City. He received his B.S. from Centenary College in 1938, M.A. from Stanford in 1939, and Ph.D. from the University of Chicago in 1946. He has taught at the University of Chicago, Brooklyn College, the University of California at Davis; and is currently Professor of Sociology at New York State University at Buffalo. A member of many professional associations, Friedenberg authored *The Vanishing Adolescent, Coming of Age in America,* and *The Dignity of Youth and Other Atavisms.*

Glasser, William William Glasser was born on May 11, 1925, in Cleveland, Ohio. He received his B.S. from Case Institute of Technology in 1945, M.A. from Western Reserve University in 1948, and M.D. in 1953. A chemical engineer at age nineteen, he became a clinical psychologist at twenty-three and a physician at twenty-eight. After medical school he received his psychiatric training at the Veterans Administration Center and U.C.L.A. Medical Center. Glasser has been a psychiatrist in private practice in Los Angeles since 1957, and is consulted extensively in the area of correction. His work at the Ventura School for Girls has gained him wide recognition, and has been the basis for much of his writing. Recently he has devoted himself more and more to education and, with the help of the Stone Foundation, he has established the Educator Training Center, of which he is Director. He has taught a large group of city and county school administrators, counselors, and teachers. He has worked directly with children in the Los Angeles City Schools and the Palo Alto schools. He authored *Mental Health or Mental Illness, Reality Therapy,* and *Schools Without Failure.*

Holt, John John Holt is presently consultant with the Fayerweather Street School in Cambridge, Massachusetts. He was born in New York City and graduated from Yale University. He has taught and observed children of all levels for over fifteen years. He has lectured on education at Harvard Graduate School of Education and has taught prospective teachers at the University of California at Berkeley. Holt's books, *How Children Fail, How Children Learn, The Underachieving School,* and *What Do I Do Monday,* as well as his articles in the *New York Times* magazine, *Harper's, The New York Review of Books, The Grade Teacher,* and many other publications have become standard works in the field of education.

Hook, Sidney Sidney Hook was born on December 20, 1902, in New York City. He received his B.S. degree from New York City College in 1923, M.A. and Ph.D.

from Columbia in 1926 and 1927, respectively; and has an L.H.D. and an LL.D. Between 1923 and 1928 he taught in New York City public schools. In 1927 he joined the faculty of New York University, Washington Square College, where he has taught and served as chairman of the Philosophy Department, chairman of the College of Arts and Sciences, and chairman of the Division of Philosophy and Psychology, Graduate School. He was a Guggenheim fellow twice and a fellow at the Center for Advanced Studies in Behavioral Sciences, Stanford, California. Hook organized the Conference on Methods in Philosophy and Science, the Conference on Scientific Spirit and Democratic Faith, and the Congress for Cultural Freedom. He has edited and authored many books and hundreds of articles, the most important being *Education for Modern Man, Marx and the Marxists, American Philosophers at Work: The Current Philosophic Scene,* and *Determinism and Freedom in An Age of Modern Science.*

Hutchins, Robert M. Robert M. Hutchins was born in Brooklyn, New York, on January 17, 1899. He attended Yale and received his B.A. degree in 1921 and his LL.B. degree in 1925. He was professor of law at Yale from 1923 to 1929 and Dean of the Law School from 1928 to 1929. Hutchins left Yale in 1929 to become President of the University of Chicago at age 30. He remained in this position until 1945, when he became Chancellor. As President, Hutchins reorganized the University's administrative system and inaugurated the Chicago plan of a four-year junior college and a liberal arts university which were independent of the professional schools. In 1951 he left Chicago to become Associate Director of the Ford Foundation, editor of the Great Books of the Western World in 1952, and President of the Fund for the Republic in 1954. He remained with the Fund for the Republic until 1961, after which time he became president of the Center for the Study of Democratic Institutions at Santa Barbara, California. He has written many books on education, including *The Higher Learning in America, Education for Freedom, The Conflict in Education in a Democratic Society, Morals, Religion and Higher Education, Some Observations on American Education, The University of Utopia,* and *The Learning Society.*

Kohl, Herbert R. Herbert Kohl is the author of *The Age of Complexity, 36 Children,* and *Teaching The Unteachable.* He received his bachelor's degree in philosophy from Harvard and a master's degree in special education from Teachers College, Columbia, and was a Henry Fellow at Oxford in philosophy. Formerly on the Staff of the Center for Urban Education and director of The Teachers' and Writers' Collaborative at the Horace Mann-Lincoln Institute of School Experimentation, he taught for several years in Harlem schools. He has recently been director of an experimental program, "Other Ways," in the Berkeley schools.

Lieberman, Myron Myron Lieberman was born on April 30, 1919, in St. Paul, Minnesota. He received his B.S. in Laws and B.S. in Education from the University of Minnesota in 1941 and 1948, respectively. From the University of Illinois he received his M.A. in 1950 and Ph.D. in 1952. He has taught at the high school level and at the University of Illinois, University of Oklahoma, Yeshiva University, and Hofstra College. In addition he has worked in educational research, publishing, and consulting. Lieberman has contributed articles to professional journals and authored or coauthored several books including *Education as a Profession, The Future of Public Education, Social Forces Influencing American Education,* and *Language and Concepts in Education.*

Margaritis, Stephen Stephen Margaritis was born in Lowell, Massachusetts, and raised in Greece. He received a Teacher's Certificate from Teachers Academy, Lamia, Greece, and received his B.A. from the University of Athens, Greece. From the University of Southern California he received M.A. in history and Ph.D. in education. Margaritis taught in public schools in Greece and in the United States. Since 1963 he has been teaching at Western Washington State College, Bellingham, Washington. He also taught at the University of Oregon, Eugene, Oregon. He has been a member of and held executive positions in several professional associations. Margaritis has contributed a number of articles to professional journals.

McLuhan, Marshall Marshall McLuhan was born on July 21, 1911, in Edmonton, Alberta, Canada. He received his B.A. degree from the University of Manitoba in 1933 and his M.A. in 1934. From Cambridge he received a B.A., M.A., and Ph.D. in 1936, 1939, and 1942, respectively. He has taught at University of Wisconsin, St. Louis University, and Assumption University (Windsor), and is currently on the faculty of St. Michael's College, University of Toronto. Since 1963 McLuhan has been directing the Centre for Culture and Technology. He also holds the Albert Einstein chair as professor of humanities at Fordham University, New York City. He has written articles and books, including *The Mechanical Bride, Studies in Communications, The Gutenberg Galaxy, Understanding Media: The Extensions of Man,* and *The Medium is the Massage: An Inventory of Effects.*

Melvin, Kenneth Kenneth Melvin came from New Zealand and was professor of education at Boston University when he died in 1969. He received his B.A. degree from the University of Auckland, New Zealand, M.A. from the University of New Zealand, and Ph.D. from the University of Otago, New Zealand. He was a Fellow at the Trinity College of Music and the London College of Music, University of London. Melvin served as head of the Department of Education, Faculty of Arts, University of Otago, and visiting professor, the Pennsylvania State University. He published articles in scholarly and literary journals in New Zealand, Japan, Great Britain, and the United States. He also published such books as *James Busby, First British Resident in New Zealand, The Mask and the Face, A Study in Adlerian Psychology, New Zealand: The Small Utopia, The Pattern of New Zealand Culture,* and *Education in World Affairs.*

Pullias, Earl V. Earl Pullias is professor of higher education at the University of Southern California. He was born in Castalian Springs, Tennessee, on March 12, 1907. He received his B.A. from Cumberland University in 1928, M.A. from the University of Chicago in 1931, and Ph.D. from Duke University in 1936. He has taught in junior high school and at Duke University and Pepperdine College. In addition he was an assistant psychologist at Duke Hospital Psychiatric Clinic and Dean of the Faculty at Pepperdine. A member of many professional societies, Pullias has received honors such as the U.S.C. Associate Award for Excellence in Teaching, 1965. He has been a member of the Los Angeles County Board of

Education since 1954, and has served as its president three times. He has contributed numerous articles to educational and psychological journals, and authored or coauthored several books, including *Toward Excellence in College Teaching, A Search for Understanding,* and *A Teacher Is Many Things.*

Riesman, David David Riesman, lawyer, educator, and social scientist, is presently affiliated with the Department of Social Relations, Harvard University, where he is Henry Ford II Professor of Social Science. He was born on Sept. 22, 1909, in Philadelphia. He received his B.A. degree from Harvard in 1931, LL.B. in 1934, research fellow, 1934–35; LL.D., Marlboro College, 1954. He has also received many honorary degrees from a number of institutions. He is a member of the Massachusetts, District of Columbia, and New York bars, and was a law clerk to Mr. Justice Brandeis of the U.S. Supreme Court. He has practiced law and taught it at the University of Buffalo and Columbia University, as well as serving as a deputy assistant district attorney in New York County. He has also taught social sciences at the University of Chicago. Riesman also served as fellow at the Center for Advanced Study in Behavioral Sciences, as a member of the advisory council for the Peace Corps, and as a member of the Carnegie Commission for the Study of Higher Education. He contributed many articles to professional journals and has written many books, including *The Lonely Crowd: A Study of the Changing American Character, Abundance for What? and Other Essays, Conversations in Japan: Modernization, Politics and Culture,* and *The Academic Revolution.*

Rogers, Carl Carl Rogers was born on Jan. 8, 1902, in Oak Park, Illinois. He received his B.A. degree from the University of Wisconsin in 1924, M.A. from Columbia University in 1928, and Ph.D. from Columbia in 1931. Rogers served as psychologist in the Child Study Department, Society for the Prevention of Cruelty to Children, Rochester, New York and as its director. He has also been director of the Rochester Guidance Center, and director of counselling services, U. S. O. Rogers was affiliated with the Western Behavioral Sciences Institute, La Jolla, California, from 1957 to 1968; he has been a member of the Center for Studies of the Person, La Jolla, since 1968. He has at various times been a member of the faculties of Ohio State University, University of Chicago, and University of Wisconsin, as well as being visiting professor at the University of Rochester, Columbia University Teachers College, University of California at Los Angeles, Harvard College, Occidental College, University of California at Berkeley, and Brandeis University. Rogers received the Distinguished Science Contribution Award from the American Psychological Association, 1956; Nicholas Murray Butler medal from Columbia, 1955; Distinguished Contribution Award from American Pastoral Counselors Association, 1967; and Professional Award from American Board of Professional Psychology, 1968. He has been a fellow at Center for Advanced Study in Behavioral Sciences, and was named Humanist of the Year by American Humanist Association in 1964. In addition he has been a member and officer of several professional associations. He has contributed articles and written many books, including *Counseling and Psychotherapy, Client-Centered Therapy, On Becoming a Person,* and *Freedom to Learn.*

Schierbeck, Helen M. Helen Schierbeck was born Aug. 21, 1935, in Lumberton, North Carolina. She received her B.A. from Berea College in 1957 and M.A. from

Columbia University in 1959. She is a member of the American Political Science Association and the American Ethnology Society. In 1958 Schierbeck joined the National Congress of American Indians, but in 1959 left to accept a Congressional Staff Fellowship and to work with the U. S. Senate Subcommittee on Constitutional Rights. In this capacity she directed staff research and analysis of American legal thought and *de facto* practices relative to constitutional rights of the American Indian. Between 1964 and 1965 she did research for the American Political Science Association on social, economic, and political problems confronting Indians. In 1966 she accepted a position at the University of Wisconsin. Here she helped to explore ideas which led to proposal for training programs for the culturally disadvantaged; she represented the University Extension in negotiations with federal and state funding agencies concerned and has served as Acting Director of the University Extension's Center for Action on Poverty. Since 1968 Schierbeck has served as Community Legal Relations Specialist with the Bureau of Indian Affairs. Schierbeck has received the John Hay Whitney Fellowship, Florina Lasker Fellowship, Congressional Fellowship, Great Lakes Region OEO Rural Service Award, and People Pour It On Pepsi Cola Award. Her research has resulted in a number of documents for the U. S. Senate Subcommittee on Constitutional Rights.

Selden, David David Selden is the current President of the AFL-CIO American Federation of Teachers. He has been a leader in the teacher union movement since he joined the AFT in 1940. Selden, who has a Masters degree in government from Wayne State University, became a member of the Dearborn, Michigan Federation of Teachers, while a social studies teacher in the Dearborn school system. He was immediately elected president of the Dearborn Federation. He also taught in Oak Hill, Florida, and Peekskill, New York. From 1948 to 1953, he served as an American Federation of Teachers field representative. Between 1953 and 1964, he was special representative and director of organization of the United Federation of Teachers, AFT Local 2, of New York City. He was the director of organization of the UFT when the union led New York City teachers to a successful collective bargaining agent election and to two precedent-setting contracts with the New York school board. At the time the contracts were negotiated, he was chief negotiator of the UFT collective bargaining committee. Mr. Selden was a member of the Urban Task Force on Education of the U.S. Department of Health, Education, and Welfare which reported in 1970, and a member of the Committee for Assessing Progress in Education (CAPE). He serves on the Executive Board of the Americans for Democratic Action and is a member of National Advisory Board of National Teachers Examination. He is the author of numerous articles on teacher organization, unionism, and current problems in education.

Skinner, B. F. B. F. Skinner was born in Susquehanna, Pennsylvania, on March 20, 1904. He received his B.A. degree in 1926 from Hamilton College. He received his M.A. in 1930 and in 1931 his Ph.D. from Harvard. He taught at the University of Minnesota and at the University of Indiana; in 1947 returned to Harvard to teach. In 1958 he became the Edgar Pierce Professor of Psychology at Harvard. He has written articles and books on psychology and education including *The Behavior of Organisms, Walden Two, Science and Human Behavior, Verbal*

Behavior, Schedules of Reinforcement, Cumulative Record, The Analysis of Behavior, and *The Technology of Teaching.*

Suppes, Patrick Patrick Suppes is Director of the Institute for Mathematical Studies in the Social Sciences at Stanford University. He was born on March 17, 1922. He received his B.S. degree from the University of Chicago in 1943, and Ph.D. from Columbia University in 1950. Suppes taught at Columbia University while completing his doctoral work; in 1950 he joined the faculty of the Philosophy Department, Stanford University. He has served as Associate Dean, School of Humanities and Sciences, as Chairman of the Department of Philosophy, and as chairman of Mathematical Social Science Board. He has been a member of several professional associations, and has received fellowships and awards including Fellow, Center for Advanced Study in the Behavioral Sciences; post-doctoral fellow, National Science Foundation; SSRC Research Award; fellow, American Association for Advancement of Science; fellow, American Psychological Association; Nicholas Murray Butler Medal in Silver (Columbia University); member, National Academy of Education; Palmer O. Johnson Memorial Award (American Educational Research Association); fellow, American Academy of Arts and Sciences; John Smith Memorial Lecturer (Victorian Institute of Educational Research, Melbourne, Australia); membré associé étranger, Société Francaise de Psychologie; AERA—Phi Delta Kappa Award for Distinguished Contribution to Educational Research, 1971; fellow, John Simon Guggenheim Memorial Foundation. Suppes has contributed more than 100 articles to professional journals and authored and edited books such as *Computer-Assisted Instruction, Studies in the Methodology and Foundations of Science,* and *Information and Inference.*

Taylor, Harold Harold Taylor was born on September 28, 1914, in Toronto, Canada. He received his B.A. and M.A. degrees from the University of Toronto in 1935 and 1936, respectively, and his Ph.D. from the University of London in 1938. He has taught philosophy at the University of Wisconsin and been a faculty member at the New School of Social Research. He was President of Sarah Lawrence College from 1945 to 1959. Taylor has also been chairman of the National Research Council on Peace Strategy; member of board of trustees of Putney School, Institute for International Order; and member of national board of Americans for Democratic Action. In recent years he has been lecturing extensively here and abroad. Taylor has contributed several articles to professional journals and authored and edited several books, the most important being *On Education and Freedom, The World and the American Teacher, Students Without Teachers,* and *The World as Teacher.*

Woodring, Paul Paul Woodring was born on July 16, 1907, in Delta, Oregon. He received his B.S. degree from Bowling Green University in 1930, and M.A. and Ph.D. from Ohio State University in 1934 and 1938, respectively. He has taught in public schools in Ohio and at Ohio State. He was also a clinical psychologist with the Detroit Criminal Courts. In 1939 Woodring joined the faculty of Western Washington State College, where he is currently Distinguished Service Professor. He has been an educational advisor of Ford Foundation and consultant for Fund for the Advancement of Education. Woodring was education editor of *Saturday Review* from 1960 to 66; he is now an Editor at Large. He has been a member of several professional associations and received several honorary degrees and awards including Tuition Plan Award, Tuition Plan, Inc.; Distinguished Alumnus award, Bowling Green State University; School Bell award, N.E.A. (two times); Educational Press Association award (three times); Educational Writers Association award; fellow of American Psychological Association. Woodring contributed several articles to professional journals, and authored books such as *Let's Talk Sense About Our Schools, A Fourth of a Nation, New Directions in Teacher Education,* and *The Higher Learning in America: A Reassessment.*